THE ROUGH GUIDE TO
The Internet

Peter Buckley & Duncan Clark

originally created by
Angus Kennedy

**ROUGH
GUIDES**

www.roughguides.com

Credits

The Rough Guide to the Internet

Text, Layout & Design:
Peter Buckley & Duncan Clark
Proofreading: Anna Leggett & Susanne Hillen
Production: Rebecca Short

Rough Guides Reference

Director: Andrew Lockett
Editors: Kate Berens, Peter Buckley,
Tracy Hopkins, Matthew Milton,
Joe Staines, Ruth Tidball

Acknowledgements

Duncan and Peter would like to thank everyone at Rough Guides. Also Angus Kennedy
for handing the book on to us, and Jonathan Buckley for arranging everything.

Inside front cover: Twitter Fail Whale Illustration by Yiying Lu / www.yiyinglu.com / @yiyinglu on twitter

Publishing Information

This fourteenth edition published Aug 2009 by
Rough Guides Ltd, 80 Strand, London WC2R 0RL
Email: mail@roughguides.com

Distributed by the Penguin Group:
Penguin Books Ltd, 80 Strand, London WC2R 0RL
Penguin Group (USA), 375 Hudson Street, NY 10014, USA
Penguin Group (Australia), 250 Camberwell Road, Camberwell, Victoria 3124, Australia
Penguin Group (Canada), 90 Eglinton Avenue East, Suite 700, Toronto, Ontario, Canada M4P 2Y3
Penguin Group (New Zealand), Cnr Rosedale and Airborne Roads, Albany, Auckland, New Zealand

Printed and bound in Singapore by Toppan Security Printing Pte. Ltd.

Typeset in Minion and Myriad to an original design by Duncan Clark & Peter Buckley

The publishers and authors have done their best to ensure the accuracy and currency of all information in
The Rough Guide to the Internet; however, they can accept no responsibility for any loss or
inconvenience sustained by any reader as a result of its information or advice.

A catalogue record for this book is available from the British Library

ISBN 13: 978-1-84836-106-5

3 5 7 9 8 6 4 2

Contents

Contents

Contents

Introduction

When *The Rough Guide to the Internet* first rolled off the press back in 1995, the Internet, or "information superhighway" as some insisted on calling it, was a mysterious and somewhat geeky phenomenon. Even if you had a computer, you probably didn't have a modem, a Web browser, Internet dialling software and all the other things we take for granted today.

In those dark days, *The Rough Guide* helped millions of people get online for the first time – with essential tips such as making sure prospective ISPs could handle the blistering speed of your 28Kbps modem! The book also provided lots of pointers on what to do once connected.

Fourteen years later, it's a very different online world – and a very different book. We still cover everything that newbies need to know to get connected for the first time, but the majority of these pages deal with tips and advice that even old hands will find useful. Want to know how to make free **phone calls** via your Internet connection, or create **your own website or blog**? Fancy pimping your MySpace page? Confused by the legal and practical implications of **P2P file-sharing** programs such as KaZaA? All will be revealed.

You'll also find tips on **staying secure** – the Internet may be much more user-friendly than it was back in 1995, but it harbours more threats to your data and privacy than ever before. Chapter 14 (p.167) deals with **viruses, worms, spyware, hackers, scams** and other evils, while Chapter 12 (p.145) provides tips on **shopping safely** and Chapter 9 (p.107) offers advice on avoiding **junk email**.

As ever, we've pointed you to a huge number of useful, interesting and entertaining websites. There are addresses dotted throughout the book, but also check out "Things to do online" (p.247), for the best sites for everything from setting up a shop to discovering your family roots.

FAQs

Everything you ever wanted to know about the Internet but were afraid to ask

Before we get into the nitty-gritty of what you can do with the Internet – and what it can do for you – let's answer a few of the most Frequently Asked Questions, or FAQs as they're called online. You'll find more detail on these subjects throughout this book.

What exactly is the Internet?

Put simply, the Internet consists of **millions of computers** connected via cables and radio waves. At the core of this giant network are a series of computers permanently joined together through high-speed connections. To connect to the Net, you simply connect your computer to any one of these networked computers via an **Internet Service Provider** (ISP). The moment you do this, your computer itself becomes part of the Internet.

Of course, the Net is not really about the computers or the cables and satellites that string them together. It's about **people, communication** and **sharing knowledge** – and it's revolutionized the way we access information, stay in touch, shop … the list goes on.

The Internet and the Web are the same thing, right?

No, but don't be embarrassed. Many long-time Net users – and almost all journalists – don't know the difference either. The **World Wide Web** (or simply "the Web") is the popular face of the

Internets and *the* Internet

Strictly speaking, what we refer to as the Internet is actually only one of many. When a number of computers are connected together (in a workplace, at home or any-where else), they're referred to as a network. If you con-nect two or more of these to-gether – to create a network of networks – the result is "an internet". But for non-geeks, this is all academic. Just as there's only one sun that mat-ters – the one that illuminates our planet – there's only one internet that matters: the giant network of comput-ers that in the last couple of decades has revolutionized many aspects of modern life. It's this internet – *the* Internet, written with an upper-case "I" – that is the subject of this book.

Internet, taking the form of billions of **websites**, each comprising one or more **webpages**. It's a bit like a huge, interactive, non-linear magazine, with **links** (or "**hyperlinks**") connecting each page to other pages.

The Internet is much bigger – and much older – than the World Wide Web. Roughly speaking, anything you do online that doesn't involve websites is part of the Net but not part of the Web. This includes everything from email to video conferencing and peer-to-peer file-sharing.

Who's in charge?

No one actually "runs" the entire Internet, but there are several major players who exert a great deal of influence. On the **theoretical and administrative levels** there is **ICANN**, which coordinates domain names (Web addresses); the **Internet Society**, which, among other things, acts as a clearing house for technical stand-ards; and the World Wide Web Consortium (**W3C**), which mulls over the Web's future. You're unlikely to encounter any of these groups directly unless you seek them out.

On the **practical level**, meanwhile, aspects such as software, network routing and wiring are largely controlled by corporations such as Microsoft, Cisco and the world's cable providers. There is no official body responsible for tying these elements together.

The **legal level** is governed by local authorities. What's OK in one territory may be an offence in another. That means if you break a local law, you could be prosecuted – irrespective of whether you're accessing something that's legal at the source. So just because you can download a pirated copy of Photoshop from a Vietnamese Web server doesn't make you immune to copyright laws at home. And while you might have the freedom to express your views about a foreign government, nationals of that state may not be so free to read it.

Indeed, some states actively censor sites that they deem problem-atic: in China, for example, the government temporarily banned the Google search engine when it realized that a search for the premier's name, Jiang Zemin, returned a link to an online game called "Slap the Evil Dictator". (Within a few years, Google and the Chinese government were on much better terms, with the search engine agreeing to incorporate censorship into its Chinese site in spring 2006.)

How was the Internet set up?

The Internet was first conceived half a century ago as a network for the American Defense Department, its primary purpose being to act as a bomb-resistant method of exchanging scientific information and intelligence. In the 1970s and 80s several other networks, such as the **National Science Foundation Network** (NSFNET), jumped on board, linking the Net to research agencies and universities.

As the Cold War petered out and personal computers became widespread, the Internet grew more publicly accessible and user-friendly, with the World Wide Web emerging as a key way for non-technical people to exploit its potential.

For a more substantial history of the Net, turn to p.299.

How many people are online and where are they?

Surveys estimate that almost 1.5 billion people use the Internet – slightly fewer than one in four people worldwide. Of course, far fewer people are regular users and access is unevenly spread around the world. In North America, more than seventy percent of the population are Internet users, compared to forty-eight percent in Europe, fifteen percent in Asia and just five percent in Africa.

What's a website?

A website is a set of webpages that represents someone or something on the Web. A website is based around a single so-called

Internet stats

For mind-bogglingly in-depth Internet demographics and statistics, try the following websites:

Internet World Stats www.internetworldstats.com
ClickZ www.clickz.com/stats /web_worldwide
PEW Internet www.pewinternet. org/topics.asp?c=1

"**domain**" – for instance, the hundreds of pages that make up the Rough Guides website each have a Web address based on the domain roughguides.com. A domain can include various so-called **subdomains**. For example:

travel.roughguides.com
internetbook.roughguides.com

What's a homepage?

Homepage has two meanings. One refers to the page that appears when you start your Web browser, the program you use to look at webpages. You can choose any webpage as your homepage (see p.68) and access it quickly at any time by clicking your browser's "Home" button.

The other use describes the "front page" of a **website**. For instance, the Rough Guides website's homepage is at www.roughguides.com. You can access every page in the Rough Guides site by following links from the homepage.

Elements within a website are also sometimes said to have their own homepage – for example, www.roughguides.com/travel is the homepage for Rough Guides travel content.

What do I need to get started?

Although you can access the Net through all kinds of gadgets, from mobile phones to televisions, to get the full Internet experience you'll need a **computer** – either a PC or a Mac (see p.26). A relatively fast computer is preferable, but most machines produced in the last five years are OK at a push. For more on choosing a computer, see p.25.

Once you have your computer, you need an account with an **Internet Service Provider**.

What's an Internet Service Provider?

An **Internet Service Provider**, or **ISP**, is a company that acts as a gateway between your computer and the rest of the Internet. Many ISPs are telephone or cable TV companies, though others only sell Internet access.

Most ISPs offer a range of different accounts priced according to download speed, usage limit and connection type – either **broadband** or slow, old-fashioned **dial-up**. For help choosing an ISP and connection, see p.30.

What about modems and routers?

Most Internet connections involve the transmission of information via a phoneline or cable connection. These wires transmit analogue information, but computers only speak the digital language of "0s" and "1s". A **modem** is a device that translates between the two, converting analogue to digital and digital to analogue: the word is a contraction of **mo**dulator-**dem**odulator.

Most computers have a standard dial-up modem built in, so you can just plug the computer directly into the phone line. Broadband connections, by contrast, require special broadband modems. These are usually provided when you sign up with an ISP.

If you want to share a broadband connection between more than one machine, or connect a computer to the Internet wirelessly at home, you'll need what has become (slightly inaccurately) described as a **router**: a device that drives the right bits of data to the various computers in your home. A router can be a stand-alone piece of equipment or built into a single box with a broadband modem.

Wireless

A router with wireless ("Wi-Fi") capability will zap a broadband connection around your home, so that you can get your computers online without cables. See p.29 for more information.

NETGEAR

How easy is it to set up a website?

It's relatively easy to set up a simple website. The process goes something like this: get online and register a domain name (Web address); create your webpages on your own computer using an HTML editing program or even a regular word processor; find some space on a Web server (a computer owned by your ISP or a third-party service); and, finally, "upload" the pages (move them from your computer to the server). For more detailed instructions, see p.209.

If that sounds like a bit too much work, there are various idiot-proof, off-the-shelf website options out there, including setting up a blog, or getting a page on a social network such as Facebook (see p.237).

What's a blog?

A blog is a frequently updated website arranged with the most recent "posts" (chunks of text, perhaps with photos) at the top of the front page. Tens of thousands of people have a personal blog, and major sites also feature a blog alongside their regular webpages. Blogs have been one of the biggest boom areas of the Internet in the last few years, and it only takes a few minutes to set up your own, even if you have zero technical skills. See p.230.

Can I make money out of the Internet?

There are many ways to try to make money via the Internet. Tens of thousands of people are full-time traders on the **eBay** auction site (see p.155). And, thanks to automatic ad systems such as Google's **AdSense**, it's very easy to try and make some money from putting ads on your own site – but you'll usually be paid according to the number of times visitors actually click on the ads, so the income will be feeble unless your site is enormously popular.

AdSense www.google.com/adsense

If you're an exhibitionist, you could try something a bit more off-the-wall. There have been many examples. One woman was successful with a (non-pornographic) site requesting that caring men around the world contribute to her breast-enlargement fund. And the man behind a website called SaveToby generated vast amounts of traffic (and money) by threatening to cook and eat his cute pet rabbit unless he received $50,000 in donations.

SaveToby www.savetoby.com

Where's the best place to get an email address?

You should get at least one **email address** thrown in by your ISP with your Internet access account (see p.108). The problem with addresses such as these is that they tie you to the ISP: if you switch to a different ISP, you'll probably lose your email account. For this reason and various others you'd be better off with a free email account from a stand-alone email provider, or even to register your own domain name. For more on choosing an email account, see p.107.

Is my email private?

In general, yes. But unless you go to the somewhat tedious effort of **encrypting your emails** (p.128), they could theoretically be read at various points. For example, whoever administers your mail account could quite easily open your messages without you ever knowing. So in effect your emails are like postcards, at the mercy of whoever is delivering them.

Tip: Once you have your genius moneyspinning website set up, there could be a whole bunch more notes to be made from merchandising – or even a spin-off book.

How can I find someone's email address?

The best way is to ask them. But many email addresses can be found on the Web (see p.131).

What if I want to cancel an email I've sent?

You can't. So you'd better think before you click "send". That said, if you use email at work you may well be able to cancel an email sent to a colleague, assuming you are both using the same mail server – your network administrator should be able to let you know whether it is possible.

Can I make phone calls via the Internet?

Yes. And you might save money, too. All you need is a broadband connection and some form of microphone and speakers (or a dedicated USB handset, as pictured). Then you can phone other computers for free, and regular telephones and mobiles around the world for a small per-minute charge. For more information, see p.133.

Can I make friends on the Internet?

It's easy to meet people with common interests on the Internet – for example through website discussion forums – and there are count-less sites and services dedicated specifically to friendship, dating and social networking (see p.237). Conversing openly with strangers while retaining a comfortable degree of anonymity often makes for startlingly intimate communication. However, translating online friendships or romance into the real world is another matter.

Will being on the Internet put me at risk?

Unless you go out of your way to invite trouble, the Internet should impose no added risk on your **personal safety**. However, the Internet **does expose your computer to all sorts of new risks**, such as viruses and attacks from so-called hackers – particularly if you're using a PC with Microsoft Windows. And there are plenty of scammers online that are keen to make you part with your money. To protect your computer and wallet against all these threats, turn to p.167.

What about my credit card number?

Your card details are generally safer when entered at a reputable online store than when you pass over your plastic in a shop. Even so, you could still theoretically be scammed, so read the advice on p.146.

What's spyware?

Spyware is, strictly speaking, software that keeps track of something you do on your computer (such as the websites you visit) and then sends this information to someone – all without you knowing about it. However, today the term "spyware" is often used more broadly to describe any program that has a hidden agenda – displaying pop-up ads, for example, or hijacking your modem and calling a premium-rate number in Honolulu. All this sounds extremely sinister, but don't be too scared. It's easy to stay spyware-free with the right tools and a bit of common sense (see p.173).

What's phishing?

Phishing is an online scam in which a fraudster persuades someone to volunteer private information – such as their online banking details. Most commonly this involves sending them to a webpage that seems to be part of a legitimate organization, such as a bank, but is actually a fake, set up with the sole intention of capturing private data. See p.175.

What if my children discover pornography?

There are loads of good, child-friendly sites on the Web. But you only need type **the merest hint of innuendo** into a search engine to

Bandwidth

Though it has a complex mathematical definition, the term **bandwidth** is most commonly used to refer to the speed of an Internet connection. Slow, old-fashioned dial-up – or "narrowband" – connections achieve a relatively low bandwidth, while faster ("broadband") connections achieve a higher bandwidth. Strictly speaking, a broadband connection doesn't actually download information any "faster". It can download more chunks of data – "bits" – simultaneously, but the speed of each bit is limited by the speed of light. Hence the term band*width* and the fact that Internet connection speeds are measured in bps (bits per second), not miles per hour.

come face-to-face with porn sites. Indeed, what once wasn't much more than schoolboys trading *Big & Busty* scans soon became one of the Internet's prime cash cows. Most perfectly normal kids will search on a swear word the first chance they get – after all, children are pretty childish. So it might not be long before they encounter a porno merchant, even if they're not already curious about sex.

What can you do about it? Well, you could try the **censoring tools** that are probably already at your disposal (see p.83), but they rarely work flawlessly and clued-up older children often work out how to circumvent them. For older kids, then, it's probably better to talk to them about the issue rather than trying to shield them.

You could also try spying on their online activities, by simply clicking on their browser's "History" button (see p.74). Should they be smart enough to cover their tracks, they're probably smart enough to know how to handle what they find.

What's downloading?

Technically speaking, whenever your computer receives information from another computer, you're "**downloading**" that information. Confusingly, however, people very often use the term to describe something more specific: the act of taking something from the Internet and saving it permanently to a computer.

To give an example, every time you view a webpage, the various components of that page – text, images, etc – are, strictly speaking, "downloaded" to your PC or Mac from a computer elsewhere on the Internet. But these pages are not stored permanently on your computer. By contrast, if you hear someone say that they've "downloaded some great images from the Internet", they probably mean that they've specifically saved them onto their computer's hard drive – not just viewed them on a webpage.

Many Internet access accounts come with a monthly "download limit", describing the maximum amount of data that you can receive each month without incurring any extra fees. Here, it's the technical meaning of "download" that matters: all the information you receive, including the text and images in webpages, constitutes "downloaded" data and contributes towards your monthly download quota.

What's an Intranet?

The mechanism that passes information between computers on the Internet can be used in exactly the same way over local networks such as those used in offices. When this isn't publicly accessible, it's called an **Intranet**. Many companies use Intranets to distribute internal documents – in effect publishing webpages for their own private use.

What are bits and bytes?

A **bit** is the smallest unit of data that computers recognize, representing either a "0" or a "1". And the Internet is all about lugging these bits from A to B. You might hear people talking about "56K" modems, for example, or an "eight megabit" (8Mb) broadband connection. What such numbers actually refer to is the number of bits being transferred each second, with K short for Kbps (1000 bits per second) and Mb short for Mbps (1,000,000 bits per second).

Inevitably, you'll also come across the confusingly similar term **byte** – this usually means eight bits, enough data to represent any number or letter. In general, data transfer speeds are measured in bits, while document sizes are measured in bytes. So a broadband setup might be two megabits, while an image taken with a digital camera might be two megabytes.

.com, .co.uk, .biz... what's that about?

Each domain name ends with a **top-level domain** such as .org, .com and .net. These are managed by ICANN (the Internet Corporation for Assigned Names and Numbers), which has introduced more

Domain codes

Common **domain types**
include the following:

ac Academic (UK)
com & co Company or
commercial organization
edu Educational institution (US)
gov Government
mil Military
net Internet gateway or
administrative host
org Nonprofit organization

And here are a few of the
more commonly encountered
country codes:

au Australia
ca Canada
de Germany
es Spain
fr France
jp Japan
nl Netherlands
no Norway
uk United Kingdom

top-level domains over the years. Each top-level domain has a specific meaning (see box) but their use isn't strict – you might come across a charity with a .com address or a company with a .net address. Very often an organization will register all the available versions of its domain and have them all forwarded to their website's front page.

In addition to a top level domain, every country has its own distinct two-letter country code. If an address doesn't specify a country code, it's more than likely in the US, but that's not a rule: there are numerous UK sites, for example, that use .com – either because they prefer it or because .co.uk has already been registered by someone else. Furthermore, some companies register a foreign domain to make their domain more memorable. For example, you might see online radio stations using .fm (actually the code for the Federated States of Micronesia) or TV companies using .tv – the island of Tuvalu.

Governments can charge foreigners a fee to use their country's domain code, and, during the Internet bubble of the 1990s, Tuvalu's whole economy was given a huge boost by this, with domain-name sales paying, amongst other things, for the country's first UN representative. For a complete list of country codes, see:

IANA www.iana.org/cctld/cctld-whois.htm

What are servers?

In Internet-speak, any computer that's open to external online access is known as a **server** or **host** (since they "host" files and "serve" them to other computers). A Web server is a computer where webpages are stored and made available for outside access – for example to your PC or Mac. And a mail server is a computer equivalent of a sorting office, distributing email between senders and recipients.

You access servers with programs known as **clients**, some common examples being Web browsers such as Internet Explorer and email programs such as Windows Mail. In general, you can simply replace the word client with "program".

What's a URL?

Roughly speaking, a URL (Uniform Resource Locator) is the same as a Web address. For more see p.67.

What's an IP address?

Every computer on the Internet, whether it's your home PC or a corporate Web server, has a unique numerical **IP (Internet Protocol) address**, which represents its official location. Each address comprises four numbers separated by dots, such as: 149.109.211.5

Some computers have a fixed ("static") IP address, but unless you have requested this from your ISP it's likely that your own computer will be assigned a different IP address each time you log on. This is called a "dynamic" or "server-allocated" address.

Since numbers are difficult for humans to remember, a network of computers called **Domain Name Servers** (DNS) translate the IP addresses into their corresponding domain names and vice versa. So you might type www.roughguides.com into your Web browser, but behind the scenes, a DNS server will translate this into something that looks more like 204.52.130.18 in order to kick-start the process that results in the relevant webpage appearing on your screen. This process is called a **DNS lookup,** and it applies to both Web content and to emails.

Tip: If you want to know your own IP address, visit: www.whatismyipaddress.com

How does an email get from A to B?

Suppose you're in Boston and you want to email someone in Bangkok. When you send your message, it goes to your local ISP. The **mail server** examines the message's address to determine where it has to go, and then passes it on to its appropriate neighbour, which will do the same. This usually entails routing it towards the **backbone** – the chain of high-speed links that carries the bulk of the Net's long-haul traffic. Each subsequent link will ensure that the message heads towards Bangkok rather than Bogotá or Brisbane. The whole process should take no more than a few seconds.

How does all the data know where to go?

For a surprisingly entertaining explanation of how networks, routers, switches and firewalls shunt data in the right direction, check out the movie at:

Warriors of the Net www.warriorsofthe.net

Getting online

Choosing a computer

What do you need?

It's possible to access the Net with almost any contraption you could call a computer, but expect some frustration with any machine more than a few years old. You probably won't be able to run much of the recent Internet software. And if you can't use your Web browser and mail program together without a lot of pauses and chugging noises coming from your hard drive, your teeth will be grinding pretty soon. So you might do better investing in something newer and faster.

Buying a new computer

Practically any new computer will be more than powerful enough for most Internet-related tasks, so don't **invest in the most powerful machine available** simply to get online. You pay disproportionately more for a top-of-the-range computer, and these days you're unlikely to actually use the extra firepower unless you get into gaming, video editing or some other processor-intensive activity. On the other hand, you may end up using the computer for more than you initially planned and kick yourself for having bought the cheapest thing you could find. A small hard drive, for example, is a pain if you want to get into downloading lots of music and video.

Minimum specs

You can squeeze online with an old **486 IBM-compatible PC** or **Macintosh 68030** series by sticking to old software, but it won't be much fun. Things don't get bearable until you hit the **Pentium II 200 MHz** or **Apple G3** mark, and they'll behave better with 64 megabytes of RAM or more. Ideally, though, you'll want something much faster.

As a rule of thumb, you'll probably get the best balance of bang per buck and longevity by picking a middle-range machine.

Mac vs PC?

One decision you'll have to make is whether to go for a **PC** or a **Mac**. PCs are made by many different companies and come in many shapes and sizes, but they usually run Microsoft's **Windows** operating system and hence all work in the same way. Macs, on the other hand, are a series of personal computers made by just one company – Apple – and they run a different operating system, **Mac OS X**. Macs only account for a few percent of the computers in the world, but they're picking up market share every day – partly thanks to their slick design (see the iMac model pictured left) and their association with the **iPod**, Apple's popular digital media player.

It was once the case that the Internet was more PC-friendly – a small proportion of websites didn't work on Macs, and most of the best Internet software was PC-only. But that's not really true any longer; in fact, the tables have turned. Not only do Macs come pre-loaded with a whole bunch of excellent Internet software, but they're far less prone to viruses and other **security threats** – see p.167 for more on this.

Macs are more expensive than PCs if measured in terms of pure processing power, but they score well above average in terms of manufacturing quality and reliability. For additional advice on Apple Macs, see *The Rough Guide to Macs & OS X*. Or for a list of the best technology websites, turn to p.262.

Laptops, netbooks & mobile phones

Almost anything you can do on a standard "desktop" computer, including all types of Internet activity, you can also do on **laptops** (aka **notebooks**). A laptop is more expensive than a desktop with equivalent firepower, but for the extra money you get a computer that you can take with you wherever you go. There are various ways to get online with a laptop when you're out and about – see p.57 to find out more.

When buying a portable computer of any kind, consider its wireless capabilities (see overleaf). And if you plan to travel a lot with a laptop, look for something small and light that comes with a healthy international **warranty**. If you don't mind a relatively small screen, a lightweight "netbook", such as those made by ASUS (pictured below) are a good bet, and will slip easily into a handbag or briefcase. Also consider **battery life**: many apparently good-value laptops can't be used for more than a couple of hours without being recharged.

Or, you could use a desktop computer at home and a PDA or smart phone (such as the increasingly popular Apple iPhone) that offers Internet connectivity when you're out and about (see p.62).

Games consoles and the Web

Several major gaming consoles can be connected to a home network and be used to surf the Web – via a regular TV screen. Nintendo's Wii (pictured) and Sony's PS3 feature built-in Web browsers, the former having hooked up with Opera (see p.70), the latter using its own homegrown software. The results are not flawless – some users have experienced problems with streaming content and certain sites – but it's perfectly functional for many tasks. For information about connecting to the Web with a mobile games console such as the PSP, turn to p.62.

Wireless: Wi-Fi & Bluetooth

When people talk about "wireless" internet, they're usually referring to Wi-Fi, or IEEE 802.11x as it's known in geekspeak. This technology allows computers and other devices to communicate using radio waves. The most common use is to spread an Internet connection across a home, office, hotel or café, allowing anyone with a Wi-Fi-enabled computer to get online. To get such a system up and running at home, all you need is a wireless router (see p.49) and one or more PCs or Macs with Wi-Fi installed.

Most new laptops and some desktops come with Wi-Fi built in. Otherwise it can be added via an inexpensive adapter: either a PC card for a laptop or an internal or external unit for a desktop (see box opposite). Wi-Fi is not as fast as a wired computer network but is more than fast enough to handle even the most blazing Internet connection.

Wi-Fi can also be used to share Internet connections, files and printers between multiple computers (see p.47). In fact, this is now the cheapest and easiest way to share a connection, and it allows you to surf the Web throughout your home – and even garden.

There are various flavours of Wi-Fi, but they all work seamlessly with each other (most of the time, at least). **IEEE 802.11b** was once the most ubiquitous but it was soon superceded by the faster **IEEE 802.11g**, which can send and receive data at 54Mbps instead of 11Mbps. If buying a computer, look out for compatibility with the next-generation standard – **802.11n** – which offers even faster speeds.

Another popular wireless technology is **Bluetooth**, which is slower and has a shorter range, but is very easy to use with multiple devices and is commonly built into mobile phones. In terms of its Internet potential, Bluetooth can be useful for connecting a laptop to a phone to get online when you're out and about (see p.60).

For the slickest wireless solution, look for a laptop with built-in access to a mobile-phone network such as 3G or GPRS (see p.60).

Adding Wi-Fi or a modem to your PC: internal, external or PCMCIA?

If you want to add a device to your computer – such as a Wi-Fi or bluetooth adapter, modem or network card – you'll generally be able to choose between three types of device: USB, PCI and PCMCIA.

▶ **USB** adapters are very simple to install – and to swap between machines. If your PC or Mac was made in the last few years, it should have at least two USB ports ready for use. Some USB devices need an external power supply, but the majority don't.

▶ **PCI** devices plug into a slot inside a desktop computer. This is a tidy and inexpensive option for desktop PCs as the device in question won't take up desk space or require an external power source. Installation is surprisingly easy, but you do have to open up your machine (or have a computer store do it).

▶ **PCMCIA** or **PC Card** adapters are credit-card-sized devices that slot into the side of a laptop and pop out easily to make way for something else. This is neater than a USB device though only an option if your laptop has the a PCMCIA slot. You can even get cards with cell phone network access built in so you can surf anywhere (see p.59).

Choosing a connection

Broadband, dial-up & ISPs

A computer is all well and good, but to get the thing online at home you'll also need an Internet connection. This means making a few decisions. First, what type of connection to go for – either broadband such as cable or ADSL, or old-fashioned dial-up. Second, which Internet Service Provider (ISP) to sign up with. Some ISPs are better value than others so it pays to shop around a little.

A quick word of warning before getting into the detail: don't use the email address that comes with your new ISP account. Free services such as Gmail (see p.110) are usually better and, importantly, they let you keep your address indefinitely – even if you switch ISP.

Broadband & dial-up: the basics

Up until a few years ago, most Internet users relied upon a **dial-up connection**. This set-up can be serviceable, if not exactly fun, for simple Web browsing, but frustratingly slow – or downright useless – for watching online video or downloading large files.

The modern alternative is **broadband**. This type of connection is not only much faster, it also frees up your telephone line and avoids you having to "dial-up" each time you want to get online. If you're still using an old-fashioned dial-up connection, then switching to broadband should be a priority. If you're new to the Internet, then don't even consider dial-up unless broadband is unavailable in your area. Let's look briefly at each of broadband's three main benefits.

Speed

This is the major difference between dial-up and broadband. Having a faster connection means that webpages load faster, **files download** more quickly, and **video and music** can be streamed with far fewer glitches. The speed is measured in bps (see below).

Data transfer speed

A "fast" Internet connection isn't strictly speaking any faster than a "slow" one; what it does have is greater **bandwidth**, meaning it can transfer more **bits** of data than a slower connection can shift each second. Hence when you're shopping around for an Internet connection, the speeds of the various broadband connections on offer are defined in terms of **bps** (bits per second). As with metres and other measurements, a "K" before the figure means "times a thousand" and an "M" means "times a million". So:

1Kbps = 1000bps
1Mbps = 1000Kbps = 1,000,000bps

It can take up to ten bits to transfer a single character of text (one "byte"), so a dial-up modem operating at 56Kbps would transfer roughly 5000 characters – around a page of text – each second. A broadband account operating at 2Mbps could download almost forty times as much in the same time. That might sound like more speed than you need, but that's because text doesn't take up many bits and bytes compared to images, sound and – most of all – video. Downloading a 10-minute video trailer, which might have a file size of as much as 50 megabytes, would take only minutes on the 2Mbps connection but hours on the 56Kbps. To measure the speed of your current Internet connection, try the sites on p.54.

plus.net

Dial-up connections are limited by the speed of the modem, the current standard being **56Kbps**. But just because you use a "56K" modem doesn't mean you'll actually get this speed: due to phone-line dynamics, something around 40Kbps is more likely to be what you get. This is acceptable enough for browsing webpages, but highly tedious when you try downloading big files or watching streaming video.

Broadband speeds vary according to the type of connection, the country you're in, and the specific package you choose. You might see packages from 150Kbps upwards advertised as broadband, but most deals offer speeds between 512Kbps and 24Mbps – that's around **10 to 500 times faster than dial-up**. With a 1Mbps connection (often written "1M" or "1 Meg") most webpages appear almost instantly, hi-fi music tracks download in a minute or two (or can even be played directly off the Internet), and it becomes realistic to download very big files – such as videos and large programs.

The high speed of broadband also makes it ideal for setting up either a wired or wireless **home network** and sharing the connection between more than one computer (see p.47). It is possible to do this with dial-up, too, but the speed will suffer when more than one person is using the connection simultaneously.

Freeing up your phoneline

When you're online with a dial-up connection, your phoneline is engaged – a major inconvenience if you're online a lot. You could have a second phoneline put in to avoid this, but you'll usually end up paying more on installation and line rental than you would for a broadband service that will not only be faster, but will also leave your phoneline free, so you can make and receive calls while online. One exception to this rule is one-way satellite broadband (see p.38), which clogs up your phoneline just like standard dial-up.

Always-on access

With a dial-up modem, each time you want to go online you'll need to spend around 30 seconds actually "dialling up". But broadband connections are typically "**always on**", so you only have to make one – almost immediate – connection when you switch on your PC, and then you'll be permanently online until you shut down. Note, though, that there are usually still caps on the total amount of data you can download each month (see box below).

Download limits: How big is a gig?

Many ISPs price their broadband Internet access (sometimes dial-up too) according to a monthly **download limit** or **download allowance**. This is the total amount of data – including webpages, emails, files, music, online radio, etc – that you can pull from the Net each month before either the service drops out or (more commonly) you're subject to an extra payment. Download limits are usually measured in **gigabytes**, aka gigs or **GBs**. One GB is roughly the same as 1000 megabytes (MB).

If the connection will be used by just one computer, mainly for regular Web-surfing and emails but not much else, then you're very unlikely to exceed even a 1GB download limit. However, the moment you start getting into downloading music or videos, streaming online radio and making video phone calls, a 1GB limit can be used up very quickly – especially if you're sharing the connection between more than one computer. After all, a single full-length video or large software suite can be the best part of a gigabyte, and a typical MP3 track is 5MB – so downloading 100 songs will "cost" you half a gigabyte.

PlusNet, a broadband ISP in the UK, provides potential customers with the following table to give a sense of how various different download allowances might break down. Obviously, this is only a very rough guide, and you're free to split your usage however you like, but it should give you an idea of what's possible.

Monthly download limit	1GB	3GB	5GB
Hours of surfing	4 per day	12 per day	20 per day
Email received	100 per week	300 per week	500 per week
Email with attachments	15 per week	45 per week	75 per week
Songs or video clips	10 per week	30 per week	50 per week
Hours of online radio	2 per week	6 per week	10 per week

Connection costs

In the UK, the US and Australia, unlimited broadband access (if you can get it) usually costs only slightly more than unlimited dial-up. However the exact cost varies widely according to where you are and the details of your tariff…

Broadband tariffs

Broadband is usually priced according speed and download limit. For unlimited – or practically unlimited – medium-speed broadband, expect to pay around $20 per month in the US, £14 in the UK and $30 in Australia. From there, prices go up for extra-fast connections and down as the download limit or speed decreases.

Note that in some countries you may be able to get a free broadband account if you sign up for certain mobile phone tariffs. In the UK, for instance, Orange and Carphone Warehouse both offer deals of this kind, and they work out as excellent value.

Installation fees

When signing up for broadband, you may have to pay a one-off set-up fee – either to "activate" your phoneline for ADSL or to fund a suitable modem or router. However, it's increasingly common for such things to be thrown in for free (except in the case of satellite Internet access, which requires the installation of a dish), and you can usually use your own router or modem if you already have a suitable model from a previous ISP account.

Dial-up tariffs

An all-you-can-eat **dial-up account** that allows you to stay online for as long as you like commonly goes for around $15–20 per month in the US. As local calls are usually free, that's all you should have to pay.

The **UK** is a more bewildering market as local phone calls are still often timed and charged. For those who spend less than a couple of

Tip: If you're paying by the minute for access, see whether your phone provider lets you put your Internet access as a special-rate number ("Friends and Family" in the UK). Also ask about the possibility of capped monthly charges to certain numbers.

hours per week online, the best-value option is a "pay-as-you-go" tariff, with which you pay for each minute that you spend online via your phone bill at a local call rate (the ISP takes a cut of these charges). Heavier users, though, should opt for a flat-rate plan. For unlimited access, expect to pay around £13 per month or £10 for evenings and weekends only.

Australian ISPs tend to offer an assortment of plans, mostly with some kind of limit on either time or the amount you can download. Expect to pay around $10–30 per month depending on your usage, or between $1 and $2 per hour.

Types of broadband

The term **broadband** describes any high-bandwidth ("fast") connection. The most common types are DSL and cable, though there are also other options, such as satellite and ISDN. Let's take a look at each in turn.

DSL (ADSL)

DSL has taken the Internet world by storm during the last five years, generally in its most common form – **ADSL**, which stands for Asymmetric Digital Subscriber Line. The "asymmetric" describes the fact that the speed at which you can download (receive) information is much higher than the speed you can upload (send). The "digital", however, is a misnomer, since technically speaking DSL is an analogue connection just like regular dial-up – but much faster.

One beauty of ADSL is that it works through standard phonelines but allows you to be online and use the phone at the same time. It achieves this by "splitting" the line (see box on p.37) into separate frequency bands for phone and Internet. For a more detailed explanation, see: www.howstuffworks.com/dsl.htm

The first question with ADSL is whether you can actually get it. The technology only works in homes within a few kilometres of a physical telephone exchange – and the exchange has to be upgrad-

Dial-up modems

Most computers produced in the last decade have a dial-up modem built in, though some manufacturers (including Apple) have dropped them on the grounds that dial-up is yesterday's technology. If you need to use dial-up but don't have a modem, you could buy an inexpensive USB model.

Tip: Bear in mind that with ADSL you will still need to rent a regular telephone line, even if you don't use it for calls. Some telcos are now offering cheap, if not free, broadband with certain line-rental packages, which can work out much cheaper than renting a phoneline from one firm and an ADSL service from another.

Future DSL flavours

The 24Mb ADSL connections now on offer in some areas of the UK are thanks to exchanges fitted with **ADSL2+** technology. More and more of these are appearing thanks to a process called **local loop unbundling**, in which supply of broadband is more fully opened up to market forces (the individual "loops" to people's houses are "unbundled" from a single telco's control). Another up-and-coming DSL flavour is **VDSL2** (Very-high-bit-rate Digital Subscriber Line 2), which leaves the telephone exchange at a staggering speed of 250Mb, but quickly deteriorates to 100Mb after travelling around half a kilometre and 50Mb after one kilometre.

ed to support the service. This rules out some rural addresses. In the UK, ADSL is available to the vast majority of homes, but that's not true in the US and Australia. (If you're close enough to an exchange but it simply hasn't been upgraded, gang together with a few neighbours and petition your telco to get their act in gear.) Most ISPs offer ADSL and will be able to tell you instantly whether it's available to your home – for a list of ISP Web addresses, see p.43. Alternatively, ask your phone company.

If you can get ADSL, the **speed** on offer depends on the technology within your exchange. As of early 2009, the standard ADSL speed in most areas of the UK is rising from 1–2Mb to 8Mb, with 24Mb available to a small number of homes. In the US and Australia, speeds aren't yet that fast, with 1–3Mb being more typical. In all these countries, so-called "broadband" ADSL as slow as 150Kbps is also on offer.

Be aware that you won't necessarily get the advertised speed – things get slower the further you get from the exchange, and even over short distances poor line quality and other interference can reduce speed. So don't be surprised if, say, an 8Mb connection turns out closer to 6Mb in reality.

Cable

If you can get cable TV, chances are you can get cable Internet too. Cable offers speeds of up to around 20Mb, though, as with ADSL, it's often offered some way below its full potential and priced according to the speed. While DSL is offered by scores of ISPs, cable is only offered by the cable providers, so it's them that you need to contact about availability and prices. In the UK, that would be:

Virgin Media www.virgin.com/broadband

In Australia, it's:

Optus www.optus.com.au/broadband
Telstra www.telstra.com

In the US it depends where in the country you are, so try your local cable provider. This site will lead you to them:

Cable Modem Directory cable.theispguide.com

ADSL or cable – which one to go for?

Until you've tried both in your own home it's hard to tell whether your local ADSL or cable services will be better. For a connection of the same advertised speed, ADSL should theoretically be superior because you get your own dedicated line; with cable, you share bandwidth with neighbours, so if everyone on your street is downloading MP3s at once, you can expect the connection to slow down. On the other hand, ADSL degrades as you move further from the exchange. If you live more than 3.5km (2.2 miles) away, you may find yourself disadvantaged – if you can get it at all, that is.

In reality, the differences are likely to be very small, so it's usually best to choose whichever service offers you the best value. If you already have cable TV, for example, you might find cable Internet cheaper, whereas if you can get ADSL bundled in with your phone-line or mobile, then that might work out best.

Fibre-optic broadband

The fastest broadband around today comes through fibre-optic cables made of super-fine strands of glass which transmit pulses of light. Such cables can operate at up to 100Mbps. Though many countries have now upgraded their national communication "backbones" to fibre-optic, few have as yet tackled the mammoth task of replacing the end-user phonelines to allow a "Fibre to the Home" (FTTH) service. That said, in some Far East countries super-fast fibre-optic broadband is already the norm and there have been very successful fibre-optic upgrades carried out in parts of Paris. In the UK, fibre-optic is currently widely available with cable rather than ADSL connections, with Virgin expecting to offer a 50Mb fibre-optic service to 13 million homes in 2009.

Line splitters

In addition to a modem, an ADSL connection requires that you fit small devices called micro-filters (aka line-splitters) to all the telephone sockets in your home. As their name suggests, they split the data travelling through the phoneline to stop the ADSL signal from interfering with the regular telephone signal. ISPs often provide a couple of micro-filters to their customers for free. If you need more, they are inexpensive to buy. An even neater option is to replace your existing home phone sockets with models that have built-in micro-filters (pictured).

Choosing a connection

Other broadband options

The catch with DSL and cable is that you need the right wire coming into your house. In many rural areas neither is available, in which case you have various other choices.

Satellite

No matter where you live, you can probably get satellite Internet access. There are two types of satellite access systems: a **one-way system** means you receive information direct from a satellite, but you send information (including the "requests" for webpages and files generated when you click Web links) via a dial-up ISP. In a **two-way system** you send information back up to the satellite.

Download speeds are sometimes capped at 512Kbps or less, though 1–2Mb is now quite common. Upload speeds are limited to standard dial-up 33Kbps in a one-way system, but can be up to 256Kbps in a two-way system. While that's fast, satellite suffers from fairly savage **latency** (time delay), so "real-time" data-heavy tasks such as online gaming and video phone calls can be problematic or impossible.

Prices have traditionally been high, but they've dropped swiftly in the last few years and some providers are now offering prices comparable to DSL or cable. However, remember to add the price of dial-up access when looking at one-way systems, and the start-up cost of buying or renting a dish and modem.

ISDN

ISDN splits a standard phone line into three channels (1x16Kbps and 2x64Kbps) that can be used and billed in various ways. It's nowhere near as fast as DSL or cable – British Telecom once dubbed their home service "**midband**" – and it's not as good value for money. That said, costs vary widely, depending on where you live and how the call charges are calculated, so it may be worth exploring if you can't get ADSL or cable.

Satellite providers

For services in the UK and Australia respectively, scan the lists at:

ISP Review www.ispreview.co.uk/broadband/sat.shtml
Broadband Choice www.broadbandchoice.com.au

In the US, the major providers include StarBand and WildBlue:

StarBand www.starband.com
WildBlue www.wildblue.com

For more suppliers, visit directory.google.com and search for "satellite internet".

38

Thanks to almost-instantaneous connection, you'll often only be charged while you're actually transferring data, and you may be able to use the phone while online (with the Internet dropping to one channel when you pick up the phone). For more info, try some major ISPs in your area, such as those listed on p.43.

Powerline Internet

Another possible framework for delivering high-speed computer networks is the powerline system. Your modem literally plugs into a power plug and recognizes Internet-specific frequency patterns. This hasn't really taken off as yet, but pilot schemes in Scotland and Virginia (www.forcvec.com/bplcoop) have been successful.

High-speed wireless access

There's little doubt that the future of broadband is **wireless**, the idea being that you just turn on your laptop – at home or anywhere else – and find yourself connected to a super-fast network. Some town and city centres are already flooded with Wi-Fi access, though in general the access fees are higher than for a private ADSL or cable account. That will change over time, however, and if you're lucky enough to be within range of a **community Wi-Fi connection** (see box), you may not have to pay anything at all.

Another wireless-broadband option is to equip your laptop with a 3G or GPRS broadband card (see p.59), which will get you decent-enough broadband wherever you can get a mobile phone signal. Some recent laptops even have such cards built-in. Again, however, the access fees for these services – usually paid via your mobile phone bill – are relatively high for day-to-day use.

Community connections

It's still a fringe interest, but community connections are gaining ground every year. The idea is simple: sharing one broadband Internet connection wirelessly between a number of houses, or even a whole town. Often they're free, with a hobbyist or two happy to supply their neighbours via their own connection. Other schemes are cooperatively run, with members chipping in a share of the connection cost and aerial, and sharing the bandwidth. There are now whole small towns that are flooded with free Wi-Fi access. To find out about wireless networks in your area, check out Wireless Anarchy or FreeNetworks. Or to find smaller-scale community Wi-Fi hotspots, see p.58.

WirelessAnarchy
www.wirelessanarchy.com
FreeNetworks
www.freenetworks.org

Dongles at home

Another option for satisfying your domestic Internet requirements is a "mobile Internet" contract from one of the major cell networks. The service is supplied over the airwaves via 3G or GPRS (see p.60), which means you need neither a telephone landline or cable service, and you can take your connection with you when you leave your home, and use it with a laptop anywhere. Such accounts come with a USB "dongle" modem, which can either be plugged straight into your PC, or into a special Wi-Fi router if you need to share the connection between several machines (pictured below). To find out more, turn to p.60.

Doubling-up dial-up

If you're really stuck for other options, you could try using two or more phonelines simultaneously, each with its own modem. This should give you a bandwidth equal to the sum of the individual connections, and it may even work out cheaper than ISDN. The hardest part is finding an ISP that supports Multilink.

Choosing an ISP

Whatever type of Internet access you choose, you'll need an account with an **ISP** (**Internet Service Provider**). When you connect to the Net, you really connect your computer to their computer, which in turn is connected to another computer, which in turn… That's how the Internet works.

The industry has matured steadily over the last decade to the point where most established ISPs deliver reasonable performance and service. However, all providers aren't equal, and it's difficult to tell good from bad until you've used them over time. Poor access will jade your online experience, so if you're not happy with the service you're getting, consider trying another.

Shopping around

When choosing an ISP, you want a reliable, fast connection and good customer support in case of problems. We've listed a few of the most popular providers on p.43, but it's definitely worth doing your own research.

The best approach is to **ask around**. If someone you know swears by an ISP, and they know what they're talking about, give it a go. Of course, there's also lots of information available online, at sites such as:

ADSL Guide www.adslguide.org.uk (UK)
Broadband.co.uk www.broadband.co.uk (UK)
ISP Guide www.theispguide.com (US)

ISP Review www.ispreview.co.uk (UK)
The List www.thelist.com (US)
Net4Nowt www.net4nowt.com (UK)
Whirlpool www.whirlpool.net.au (Aus)

What to ask (or at least think about)

Before signing up with any ISP, ask – or at least ponder – the following questions. Some will not apply to you, but it's worth scanning the lot just to make sure. Then get online (at a friend's home or Internet café if necessary) and compare what's on offer. The major providers listed on p.43 are a good place to start.

▶ **Do you have to pay via your phone bill** for your time online? If so, factor that in – and make sure only local call rates apply.

▶ **Is there a download limit?** If so, how much is it? And how much extra will you be charged if you download more?

▶ **Are there any other restrictions?** A few bargain DSL providers ban file-sharing networks (see p.202), for instance.

▶ **Do they throw in a free modem and/or router?** If not, how much will they charge? Can you use your own hardware?

▶ **Is there a minimum subscription period?** Some ISPs, especially budget broadband providers, require you to sign up for a minimum period – usually a year. This is standard if you receive a free modem or router when you sign up.

▶ **Can you change plan?** How much will it cost if you want to upgrade your speed or increase your download limit?

▶ **Is there a startup, installation or activation fee?** If so, how much? And, perhaps more importantly, will they charge a cancellation fee or apply any other penalties if you ever decide to leave?

Free trials

Some ISPs offer free trials, enabling a certain number of gratis days or hours with an ISP. If you take up one of these offers, avoid using the email account provided, as the moment people have your address you'll feel under pressure to stick with the ISP. And when the trial ends, if you're not absolutely delighted, be sure to cancel your account, or you might be billed. In the case of AOL trials, completely uninstall their software (see p.183) if you choose not to sign up – it has a history of causing problems.

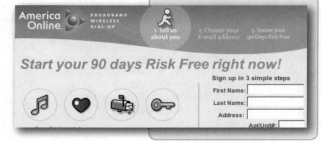

Choosing a connection

▶ **Does the package include any Internet phone calls?** How much will it cost and are there any free minutes included? See p.137 for more information.

▶ **What are the hours for phone support and how much does it cost?** Free phone support until the mid-evening is standard except in the UK, where rates range from national to premium.

▶ **Is there a backup number?** Cable and ADSL connections occasionally just drop out – for a minute, an hour or even a day. When this happens, you'll appreciate a backup dial-up number so you can connect via a standard modem until the problem is fixed. A dial-up number can also sometimes be useful for connecting away from home.

▶ **How much Web space is included?** Most ISPs include some megabytes of server storage so you can publish your own website or store files online. Check whether the ISP will put pop-up ads or banners on your site, and if they'll charge you for going over your space limit. Don't make this a decider, though, as you can always sign up with a free Web-space provider later (see p.221).

AOL

AOL (short for **America Online**, though the company is active internationally) has been around since the 1980s, but only in 1996 did it start offering access to the whole of the Internet. Before then, it specialized – like other so-called "online services" – in providing access to its own in-house content, chatrooms and other services.

Today, AOL is more similar to other ISPs, but certain things still set it apart, the most obvious being that it encourages you to use its own special access software ("AOL") instead of a standard Web browser and email program. This software is generally very much dumbed-down for the new user – and though you might

find this an appealing prospect initially, it will probably soon become a shackle that will hinder your progress online. Also be warned that an AOL email address is considered deeply uncool by most Net-savvy people.

AOL's popularity was in large part down to a huge marketing budget that pays for tie-ins with high-street retailers and the distribution of millions of free-trial CDs, usually offering "1000 free hours" or some such deal. These CDs have annoyed many people to the point that one campaign seeks to collect 1,000,000 of them and dump them on AOL's HQ.

AOL www.aol.com
No More AOL CDs www.nomoreaolcds.com

▶ **Do you get a static IP address?** Whenever you're connected to the Internet, your computer has a numerical IP address (see p.21). Most ISPs allocate IP addresses "dynamically", meaning that you'll get a different one each time you connect to the Net. However, you may be offered a "static" IP address – either as part of a connection package or for an extra fee. In general, this will only be useful if you want to host a website (see p.224), connect to your office via a "virtual private network" (ask your administrator if it's an option) or for certain types of Internet gaming.

▶ **Do they run a games server?** This will decrease the lag time that can slow down online gaming.

Some major ISPs

The list below contains some of the major ISPs in Britain, North America, Australia and New Zealand. It's by no means complete and **inclusion shouldn't be taken as endorsement**. But if you compare what these providers offer, you should get a reasonable idea of what's available.

UK

BT www.bt.com/broadband
Demon www.demon.net
Orange www.orange.co.uk
Pipex www.pipex.net
PlusNet www.plus.net
TalkTalk www.talktalk.co.uk
Tiscali www.tiscali.co.uk
Virgin www.virgin.net

North America

AT&T www.att.net
Comcast www.comcast.com
EarthLink www.earthlink.com
Golden (Can) www.golden.net

Inter.net (US/Can) www.inter.net
Qwest www.qwest.com
Road Runner www.rr.com
Verizon www.verizon.com

Australia and New Zealand

Big Pond www.bigpond.com
Clear Net (NZ) www.clear.net.nz
Dodo www.dodo.com.au
Internode www.internode.on.net
Netspace www.netspace.net.au
Optus Internet www.optus.com.au
iiNet www.ozemail.com.au

Switching ISPs

If you plan to switch ISPs, remember that you may need to give a month's notice to your current provider – which can be two months in practice, since you usually pay at the start of the month. As with gas and electricity companies, switching ISPs can be something of a headache, though in the UK changing ADSL providers has become less painful thanks to a process in which each switching customer gets a Migration Authorization Code (MAC). This number has nothing to do with Apple Macs, nor MAC addresses (the "Media Access Control" numbers that allow computers to find each other on a network). It's just a code that helps ISPs provide an uninterrupted service when you switch from one account to another.

Get connected

Once you've chosen an ISP, you can either sign up online (perhaps using the free referral service built into Windows), get a CD from the ISP, or set it up manually. Read on to find out more…

Setting up

Making the connection

Once you've signed up for an account with an ISP, you're nearly ready to connect. However, there may still be some delays. If you're getting a router or modem from the ISP, it might take a few days to arrive. Also, you might need to wait for your telephone line to be "activated" (for ADSL broadband) or for a cable engineer to visit your home (if you're having a cable connection installed for the first time).

Once everything is in place, getting the connection to actually work will hopefully be as simple as following a few simple instructions for the ISP. However, it's worth reading through this section in case you do run into problems, and also to avoid such common pitfalls as installing software that isn't needed and, in the case of a wireless set-up, leaving yourself open to security threats.

The following sections look at broadband and dial-up set-ups respectively. We cover routers within the broadband section. Note, however, that it is possible to use a router with a dial-up account.

Broadband set-ups

The set-up process for broadband depends on whether you're dealing with an ADSL or cable connection and also on the kind of hardware you're installing – just a modem, a modem and a router, or wireless modem-router.

Setting up with a broadband modem only

With a modem-only broadband set-up, things should be relatively simple, though it pays to read the instructions that came with your modem carefully. For example, people installing USB ADSL modems (popular in the UK) often get confused after failing to observe the instruction to install the software that came with the modem *before* physically attaching the device to the computer. (If you fall into this trap, you'll have to detach the modem, uninstall the software and start again.) Once you have the modem attached, you'll probably need to enter the configuration details provided by your ISP. If you run into problems installing a broadband modem, check the following:

▶ **Are your micro-filters installed and working?** Micro-filters (aka line-splitters) are the devices that filter the data coming through a phoneline set-up for ADSL so that the broadband data ends up in your modem and telephone data ends up in your ear. They are generally supplied with ADSL modems, though some modern phone-socket boxes have them built in (see p.36). They need to be fitted to every socket used for either a telephone, Internet or both. You don't need filters if you're setting up cable Internet.

▶ **Are your authentication details correct?** Check that you're entering the correct username and password. You might have been given a different username for your connection account and your email account. If they're right, but you receive an "authentication error" message when you try to connect, then the problem is most likely with your ISP and you will need to get in touch with them.

▶ **Is your modem working?** Disconnect your modem and leave it unplugged for a minute or so, then plug it back in and reboot both the modem and the computer. Find the manual that came with your modem and try to make sense of the little indicator lights. To be absolutely sure the problem is not related to your modem, try another one – or get a friend to try yours.

▶ **Is your virus software happy?** Your computer's virus software (often bundled with new PCs) might throw up a stream of warnings and prevent you from getting online when you try to set up a new Internet connection. If this happens, disable or uninstall (see p.183) the software, get your connection up-and-running, and then reinstall your virus software, being sure to download all updates from the manufacturer's website. For more on virus software, see p.173.

Still no luck? Call your ISP or get online with a dial-up modem and search for advice on the Web. See p.262 for a list of good techie sites.

Setting up with a wireless router

Wireless routers are now extremely common and many ISPs will include one with each new account. In the UK, the typical arrangement is that the ISP sends you a wireless router with all your log-in and password details pre-loaded. This way, you just plug the router into a power source and choose the relevant Wi-Fi network when your computer detects it. To do this on a Mac use the fan icon (at the top-right, by the clock). On a PC, if the list of available wireless networks doesn't pop up automatically, choose Connect To in the Start menu and select the wireless option. Finally, if required, enter the password printed on a label on the bottom of the router.

Buying and setting up your own wireless router

If your ISP didn't provide a wireless router, or you want to add one to your existing broadband set-up, then you'll need to purchase and set it up yourself.

Wireless routers typically cost around $75/£50. When purchasing, you first need to decide whether you need a router with a modem built in: if you already have a broadband modem that has an **Ethernet socket** on it, then a standard router should be fine. If not – if you have an ADSL modem with only a USB connection, for instance – then your best bet is to replace it with a router with a built-in ADSL modem.

Other things to consider are the number of Ethernet sockets and the range and speed of the wireless functions. All wireless routers will be fast enough to get the most out of your Internet connection, but the latest, faster versions (such as 802.11n) can speed up file-sharing between computers (but only if the computers also have 802.11n).

The most established router manufacturers are Netgear, Linksys, Belkin and D-Link.

Routers: the basics

A router, or hub, is a device that distributes an Internet connection between various computers. The router connects to the Internet via a modem (which may be a separate device or combined in the same unit) and each computer connects to the router, either via cables or, in the case of a wireless router, via a radio-wave technology known as Wi-Fi.

The traditional way to connect computers and routers is with **Ethernet cables.** These are very secure and reliable but can be inconvenient (and expensive) when the computers on the network are located in different rooms.

Wi-Fi, by comparison, lets you connect throughout the home and garden. It's not quite as fast or secure as Ethernet, but you'll only notice the speed difference if you're moving large files between the various computers on the network, and security shouldn't be an issue if you follow the advice in this chapter.

It's perfectly possible to combine Wi-Fi and wires on the same network. Most routers offer Ethernet ports as well as a Wi-Fi signal. As for computers, most recent models have Ethernet and Wi-Fi built right in. For machines that lack one or both, inexpensive adapters are available in USB, PCI or PCMCIA formats (see p.34).

Setting up

Setting up a router can be painless but it can also throw up problems, so don't get too dispirited if you're struggling to set yours up. First, if you have a separate modem, then make sure it's working by connecting it directly to a computer, missing out the router. Next, you'll need to plug in the router (to both a power source and the cable that will feed it the Internet) and access its configuration section. This is usually done by "connecting" your computer (either with an Ethernet cable or wirelessly), opening a Web browser window and entering the admin IP address listed in the router's instruction manual – just as if it were a website address. You'll then be able to log-in to the router and access all the settings. Once you've got the connection working, be sure to think about security, as described below. For more on routers and networking, see:

How Stuff Works www.howstuffworks.com/home-network.htm
Practically Networked www.practicallynetworked.com

Using your computer as a wireless router

Though most people use a router to provide their wireless Internet, it is possible to get by without one. All you need to do is set up a peer-to-peer network. In this arrangement, one computer connects to the Internet and shares the signal with other computers in the home. The computer that's connecting directly to the Internet is effectively acting as a router.

For instance, you might have one computer connected to the Internet via a cable or DSL modem distributing that signal to other computers via Wi-Fi. Conversely, you might have one computer connected to the Internet via a wireless signal distributing the connection to another computer via a network cable. Note that you do have to use two separate channels – a computer

can't receive and share a signal just using Wi-Fi or just using Ethernet.

This kind of set-up works perfectly well. The only disadvantage is that the computer which connects directly to the Internet has to be switched on in order for the others to get online.

Setting up a peer-to-peer network is relatively simple. In Windows, open the Network Setup Wizard from the Communications folder (under Start > More Programs > Accessories) and follow the prompts. If it doesn't work straight off, run the wizard on the other machine, too. In Mac OS X, open System Preferences and select Sharing, then Internet.

Wi-Fi and security

Because Wi-Fi can work through walls, your network won't stop at your front door. This is great news for surfing in the garden, say, or sharing an Internet connection between various apartments in a building. However, if the router has no security features enabled, anyone within a few hundred feet could connect to your network. They could then potentially download large files, slowing down your connection and using up your allocated monthly bandwidth; download illegal material or carry out illegal acts that would be traceable to your ISP account; spy on your Internet activity; and possibly even access personal data on your computers.

There are two main ways to secure a wireless network. You can use one or both of these techniques.

Add a password

Some routers come with a password already set up, but in other cases you'll have to log-in to the set-up section of your router and configure it yourself. This usually involves opening a Web browser window, entering the admin IP listed in the router's operating instructions, and looking for the relevant settings. You may find a few different types of password protection on offer:

▶ **WEP** (Wired Equivalent Privacy) is offered by all routers but isn't very secure. Anyone technically minded can find and run software capable of cracking the password.

▶ **WPA & WPA2** (Wi-Fi Protected Access) are newer standards that are both incomparably more secure than WEP, so always choose one of these options when available.

Access lists

A WPA password is enough for most people, but for maximum security you may also want to tell your router to refuse Internet access to all computers other than those you have specifically approved. You give your router an **access list** containing a ten-digit

<div class="sidebar">

How to find your MAC address

▶ **In Windows Vista** Click in the Start Search box and enter cmd. In the window that appears type ipconfig /all and press Enter.

▶ **In Windows XP**, click Start, then Run, type ipconfig /all followed and press Enter.

▶ **On a Mac** Open About This Mac from the Apple menu and click on Network. Click AirPort or Ethernet and the MAC address is listed below under Ethernet Address.

</div>

identity code – a so-called **MAC address** – for each approved computer. It then bars access to all other computers. Note that if you use an access list *without* a WPA password, you won't be protected from people potentially spying on your Internet use.

To set things up, look for an Access List or MAC Filtering option in your router's configuration settings and enter the address of each computer. See the box (left) to find out how to get the addresses.

Setting up dial-up

Setting up a dial-up connection usually just means receiving a few account details from your ISP and plugging them into your computer. It's preferable to do this manually rather than to install special software from the ISP. Such software, whether a download or on CD, is generally unnecessary and might do annoying things such as set your ISP's website as your browser homepage.

Plugging in the details

The minimum account details you need to get a dial-up connection working is a **username**, a **password** and an **access phone number**. However, some ISPs will also provide you with an IP address, two domain name server (DNS) addresses and a proxy server address (see p.53). They may also provide email account details, but this can be set up separately (see p.108).

Once you're armed with the necessary details, you're ready to enter them into your computer:

▶ **On a PC** In Windows Vista or XP, you need to open the "Connect to the Internet" option and choose "Set up my connection manually". You'll find this option via Start > Control Panel > Network and Internet > Network and Sharing Center > Set up a connection or network (on Vista) or in "Network Connections" > "Create a new connection" (XP). Once you've plugged in the details and pressed OK, an icon will appear from your new connection in your Network Connections panel and/or on your Desktop.

Adding extra ISP accounts

In Windows, you can add as many ISP accounts as you wish. However, if you want one to be your main (default) account, you'll need to specify in Internet Options, which you'll find under the Tools menu in Internet Explorer. In Mac OS X, you can add a "new configuration" using the Internet Connect application.

▶ **On a Mac** Open System Preferences, select Network and choose the Internal Modem from the "Show" menu. Alternatively, open Internet Connect from the Application menu.

You can edit the details at any time by right-clicking the connection's icon and selecting Properties (in Windows) or by returning to the Network panel in System Preferences (on a Mac).

Connecting and disconnecting

On a PC, you can connect to your new dial-up account by clicking "**Connect To**" in the Start menu and choosing the connection you just set up. To finish your dial-up session, right-click on the twin computers icon in the Windows System tray (by the clock) and choose "**disconnect**". Alternatively, double-click the connection's icon and then choose the "disconnect" button.

On a Mac, you'll find connect and disconnect options next to the little phone icon at the top of the screen (next to the clock).

Troubleshooting dial-up connections

If you **didn't succeed in connecting to your provider**, there's probably something wrong with your Dial-up Networking or modem configuration. The most common errors are:

▶ **No modem detected** Is your modem installed properly? To diagnose a modem in Windows, click on the "Modem" icon in the Control Panel. Alternatively, check your modem is working by setting up a new dial-up connection with the phone number of a friend or your own cell phone. If the target phone rings, you'll know your modem is functioning.

▶ **Dial tone not detected** Is your computer correctly connected to your phoneline? Do you have a voicemail service that interrupts the dial tone to let you know there are new messages waiting (which can confuse your modem)? If neither of these is the problem, try disabling "Dial Tone Detect" or "Wait for Dial Tone" under the modem settings in the Windows Control Panel.

Tip: If you find your PC trying to connect at inopportune moments – such as when you're reading your mail offline – go to the Connections tab in Internet Options (in Explorer's tools menu) and choose "Never dial a connection".

Finding the settings

To access all the connection settings for an ISP account in Windows, open Network Connections on the Start menu (or "Dial-up Networking" in My Computer in older Windows versions), right-click on the troublesome connection and choose "Properties". In Mac OS X, everything's under "Network" in System Preferences; in earlier Mac systems, look under Remote Access, TCP/IP and Modem in Control Panels.

```
 ▱▱  Dial-Up Networking was unable to complete the connection.

 Error: 680
 ┌─────────────────────────────────────────────┐▲
 │There is no dialtone.                          │
 │Make sure your modem is connected to the phone line properly.│
 │                                               │▼
 └─────────────────────────────────────────────┘
```

▶ **No answer** Check you're using the right phone number.

▶ **Busy/engaged** Access providers' lines occasionally fill up at peak hours. Keep trying until you get in. If this happens often, complain, or move ISPs.

▶ **You got through but were refused entry** Check your username and password.

▶ **You can't access a specific website** See p.85 for more help.

▶ **You're online but can't access any websites** Disconnect and check that you haven't mis-entered the DNS or proxy settings that your ISP may have provided.

Proxy settings

Many ISPs run a server that "caches" (copies) popular websites. If you specify this machine's address as your proxy server, it might make browsing faster as you'll be downloading from somewhere relatively close to you (though its real purpose is to reduce traffic across your ISP's links to the Net).

Because you're downloading a copy of the site, it might not be the latest version, but hitting Refresh should bring down the page from the source. If you have a proxy server specified, you'll find its address

under the Connection tab in Internet Options (in Internet Explorer's Tools menu). On Mac OS X, look under Proxies in Network (within System Preferences).

Proxies often get in the way more than they help, so if you have a choice, experiment with and without it: make a note of the address, then remove it, and see how your connection improves or worsens. Depending on your ISP's policy, however, you might find that you won't be able to browse at all without the proxy address specified.

Speed issues

If things are painfully slow when you're trying to access a specific website, then it could be a problem with that site as opposed to your connection. So first of all, try a few other sites. If they all seem slow, you might want to test your connection speed, using a free online tool such as:

Bandwidth Place www.bandwidthplace.com/speedtest
Think Broadband thinkbroadband.com/speedtest.html

When interpreting the results, don't be surprised if your connection is up to around a third slower than you'd expect (eg 35Kbps with a standard "56k" dial-up connection). This isn't very unusual and is likely to be to do with your specific phoneline. But it's also possible that there's a problem with your ISP, especially if it tends to be slower at peak times such as early evening – or if you've ever previously achieved a faster connection via the same phoneline. Ask your ISP for advice, and if they can't help, consider trialling another provider.

If you'd really like to know what's slowing things down, you'll need to turn to some network diagnostic tools. The staples are **Ping**, which works like a radar to measure how long it takes a data packet to reach a server and return; and **TraceRoute**, which pings each router along the path to see which one's causing the holdup. You can use these in Windows XP by clicking Run on the Start menu and typing, for example, ping www. roughguides.com or traceroute www.roughguides.com. In Mac OS X, open the neat little Network Utility tool from Utilities, within Applications – this also features a WhoIs tool (for looking up domain ownership) and other tools.

However, if you want more capability, or help interpreting the results, browse the software download

sites (see p.183) for some suitable programs. Some packages, such as **VisualRoute** (www.visualroute. com), add another level to TraceRoute by identifying who owns the routers and then mapping it all out in Hollywood style.

For tips on maximizing the speed of a broadband connection, see:

Speed Guide www.speedguide.net
Cable-Modem.net www.cable-modem.net
Cable-Modems.org www.cable-modems.org
Navas Cable Modem/DSL Tuning Guide cable-dsl.home.att.net

If everything works fine but **your connection often drops out**, you'll need to check each link in the chain between you and your provider. Unfortunately there are a lot of links, so it's a matter of elimination.

▶ **Does it happen only after an extended period of inactivity?** Then it could be an automatic defence mechanism at your provider's end or in your settings. On a PC, enter the connection settings and look under "Options" or "Dialling" for "Disconnect if idle for…". On a Mac, Network in System Preferences, click on the PPP tab and look under "PPP Options".

▶ **Do you have telephone Call Waiting?** If it's enabled and you're called while online, those little beeps may knock out your connection.

▶ **Pick up your phone.** Does it sound clear? Crackling sounds indicate a poor connection somewhere. Modems like a nice clean line.

▶ **Do you share a line or have more than one handset?** Picking up a handset while online will drop your connection.

5 Connecting on the move

Cafés, laptops, hotspots & phones

Over the course of the last two decades, the Internet has become an increasingly mobile phenomenon. Laptops and netbooks are ever more popular and they can be connected to the Internet in various ways when you're out and about – from Wi-Fi hotspots to Ethernet networks. And the emergence of PDAs, games consoles and mobile phones equipped with full Web browsers has meant that Net addicts really can stay permanently plugged into the online world. Then, of course, there's the old-fashioned "Internet café" and other public access facilities. This chapter takes a brief look at all these various ways to connect on the move.

Public Internet access

The term Internet café was coined in 1994 by the proprietors of Cyberia, a small establishment in London's West End that combined computers and coffee. Since then, so-called cybercafés – with hot drinks or without – have cropped up in every corner of the globe. Today, they're mostly aimed at tourists; but others have been important, and at times controversial, sources of information for people in countries where press freedom is limited.

Besides the traditional Net café, in many countries you'll also come across Net-enabled **public telephones**, free or coin-operated "**Netbooths**", and wireless **hotspots** for connecting a laptop in places such as airports, hotels and shopping malls (more on hotspots below). If you hunt around you might even find free access offered somewhere, such as your local **library**.

Many public access points offer printing and faxing, and some also provide wireless access for laptops, discount phonecalls, networked gaming and more.

Finding public access

You shouldn't have any trouble finding a cybercafé. There's sure to be at least one close to the main street or tourist district in any town. If not, try asking at a hotel, post office, library or computer store. Or, if you're going on holiday, and you're organized enough to check before you set off, look up the following directories:

Cybercafé Guide www.netcafes.com
Cybercafé Search Engine www.cybercaptive.com
easyInternetCafé www.easyinternetcafe.com
Internet Café Guide www.netcafeguide.com

Connecting a laptop on the move

As an Internet station in the home, a **laptop** or **notebook** computer works exactly like a standard desktop machine. But laptops are designed to be taken on the road, and they can be connected to the Net in various ways when you're away from home:

#1: Via Wi-Fi

If you have a laptop or PDA with wireless capability you can connect wirelessly anywhere you find an accessible Wi-Fi network. This might be a friend's house, a café or hotel, or even a city-wide network.

Collecting your mail from any computer

You can send and receive your mail from any computer connected to the Internet. Many people assume this applies only to webmail accounts such as Yahoo!, Gmail and Hotmail, but it's also true of the accounts usually accessed at home via an email program. So if you can get to a cybercafé or hotspot, you can stay in touch, no matter where you are in the world. To find out how, see p.107.

Tip: If you connect your
laptop via a wireless hotspot,
a friend's computer or an
office network, you may find
that your email program
can receive, but not send,
messages. This is normal, and
relates to your outgoing mail
server. To solve the problem,
temporarily change your mail
setup (see p.114) to incorporate the outgoing mail of the
connection you're using.

Though none is comprehensive, there are various online directories of hotspots, such as:

Hotspot Locations www.hotspot-locations.com
WeFi www.wefi.com
WiFinder www.wifinder.com
Wi-Fi Free Spot www.wififreespot.com
ZONE Finder www.wi-fi.jiwire.com

Many commercial hotspots are pay-to-use. You either pay the person running the system (over the counter in a café, for instance)
or sign-up directly via your laptop. If you use such services a lot,
you may save time and money by signing up with a service such
as **Boingo**, T-**Mobile** or **Wayport,** which allow you to connect at
thousands of hotspots for a monthly fee.

Boingo www.boingo.com
T-Mobile www.t-mobile.com/hotspot
Wayport www.wayport.com

Many hotspots, however, provide free access for all. Some do this intentionally, others simply by having an unencrypted network that a laptop user can "sniff" out and use from the pavement outside. (Motoring around to find free Wi-Fi points, whether from hotspots, homes or unwitting offices, is known as **wardriving**. **Warchalking**, meanwhile, though not a trend that ever quite took off, involves writing chalk runes on the street to alert others to locations where they can get online for free.)

#2: Via an Ethernet cable

Most modern laptops have a built-in Ethernet port. This will usually be all you need to get online via an office network, and it can also allow you to share an Internet connection at a friend's house where there's no router. Simply plug a network cable between their computer and your laptop, turn on Connection Sharing (see p.47), and you have an impromptu network, allowing you both to be online at the same time. If your laptop lacks an Ethernet socket, you can add one with an inexpensive adapter – either a PCMCIA **network card** or a **USB device** (see p.34).

#3: Through a phone socket

Some dial-up ISP accounts only allow you to dial-in via your own phoneline, but in other cases there's no such restriction. So if you use a dial-up connection at home, you may find you can simply hook up your laptop to any phone number in the country and get online as normal. Even if you use broadband, your ISP may be happy to provide a dial-up phone number, which you can set up in the normal way (see p.51).

The same technique should also work further afield. Assuming your modem is compatible with the phone system of whichever country you're in, you should be able to simply add your home country's international dialling code to your dial-up phone number and connect as normal (see p.51 to find out how to edit the phone number).

Tip: If you're travelling off the beaten path with a laptop, consider your modem: technically, you could be breaking the law if it isn't approved in the country in question; and digital phone systems can fry analogue modems. So if you're travelling a lot, consider a special global modem card with built-in line guards, tax impulse filtering, widespread approval and software to tweak your modem to the tastes of almost any telephone network. You may also need an adapter to hook up to a foreign phone socket.

"Tethering" via a mobile phone

It is possible to connect a laptop to the Internet via a cell phone; a process that's often referred to as "tethering".

The basic requirement is a **data-compatible handset,** ideally one with fast connection technology such as GPRS or 3G. You also need some way to connect the phone to the computer. This might be a cable, possibly in conjunction with a special modem. But a slicker option is to connect the phone and computer wirelessly using **Bluetooth** (see p.27). Bluetooth is featured on most recent laptops and data-compatible phones, allowing them to talk to each other quickly and reliably; inexpensive USB adapters are available for older laptops. It's also possible to connect a phone and laptop via infrared, but it's notoriously problematic.

Ask in any phone shop to get the full lowdown. However, keep in mind that tethering is frowned upon by some cell service providers, and even if your mobile is data compatible you might quickly run up some hefty usage bills using it with a computer. You might even find that you have broken the terms of your cell contract. A similar option is to get either a PCMCIA card or USB dongle 3G mobile Internet account (see right).

The problem with connecting this way – if it works at all – is that if you add an international dialling code to your dial-up details, you're making a long-distance call each time you connect, so it might get pricey – especially if you're using a hotel phone socket. A better option is to find out if your ISP has local dial-up numbers in whichever countries you're visiting, allowing you to avoid any long-distance charges. You may hear this described as **global roaming**, with each local number described as a **Point of Presence** (POP). Some ISPs offer global roaming for free but hit you with a fee each time you dial in from abroad; others charge you a flat-rate monthly surcharge to use the service and then you just pay local call charges.

However you do it, to avoid nasty surprises **check the rates** and access details before you set off. Also consider testing the foreign dial-up numbers: better to pay for a quick international call than wait until you're wrestling with a hotel phone system and a directory enquiries agent who can't understand a word you're saying.

If you plan to spend long hours on the Web somewhere where there's no Wi-Fi it might be better to **sign up with a local ISP** in whichever country you're heading to.

#4: Through a mobile Internet account

An increasingly common and increasingly affordable option for laptop-users is a mobile Internet account from one of the major cell service providers.

For roughly the same amount of money as a domestic broadband account you get your Internet service supplied over the **GPRS** and **3G** airwaves, generally via a USB device called a dongle (which looks very much

like a USB flash drive), but sometimes in the form of a PCMCIA card (pictured right). Such services give you Internet access pretty much anywhere that you can get a phone signal, and the download speeds are significantly faster than those achieved by smart phones and PDAs using the same networks. On the downside, most cell service providers currently offer relatively stingy download caps and long tie-in periods – an unattractive prospect for a technology destined to drop in price rapidly over the next couple of years.

One other advantage of a mobile Internet account is that you can use the dongle both when you are out and about and when you are at home (see p.40).

An even neater variant for getting a laptop connected anywhere with a mobile Internet account is a machine that comes GPRS- or 3G-ready. Such laptops have a SIM card and antenna built in and when you buy the laptop you sign up for a contract. This set-up is primarily aimed at the business market at present and, as you might expect, is not cheap, especially if you travel and want to use overseas networks. In Europe, both Dell and HP have hooked up with Vodaphone to offer such a service, so visit their sites to find out more.

The Nokia D211 (see www.nokia.com) – a PCMCIA card with fast data-compatible mobile Internet access built in.

The Net in your pocket: phones & PDAs

Internet phones range widely in terms of useability and features. Plain-old mobile phones with **WAP** (**Wireless Application Protocol**) feed close to the bottom of the gadget pool – hence common alternative interpretations of the acronym, such as "Worthless Application Protocol" and "Wait And Pay". If you're patient and dexterous, you can tap into the Net to collect and send email, and browse online information in a very limited way

61

from certain sites. Keep your expectations low, though, or you'll be disappointed.

More recent phones based on **GPRS** (sometimes dubbed "2.5G") and, even better, **3G** (Third Generation, also called UMTS) are much better, some of them offering a fully featured Web browser and decent connection speeds. 3G technology is still young, but with potential data speeds as fast as many home broadband connections, it looks set to revolutionize the way we access data on the move.

The best and best-known Web-browsing phone at the time of writing is Apple's **iPhone**, which offers a 3G data connection, a super-high-res screen and a Web browser that's easy to use and can do almost anything. The iPhone also has a great mail program, a handy Google Maps tool and many other Internet features. The **BlackBerry**, popular with corporate types, is another choice with a strong tool kit.

After years of rip-off prices, mobile Internet is finally priced quite cheaply. A phone contract that includes unlimited Internet as well as many free calls costs approximately double a home broadband connection. For much more information on Apple's super-phone, see *The Rough Guide to the iPhone*. Or find out more at:

Apple iPhone www.apple.com/iphone
BlackBerry www.blackberry.com

Portable games consoles

One final option for mobile Internet access is a portable games console such as Sony's PlayStation Portable (aka the PSP, pictured). However, it can be quite a fiddle to browse the Web using the PSP controls and you'll have to find a Wi-Fi hotspot to connect. For more information, visit www.playstation.com

Surfing & searching

Browsing the Web

6

The world at your fingertips

The World Wide Web is the Internet's glossy, glamorous, point-and-click front door: a colourful assault of opinion, shopping, music, news, art, books, travel, games, job agencies, movie previews, radio broadcasts, self-promotion and much, much more. The biggest breakthrough in communications since TV, the Web has sparked off a publishing revolution, both professional and DIY. It's better than the best encyclopedia, the best shopping mall, the best newspaper … and for the most part it's free.

Though "surfing" or "browsing" the Web is extremely easy, there are plenty of useful tricks that most people aren't aware of – from choosing a better Web browser to blocking annoying flashing ads. This section reveals all. For more inspirational ideas for things to actually *do* on the Web, turn to p.249, or for tips on searching effectively, flick to p.92.

Web basics

As already mentioned, **the Web and the Internet are not the same thing**. The Internet is a giant global network of computers – including yours, when it's online. The Web, meanwhile, consists of billions of **webpages** that live on computers attached to the Internet. These webpages are special documents containing text, pictures, video clips and more. Each page has its own unique **address** (see box opposite) and can be viewed with a piece of software called a **Web browser**.

Your first time online – what you need to know

These days, all computers come with at least one Web browser pre-installed and ready to go. On a PC, it's **Internet Explorer**, with the blue "e" icon. On a Mac, it's **Safari**, with its light-blue compass icon. If you're absolutely new to the Web, you should use one of these to find your feet.

▶ **Entering addresses** Open your browser and ignore whatever appears. See the white bar running horizontally at the top? That's the **Address bar**. This is where you enter Web addresses. To see how it works, click inside it, delete whatever is there, type www.yahoo.com and hit Enter or click Go.

If all works well, your browser will retrieve the page – in this case the Yahoo! search engine and directory – and display it on your screen.

▶ **Links** Webpages are written in HTML – HyperText Markup Language – which allows pages to contain links, or **hyperlinks**, to other pages, images or downloadable files. Usually, when you pass over a link your cursor will become a pointing hand and the target address will appear in a bar at the bottom of your browser. It's easy for site designers to override all this, though, should they choose. Try moving your mouse cursor around and clicking on a few links.

Along the top of most Web browsers you'll find the following buttons. You can add and remove buttons by customizing your toolbars (see p.77).

Behind the scenes

When you type a Web address into your browser, a signal is sent to a **DNS server** (see p.21), which will convert the address into a numeric IP address. Once it's converted, the browser will contact the website's server and request the page.

Tip: By default, links in text are underlined and colour coded: blue if they point to pages you haven't yet visited, or purple if they point to pages you have. Your browser uses the information in your History (see p.74) to work out which links should be which colours – though individual websites often override these settings.

How to read a Web address (URL)

Though many Net users have never really considered it, a webpage is basically just a type of computer file. (We say "basically", because a single page can contain more than one file, but that's beside the point.) In the same way as you would save a word-processing document on your hard drive, a webpage is a file saved on a hard drive of a Web server: a computer set up to deliver webpages over the Internet. And, just like the documents on your hard drive, webpages on servers are arranged into folders, or "directories".

All files available on the Internet – including webpages – have a unique "address". In the jargon, this is called a **URL** (Uniform Resource Locator), and URLs can be broken into three parts. Reading from left to right, they are:

▶ the **protocol**, such as http://, ftp:// or news:

▶ the **domain** or **host name**: everything before the first single forward slash.

▶ the **file path**: everything after and including the first single forward slash.

Consider, for example, this imaginary web address:

http://www.star.com.hk/Chow/Yun/fat.html

▶ the **protocol** is http://, which stands for HyperText Transfer Protocol. All webpages start with this, even though you could enter the address into your browser without it.

▶ the **domain** is www.star.com.hk from which we can have a good guess that the webpage in question is within the website of a commercial organization called Star, based in Hong Kong. See p.19 for more on domains and country codes.

▶ the **file path** is /Chow/Yun/fat.html. The bit after the final slash is always the actual file name of the webpage itself – in this case fat.html. Working back, we know that it's within a folder called "Yun", which is in another folder called "Chow".

Sometimes, when you're looking at a webpage, you'll only see the protocol and domain – not the file path – in your browser's address bar. Often this is because of some clever programming by the site designer. But usually it's because you're on a homepage. For example, when you look at the Rough Guides homepage – http://www.roughguides.com – you're actually viewing http://www.roughguides.com/default.html. Homepage file paths are hidden to keep everything looking neat.

▶ **Back & Forward** Lets you move quickly between pages you've already visited. With a slow connection, this can be especially handy, as the pages will load quickly from the browser's cache (see p.80) rather than being downloaded afresh.

▶ **Home** Takes you to your homepage, which is the page your browser tries to access whenever you open a new window. You can choose any page as your homepage (see box, p.68).

▶ **Stop** lets you cancel a page request because it's taking too long to load or you've made a mistake. In Safari, the refresh button becomes the stop button whenever a page is loading.

▶ **Refresh** let's you reload a page, either because it didn't load properly, or because you think something may have changed on the page since you last loaded it (such as on a frequently updated news site). If your ISP requires you to use a proxy server (see p.51), refresh is also useful for making sure you're looking at the "live", not "cached", version of a page.

Right-clicking

Further controls can be accessed with the **right mouse button**, which will yield a little menu of options when clicked. The menu will change depending upon what you click. For instance, if you click on a link, you'll have the option of opening the target page in a new window. Click on an image and you'll see the option to save it to disk. You'll also find Back, Forward, Refresh and Print in there.

If you're using a **Mac** with a one-button mouse, you can access the "right button" menus by holding the Control key as you click.

Which browser?

Your Web browser is the key component of your Internet toolkit. It's not only the window through which you view webpages but a package for downloading files, viewing news feeds and much more. As we've already seen, your computer already has a Web browser installed, but that doesn't mean it's necessarily the best one to use. So before we look in more depth at all things www, here's a quick run through the main browsers. Don't be afraid of trying a few out to see what suits you best – you can always uninstall them, or use different browsers for different tasks.

Of the browsers described over the next two pages, we feel that Firefox is the best around at the time of writing, so the remainder of this chapter focuses on it primarily.

Lose the homepage

Every time you start your browser, you'll probably find that it automatically looks for a page that you haven't requested – usually part of the website of your ISP or the browser's supplier. This is deeply annoying, but can easily be sorted out: all you need to do is change, or get rid of, your browser's **homepage**. In Internet Explorer, you'll find the solution under the General tab of Internet Options (in the Tools menu); in Safari, look in Preferences (in the Safari menu); in Firefox open Preferences and look under General.

You can change the homepage to any address you like, even one located on your own hard drive. If you do want to start a session with a particular page, such as your favourite **search engine**, **blog** or **news site**, choose that. Otherwise, opt to start with a blank page. That way you don't have to wait for anything to load each time you open a window, and it won't cause problems when you open your browser while offline.

Internet Explorer

Microsoft's **Internet Explorer**, or **IE**, is far and away the world's most widely used browser. Recent versions are decent enough, but IE's popularity is mainly down to the fact that for years it has come pre-installed on nearly every new PC as a part of Microsoft Windows. IE has traditionally trailed behind its competitors in terms of features and security. The most recent version, IE8, closed the gap somewhat, but Firefox is still a superior option.

Internet Explorer www.microsoft.com/ie

Safari

Pre-2005 **Macs** also came with IE, but the standard Mac OS X browser now is Apple's own **Safari**. In most ways, it's an excellent browser – especially **Safari 4**, the version that was released in 2009. Safari is also now available to Windows PC users. It's fast, intuitive and nice-looking, with a Google search box built in. It also features excellent tabbed browsing, top-class newsfeed tools and an iTunes-style Cover Flow view for browsing your bookmarks. Still, whether you use a Mac or PC it's worth checking out both Safari and Firefox (see below) to see which suits you better.

Safari www.apple.com/safari

Firefox

First released in 2004, Firefox is an excellent browser created by the Mozilla Foundation as an open-source product with the help of volunteer programmers around the world. Firefox has a huge range of features, and even if you discover something that it can't do, you'll often find that the desired function can be easily added via an extension (see p.84) or some other customization.

Furthermore, most experts agree that Firefox leaves PC users slightly less vulnerable to potentially harmful scripts and other Web-based nasties than does Internet Explorer. With a built-in

Google search box, customizable address-bar searching, excellent privacy tools and many other handy extras, this is the best choice for PC and Mac users at the time of writing. Download it from:

Firefox www.getfirefox.com

Opera

Hailing from Scandinavia, **Opera** introduced many now-standard features (such as tabbed and multi-page bookmarks) years before its competitors. And it still has many unique extras, such as a fully featured mail program built right into the browser window. It's also very fast and worth trying.

Opera www.opera.com

Chrome

Chrome is one of Google's most recent additions to its armoury, and though still very much in its infancy is definitely worth considering. One interesting feature is the fact that when you open a new tab or window in Chrome you are shown nine thumbnails of your most frequently visited sites in place of the "home" feature that most browsers use.

Chrome www.google.com/chrome

And more …

There are many other browsers out there. To find them, as well as read news, reviews, tests, comparisons, tips and downloads on a wide range of platforms, see:

Browser News www.upsdell.com/BrowserNews

For a discussion of the "beta" test versions currently in progress (see p.178), try:

BetaNews www.betanews.com

Older browsers

If your computer doesn't have the operating system or specs to run an up-to-date browser, you could try an earlier release. You won't find old versions on the manufacturers' websites, but you'll find just about every browser ever released at:

Evolt browsers.evolt.org

Important: update your browser

Whichever browser you use, be sure to keep it up to date – partly to gain any extra features, but more importantly to ensure that you're not exposing yourself to any security risks. Many people assume that as long as they don't open any dodgy email attachments, they'll be safe from viruses, hackers and other such evils, but with an out-of-date browser it's possible to catch something nasty just by visiting a malicious webpage. With recent PCs and Macs, updates will be offered by automatically and should be accepted. On older PCs, you may need to use Windows Update (see p.170).

Setting your default browser

When you launch a browser that you've downloaded and installed, it may ask you whether you'd like to set it as the default browser for your system. Whichever browser you set as the default is the one that will open when you click a Web link in a non-Web application – your email program, for instance.

Entering addresses

As we've seen, the standard way to enter a Web address is via the Address bar. But there are many other ways to do the same thing. For instance, in Windows you could use the Address bar of Windows Explorer (eg the **My Documents** window) or the "Run" tool – which you'll find on the Start menu in Windows. Run can be reached quickly by hitting the Windows key plus R.

You can also "paste" an address into any of these places, if you've "copied" it from elsewhere. To copy and paste look under the Edit menu of nearly any program or use a keyboard shortcut: hold down control (or Apple on a Mac) and press C for copy and V for paste.

Tip If you use a PC, you can change the default browser whenever you like within Internet Options, which you'll find in the Tools menu of Internet Explorer. On a Mac, you can do the same via Safari: you'll find the option under Preferences, within the Safari menu.

Run [?] [X]

Type the name of a program, folder, document, or Internet resource, and Windows will open it for you.

Open: www.roughguides.com

[OK] [Cancel] [Browse...]

71

Non-http addresses

Non-http addresses

If you enter a non-http address into a Web browser, the browser examines the protocol in question and decides what to do. Some other protocols include ftp:// for **FTP** (see p.181) and telnet:// for **Telnet** (a nearly obsolete but still existent system used occasionally for library catalogues, among other things).

To access files stored on your PC's hard drive, enter a drive letter followed by a colon (eg c:). On PC or Mac, you can also launch any file by entering file:/// followed by the file's location.

Tip: If you want to return to a page you visited a while back, instead of clicking on the back button over and over again, click and hold the button and select the page you want from the list that appears. Right-clicking the button will have the same effect.

What about the http://?

Although the formal way to write a Web address is to start it with the http:// protocol (for example, http://www.google.com), you don't need to enter the http:// part into your browser, as it will be automatically added if you miss it out. For that reason, you'll often see Web addresses expressed without it – including in this book. Omitting the "protocol" will only cause problems if the address in question isn't a Web address – that is, if it's an address that starts with something other than http:// (see box).

You can frequently get away without writing the www too, depending on the browser you're using and the site you're trying to access.

Address guessing

Once you've been online for a short time you'll notice that your browser will start trying to guess the address you're entering. It will present a drop-down list of all the sites it knows that match what you've typed so far. These are supplied by your **History** (see p.74). And the link that it thinks is most likely the one you're entering will appear in grey in the Address bar. Clicking Enter will go to that address. Otherwise ignore it and keep typing, or use your mouse or arrow keys to select one of the other addresses in the list.

```
Explorer

Address   www.pi
          http://www.pies.com
          http://www.pinacolada.com
          http://www.pineapples.com
          http://www.pizza.com
          http://www.pizza.com/pages/1/index.htm
```

Address bar searching

If you enter a word or phrase – rather than a properly formed address – into your browser's Address bar, it may try to guess or search for the site. In Firefox, this works brilliantly, taking you directly to the first site that would have come up if you'd searched for that phrase on Google – also known as an "I Feel Lucky" search.

Finding pages later

Bookmarks

Whenever you find a page that's worth another visit, consider adding it to your **Bookmarks** (known as Favorites in some browsers). Then next time you want to visit the site, you don't have to type in the address: you can just select the name from the menu. You'll find the option to do this under the Bookmarks menu – or use the Firefox shortcut Ctrl+D (on a PC) or Apple+D (on a Mac).

When you bookmark a page, you'll be given the option of saving it directly into the menu, or into a folder – try to get into the habit of using folders to group related things together or you'll end up with a huge menu in which it's hard to find anything. You can tidy up your list at any time by choosing **Organize Bookmarks** from Firefox's Bookmarks menu.

Use your toolbar

The Bookmarks menu is great for storing a large archive of links. But for pages you use nearly every day, there's a better option: put them on a toolbar where they'll always be visible and easy to access. By default, this toolbar – known as the **Bookmarks or Links** bar – is located below the Address bar. If it's not there, you'll find an option to switch it on within Firefox's **View** menu, under Toolbars.

While it might look like any old toolbar, this bar is actually a special folder within your Bookmarks. That means you can add to

> **Tip:** The domain name part of a Web address (see p.11) is usually written in lower case. But domains are actually case insensitive. In other words, entering: www.Dogs.com
>
> …is the same as entering: www.dogs.com
>
> However, the file path section of the address is case-sensitive, meaning that: www.dog.com/bark
>
> …won't work if the address should be: www.dog.com/Bark

Page shortcuts

Another way to save an address for viewing later is to simply drag and drop the page icon – that's the icon to the left of the address in the browser – onto the Desktop or any other location on your hard drive. This way you can click on the link without even opening your browser first. For true instant access, try dragging a shortcut to a page onto your Quick Links toolbar (next to the start button in Windows) or the right-hand section of your Dock (the icon-laden strip at the bottom of the screen on a Mac).

it, or organize it like any other Bookmarks folder. You can also drag and drop links directly onto it from the Address bar.

If you use this toolbar a lot, and it's getting over-full, you can save space by creating subfolders with the main Folder of links. These will work like drop-down menus.

Forgot to bookmark?

Whenever you visit a site, your browser stores its name and address in a list called **History**. This is very handy if you want to return to a page that you've recently visited but you can't remember the address and didn't create a bookmark. To view the contents of your History, hit the History button in Firefox's View menu.

Like Internet Explorer (but unlike Safari), Firefox let's you sort your History by date, name or order of visits, or search through the contents of the pages listed. They also allow you to choose how long a History you want to your browser to record. A long History can be very useful, but it may also slow things down a bit, especially on an old computer, so it's wise to keep the expiry time to twenty days or less. To edit the History options, open Firefox Preferences (from the Firefox or Edit menu) and click Privacy.

Save a page

Bookmarks are just pointers to Web addresses, so when you click on one the page that appears may have changed since last time you visited. This is fine in most cases, but if you want to be able to return to a specific version of a page – let's say the front page of a news website, which might be updated every hour – then you'll need to **save** the information to your hard drive.

To do this, press Save in your browser's File menu. The resulting file or files can be opened in your browser, complete with working links. Or, if you just want to capture an image of a webpage, a neater approach is to save the page as a PDF (on a Mac, click Print and then press Save as PDF) or a screen-grab image (on a PC, press the Print Screen key, open Word and press paste).

Beyond Bookmarks: Delicious, Stumble & Digg

One problem with bookmarking pages in the standard way is that you can only easily access them from the computer where you created them. There are various tools for synchronizing your bookmarks between more than one machine (such as MobileMe for Macs), but a simpler solution is to use an online bookmarks tool.

One option is **Delicious** – a "social bookmarking" tool. The social aspect lies in the fact that you can view other people's bookmarks and they can see yours. It's a great way to discover new and interesting sites. You can either check out what your friends have been bookmarking, or go to the site homepage to see what Delicious users in general are bookmarking.

Delicious allows you to tag each of your own bookmarks with customizable keywords, so you can quickly navigate your list of favourite sites by various different categories.

StumbleUpon, a "personalized recommendation engine", also allows you to store bookmarks online for other users to discover. But it also adds an element of surprise, in the form of a "Stumble" button that takes you to a random new page based on your own tastes.

Also worth investigating is Digg, an online bookmark aggregator where users submit favourite links and news stories, and then sit back and watch as their link is voted up or down in the community's list; it's a little like a news Hit Parade, with the most interesting and topical material making it onto the Digg homepage.

Delicious www.delicious.com
StumbleUpon www.stumbleupon.com
Digg www.digg.com

Other similar services include Reddit, Fark, Google Bookmarks, and a feature built into Facebook. You'll often find a link for some or all of these services under each post or story on a blog or news website.

75

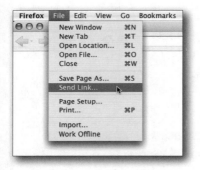

Send addresses to friends

One thing you'll inevitably want to do at some point is share an online discovery with friends. One way to do this is to copy the site's address into an **email**. Alternatively, you can send a link or a whole page using the link in the File menu. Sending a link is neater and avoids the risk that the message will come through as mumbo-jumbo if the recipient's email system doesn't allow proper HTML.

If you want to **send a whole list** of links, try exporting your bookmarks – or a folder of bookmarks – as an HTML file and sending that file as an email attachment. You'll find this option in the File or Bookmarks menu. The recipient can either view the file like a webpage or import it into their own bookmarks. Alternatively, use an online bookmarks manager (see box on p.75) and simply point your friends to that.

Viewing multiple pages

One thing that marks out experienced Web users is that they very often have multiple webpages open simultaneously. It makes a lot of sense to work this way: you might have your webmail open in the background, for example, while you read a blog in the foreground. Or you might fire open all the interesting-looking stories from the homepage of a news site; by the time you've read one, the others will have loaded, so you won't have to wait around.

Windows & tabs

The traditional way to open multiple webpages simultaneously is to open each page in a **new window**, but modern browsers also give you the more manageable option of having the various pages active within a single window, with **tabs** at the top to let you switch between them.

You can open a link into a new window or tab by **right-clicking** (Ctrl+click on a Mac) and selecting the relevant option in the mouse menu. But it's worth getting used to the various shortcuts for opening new pages both in front of and behind the current window or tab – and also for toggling between the various open pages. In Firefox, they are:

	PC	Mac
New window	Shift+click	Shift+click
New tab (foreground)	Ctrl+Shift+click	Apple+Shift+click
New tab (background)	Ctrl+click	Apple+click
Toggle between windows	Alt+Tab	Apple+~
Toggle between tabs	Ctrl+Tab	Ctrl+Tab

More basic tricks

Download images, programs or other files

To save an image, right-click (Ctrl-click on a Mac) on it and choose **Save Image As…**. You can also save an image as your **Desktop wallpaper**, but try clicking the image first to see if it links to a higher resolution version.

As for any other kind of file – such as movies, music clips, etc – usually all you'll have to do is click on a link to set the download in motion. But if your browser plays or displays it, rather than downloading it to your hard drive, right-click the link and choose **Save Link As** or **Download Linked File.**

Change the buttons & bars

You can customize the way the buttons and bars appear on your browser, adding things that are missing or removing things you don't use. To access these settings, right-click the toolbar (Ctrl-click on a Mac) and choose **Customize**.

On a PC, you can also move the bars around to your liking, by dragging and dropping them using their left-hand edges. However, you may need to right-click a toolbar and select "Unlock" first.

Find something on a page

To search for a word or phrase within a webpage, choose "Find" from the Edit menu, or use the shortcut **Ctrl+F** (PC) or **Apple+F** (Mac). In Firefox, you can then jump to other occurrences of the same word or phrase by clicking **Ctrl+G** (PC) or **Apple+G** (Mac), or highlight all occurrences of your search term in the current page using the buttons at the bottom of the window.

AutoComplete

As well as suggesting addresses from your History, browsers can also **suggest form entries**, such as search engine terms, usernames and passwords. You can turn this feature on and off, clear the stored data and more in Firefox's Privacy settings. Click Options (in the Tools menu on a PC) or Preferences (in the Firefox menu on a Mac).

Change the text size

You can change the size of the text on a webpage by looking in the View menu. PC users should also try holding down **Ctrl** while rolling the **mouse wheel**. And Mac users can hold down the Apple key and press the plus and minus keys.

The only problem is that increasing or decreasing the text size can do strange things to a webpage's layout. If you want the text to appear bigger without this happening, you could try decreasing your **Screen resolution** – in Display, under Window's Control Panel or Mac OS X's System Preferences. Alternatively, use

Tip: Clearing your Temporary Internet Files can also be useful when your browser is playing up and not loading pages properly. It's sometimes an instant fix.

Internet Explorer 7, which allows you to scale-up the whole page instead of just the text.

Print a page

Printing a webpage is simple: turn on your printer and select Print from the File menu. What many people don't notice, however, is that you can alter the various **layout options** – which can be useful, as webpages often look messy on paper, and have headers and footers that you might not want there. To tweak the layout options on a PC, select **Page Setup** from the File menu and, when you're done, use **Print Preview**. On a Mac, press Print as normal and then explore the various drop-downs, followed by the **Preview** button.

> **Tip:** The standard shortcut keys for printing from most applications are Ctrl+P (PC) or Apple+P (Mac).

Copy & paste

To copy text from webpages, highlight the words or lines you are after, choose **Copy** from the Edit or right-click mouse menu, then switch to your word processor, text editor or mail program and select **Paste**. Alternatively, use the standard shortcuts: hold down the **Control** key (or Apple key on a Mac) and press **C** for copy and **V** for paste.

Uncover the source

If you're interested in **learning Web design**, or just understanding exactly what a webpage actually is, you'll find it informative to peek at the raw HTML code behind the pages you like. To do so, choose **Source** or **View Source** from the View menu. For more on webpage design, see p.209.

Browsing offline

If you're paying by the minute to be online, or you want to be able to browse webpages where there's no Internet connection – on the train to work, for instance – consider **gathering pages** rather than reading them there and then. When you use Firefox (or IE), the pages you load go onto your hard drive and are available for reading offline later. That means you can quickly visit a bunch of sites and run back through your session after you hang up. To do this, choose **Work Offline** from the File menu.

Once in offline mode, you can **call up sites** by typing in their addresses or following links – just as if you were online – or by clicking on their entries in your History. The contents of the pages are stored temporarily in a so-called **Cache**. These exist partly to enable offline browsing, but primarily to speed up online browsing: if you return to a page, your browser will load the saved version rather than downloading it again from the Net.

If you're serious about ripping the contents from a site for offline use, look no further than **Offline Explorer (30-day free trial, $30 to buy)**, a feature-packed tool designed specifically for the job. You can set it up to extract only certain types and sizes of files, and configure all manner of keyword restrictions in the server and directory names. For example, you could visit a music site before you retire for the evening, right-click on the page, choose "Download page with Offline Explorer", set the parameters and wake up to a folder full of MP3s.

Offline Explorer www.metaproducts.com

Privacy & security

Hide your tracks

Because your browser records all your online activities, it's easy for someone to find out where you've been spending your time. As we've seen, every site you visit is stored (for a time, at least) in your **History**. So if you open your History folder you'll instantly see where you've been. The same evidence can also show up in the **Address bar**; just click the down arrow on the right-hand side of the bar to reveal a list of recent sites. The contents of those pages are "cached" (saved) onto your hard drive, and it's very likely the sites deposited their own telltale **cookies** in the special cookie folder (more on cookies on p.81). If you've entered anything into a form such as on a search engine, double-clicking in that form may reveal a list of previous entries. And, finally, in Firefox and Safari, your download manager also keeps records of things you've saved to your hard drive.

If you want to cover your tracks you must either delete all these files and records, or ensure they're not recorded in the first place. This is easily done in your browser's preferences panel. In Firefox, open Tools/Options (PC) or Firefox/Preferences (Mac), click on Privacy and select Clear All. Alternatively, look through the various options and delete things selectively.

Note that while these measures are fine for stopping the average punter seeing what you've been doing online, they're not airtight. A record of a site you've visited could find its way into some obscure part of your operating system. And deleting a file doesn't actually remove all traces of it from your hard drive. To do that you need a special program such as the free **Eraser** (www.heidi.ie/eraser). The same folks also make a completely standalone browser that promises to leave no records anywhere (www.heidi.ie/NoTrax).

Finally, bear in mind that every site you visit may be recorded by your ISP.

Cookies

A **cookie** is a small text file placed on your computer by a Web server as a kind of ID card. This means that next time you visit the same site, it will know you. Actually, it doesn't quite know it's "you": it recognizes your individual browser. If you were to visit on another machine or with a different browser on the same machine, it would see you as a different visitor. And if someone else were to use your browser, it couldn't tell the difference.

Some websites use cookies simply to recognize repeat visitors. On the next level, if you **voluntarily submit further details**, they can store them in a database against your cookie ID and use it to do things such as tailor the site to your preferences, or save you entering the same data each time you check in. This won't be stored on your computer, so other sites can't access it. And they won't know anything personal about you.

> ### Privacy in Safari
>
> Mac users concerned about privacy may want to use Safari for their browser and run it in Private Browsing mode. While this option is checked in the Safari menu, no browsing records will be recorded.

Kill the ads

Banner and pop-up ads provide an important part of the finance that keeps many websites afloat. But that doesn't make them any less annoying. Thankfully, all decent browsers now have pop-up ad filters built in: if they're not turned on, click the option in the File menu Options/Preferences (Firefox) or (Explorer/Safari). These do the job very well, and in Explorer and Firefox you can create exceptions to allow certain sites to deliver pop-ups. This is useful, as some webmail systems, for example, employ pop-ups in a useful way that has nothing to do with ads.

Pop-ups may be the most annoying of all, but banner ads, especially animated ones or those slap bang in the middle of a news story, can be almost as bad. If they bug you, it's not too difficult to get rid of most of them. If you use Firefox, simply install the free AdBlock Extension (see p.84). Then, when you see a banner, right-click (or Ctrl+click on a Mac) and choose "Block ads from…" (as pictured). Banners from whichever server dished up the ad in question should no longer appear in any webpages you view using Firefox.

It you use Internet Explorer, this isn't an option, though it is possible to filter webpage ads by editing the host file

– a simple-text document that in Windows Vista or XP can be found in a folder named "etc", which lives here: C drive > windows > system32 > drivers.

The idea is to "map" an ad server to one of two special IP addresses: 127.0.0.1 or 0.0.0.0. Once that's done requests to that ad server from your browser are rerouted, stopping the ads from loading. The most common ad server to block is Doubleclick, which is achieved by adding the following to your host file:

0.0.0.0 ad.doubleclick.net

Something similar can be achieved in Mac OS X, though it's much more complicated. For instructions, see: corz.org/serv/tricks/hosts.php

These standard types of cookie are uncontroversial. But there's also another type – so-called **tracking** or **spyware** cookies – that have privacy implications. These cookies are placed on your machine by sites other than those that you're currently browsing – from a pop-up ad, say – and they serve to gather information about your surfing habits, often with the aim of sending targeted advertising your way.

If you want to avoid tracking cookies, you could tell your browser to accept cookies only from the sites that you've navigated to (not pop-ups, for example). In Firefox, open Options or Preferences, click Privacy, then Cookies, and check the "for the originating site only" box. You can also turn cookies off completely, though this can make day-to-day Web use much less convenient. For more on cookies, see:

Cookie Central www.cookiecentral.com

Censoring Web material for kids

If you're a parent and you'd like to be able to leave your young child online without worrying about them stumbling upon porn and the like, experiment with the tools at your disposal. Recent versions of both Windows and Mac OS X offer parental control options. You set up a new user account on the computer for each child and then use the parental settings to specify which site you want them to be able to visit. You'll find these options within the Control Panel in Windows Vista or within Accounts in Mac OS X (version 10.4 or later).

There are also several third-party programs and browsers available that can impose all kinds of restrictions. For instance:

BumperCar www.freeverse.com/bumpercar2 (Mac)
NetNanny www.netnanny.com (PC)

Bear in mind that older, tech-savvy kinds will probably find a way to circumvent online censorship.

Cookie crushers

To find and remove tracking cookies on a PC, download Spybot S&D (see p.173). For Macs, there are few spyware cookies in circulation, but if you want additional peace of mind, try MacScan available from:

macscan.securemac.com

Browser plug-ins

Although modern browsers have a good selection of tools built-in, you may sometimes want to enhance your browser with a **plug-in** or **extension**. This might be anything from a program to play back a specific kind of video file to a piece of software that adds ad-blocking or translation tools to your browser's menus.

Essential plug-ins

A few plug-ins are definitely worth having: **RealPlayer** for streamed music and video, including online radio; and Macromedia's **Shockwave** and **Flash players** for animations and multimedia effects on webpages. Even if they came with your browser, download the latest free versions. PC users should also grab **Quicktime**, while Mac owners might find **Windows Media Player** useful.

Real www.real.com
Flash Player www.adobe.com/flashplayer
Shockwave Player www.macromedia.com/shockwave
Windows Media Player www.windowsmedia.com

PC users should also grab a plug-in for viewing PDF (portable document format) documents within your browser. The standard choice is:

Adobe Reader www.adobe.com/reader

Firefox extensions

One of the great things about Firefox is that, if you ever find something that it can't do, you can usually find a free **extension** to add whatever functionality you're after. Similar tools are available for all browsers, but because Firefox is open-source (any programmer can see its underlying code) and created by a community

ActiveX controls

ActiveX controls are similar to plug-ins, but their scope is far greater. When you arrive at a site that relies on an ActiveX control, it checks to see if you already have it, and (if not) installs it automatically after you approve the publisher's certificate. As a rule, **don't accept certificates unless you're totally satisfied the publisher is reputable.**

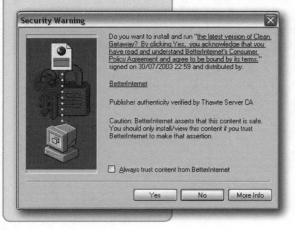

of volunteers, it's particularly strong in this area. Simply go to the Tools menu and select Add-ons. When the box pops up, choose Get Extensions and you'll be taken to a webpage where approved (safe) Extensions are arranged by category. If you find something you'd like to install, click on the relevant link and, once everything's up and running, you can usually tweak various preferences by visiting the Extensions panel, opened via the Firefox Tools menu.

When a Web address won't work

It won't be long before you come across a Web link or address that won't work; it's very common and usually not too hard to get around. Many of the addresses in this book will be wrong by the time you try them – not because we're hopeless, just because they change. It's the nature of the Internet. The most useful thing we can do is show you how to find the correct address.

When a page won't display, the first thing to do is work out where the problem lies. First check your connection by trying another site that's very unlikely to be unavailable (such as www.google.com). If no pages will open, you'll need to locate the problem (see box, right). Otherwise, you know your connection is OK and you can continue to try and locate the problem.

There are various reasons why you might not be able to access a specific page. But very often there are steps you can take to access the information you're after. You'll probably be able to work out what the problem is by looking at exactly what happens – such as the error message that your machine may flash up. Here's a run-through of the most likely symptoms you'll encounter:

File not found – 404

▶ **Symptom:** An error message saying "File not found – 404 error", or you get directed to another page within the site in question that tells you something like "The page you requested cannot be found".

When no sites work

If you can't connect to any websites, close and then reopen your browser. It might only be a software glitch. If that doesn't fix it, check whether other Internet programs are working. For example, if you use a separate email program, try checking your mail. If it fails, you know there's something wrong with your connection. Disconnect from the Internet, switch any modems or routers off and back on and try again.

If, on the other hand, your mail program works OK, you know that the connection between you and the ISP is OK. In this case, check you have the right proxy and DNS settings (see p.53); if so, make a note of them and try removing them. Still no joy? Ring your ISP and see if there's a problem at their end, or try diagnosing it yourself by testing a popular site – say, www.yahoo.com – with a tool such as Ping (see p.54). If this fails, either your provider's connection to the Internet is down or there's a DNS problem. You'll need to speak to your ISP to sort it out.

▶ **Problem:** The host you are trying to access is responding, but the specific webpage you are trying to access isn't there. It has probably been moved or removed. If www.roughguides.com/boguspage.html brought up this message, for example, you'd know the /boguspage.html section was the problem.

▶ **Solution:** If you typed the address in manually, make sure you did it correctly – including upper-case or lower-case letters. Still no luck? Refer below to "Finding that elusive page".

Server not found

▶ **Symptom:** An error message saying "The server cannot be found", "The page cannot be displayed" or "DNS lookup error".

▶ **Problem:** Unless you typed in the address incorrectly, the website you're trying to access probably doesn't exist or is temporarily unavailable. The latter may be due to maintenance on the server where the site lives, or because too many people are trying to access it at once.

▶ **Solution:** Check the address, and try adding or removing the www part of the address (so try roughguides.com instead of www.roughguides.com, for example). If not, try later – perhaps even days later – and in the meantime search for a cache of the page (see p.88).

Blank window

▶ **Symptom:** A page or frame instantly comes up blank.

▶ **Problem:** Your browser hasn't tried to fetch the page.

▶ **Solution:** Hit "Refresh". If that doesn't work, reboot your browser and re-enter the address. Failing that, clear your Temporary Internet Files or cache (see p.80). If you're using Internet Explorer and the problem appears to be related to security – such as the acceptance of an ActiveX control – check your security settings within Internet Options/Preferences, disable Content Advisor and consider adding the site to your Trusted Sites list.

A webpage won't load on a specific computer

▶ **Symptom:** You can reach a page on another computer but not your own.

▶ **Problem:** Your Windows Hosts file could be the problem – especially if you've ever installed any browser acceleration software.

▶ **Solution:** Get rid of the offending acceleration program via "Add/ Remove" in the Windows Control Panel. Then locate the file called Hosts within your hard drive (look within system32\drivers\etc). Open it with Notepad and remove any lines not starting with # except for the local host entry. Save the file and exit.

Not authorized

▶ **Symptom:** An error message saying: "Not authorized to view this page", or words to that effect.

▶ **Problem:** Some sites, or files within sites, require a password to be accessed, or can only be reached from certain systems, such as from a company network.

▶ **Solution:** Train to be a hacker.

Finding that elusive page

If you can connect to a website but the individual page isn't there, here are a few tricks to try. Check capitalization, for instance: book. htm instead of Book.htm. Or try changing the file name extension from .htm to .html or vice versa (if applicable). Then try removing the file name and then each subsequent directory up the path until finally you're left with just the host name. For example:

When a webpage looks scrambled

If everything looks weird on screen – bad spacing, images overlapping, etc – the problem could be that the web designer hasn't tested the site on more than one browser. Some sites, for example, look fine on Explorer but are badly coded and won't display properly on, say, Safari or Firefox. The solution is to try viewing the page through another browser.

No joy at www.roughguides.com/old/Book.htm?
Try… www.roughguides.com/old/book.htm
then… www.roughguides.com/old/Book.html
then… www.roughguides.com/old/book.html
then… www.roughguides.com/old
then… www.roughguides.com

In each case, if you succeed in connecting, try to locate your page from whichever links appear.

Going back in time

If you haven't succeeded, there's still hope. Try **searching for the problematic address in Google** (www.google.com), and you may find that, though the actual page is no longer available, you can still access Google's **cached copy** – if so, a link saying "cache" will appear under the search result. You could even use the shortcut, searching for:

cache:www.roughguides.com/old/Book.htm

If that doesn't work, you could try searching in the relevant domain (website) for a keyword from the name of the file or from what you expect the file to contain. So, continuing the above example, you could search with Google for:

Book.htm site:roughguides.com

Also remember that you can use a search engine to look only within URLs (see p.67). So if the elusive page has an unusual name, let's say worldcupstats.html, you could Google:

inurl:worldcupstats.html

If you still haven't found it, try browsing a saved version of the relevant site at the amazing Internet Archive, which has versions of websites going back years.

Internet Archive www.archive.org

Troubleshooting your browser

Like all other programs, Web browsers occasionally freeze or crash. The first thing to try, when any program stops responding, is the **three-fingered salute**: in Windows hold down the **Ctrl+Alt+Del** keys; on a Mac, press **Apple+Alt+Esc**. This should bring up a dialog box listing all your currently open programs. Select the entry for the misbehaving browser and press **End task** or **Force quit**. Once you've confirmed your decision, this should close the browser. If that doesn't help, and your computer won't even switch off, force-reboot your machine by holding down the power button for five seconds.

Update, scan, reinstall

If your browser continues to give you grief, empty its cache (see p.80). If that doesn't work, update your system (see p.170), check for an updated version of the browser, and scan your computer for **spyware and viruses** (see p.173).

Still no joy? If you're using anything other than Internet Explorer, you could try uninstalling the browser (via Add/Remove Software in the Control Panel on a PC, or by simply deleting the relevant file in the Applications folder on a Mac) and reinstalling a new version.

Alternatively, look online for support. Good places to start are:

Internet Explorer Support www.microsoft.com/windows/ie/support
IE Infosite www.ieinfosite.co.uk
Firefox Help www.mozilla.org/support/firefox
Safari Support www.apple.com/support/safari

Googling

And other ways to search

The art of finding things quickly and efficiently is perhaps the single most useful Internet skill. Going straight to the content you want, instead of stumbling upon it after ten minutes of looking, can make the difference between the Internet seeming like a giant waste of time and the ultimate time saver. Google – the world's most popular search engine – has made finding things much easier in the last few years, but few people use it as efficiently as they might.

Search engines: the basics

When the Web first took off in a big way, the most important tools for locating things online were **directories**: human-edited archives of useful links, arranged into categories. Directories still exist (see p.100), but these days they're almost irrelevant compared to **search engines** – such as Google – which allow you to locate pages from across the Web that contain words or phrases of your choice.

How search engines work

The better search engines can riffle through **billions of webpages** in a fraction of a second and produce thousands of results, or "hits". The reason it's so quick is that you're not actually searching billions of webpages. You're searching a database of webpage extracts stored on the search engine's server.

This database is compiled by a program that periodically "**crawls**" around, or "**spiders**", the Web looking for new or changed pages. Because of the sheer size of the Internet and a few factors relating to site design, it's not possible for the crawlers to find every word on every page. Nor is it possible to keep the database completely up to date. That means you can't literally "search the Web" – you can only search a snapshot taken by a search engine. It also means that different search engines will give you different results, depending on how much of the Web they've found, how often they update, how much text they extract from each page and how they prioritize the results that they find.

Why Google?

There are dozens of search engines (see box overleaf), but only a few are worth trying. In fact, you'll rarely need more than one. But, since you'll be using it often, make sure it's up to speed. You'll want the **biggest, freshest database**. You'll want to **fine-tune your search** with extra commands. And you'll want the most hits you can get on one page with the most **relevant results on top**. For the last half decade or so, that's been **Google**:

Google www.google.com

Google has an uncanny knack of getting it right in the first few hits, and it also provides access to "**caches**" of pages that have disappeared or changed since its crawl, or which are otherwise unavailable. This is great when you can't get a link to load (click on "cached" under a search result to see how this works).

Google has become so popular that "to google" something is now a commonly used verb. But most users hardly scratch the surface of what it can do.

> **Tip:** By default, Google (like many other search engines) only displays ten results at a time. If you'd rather see more, click the Preferences link visible on any Google search page and register your choice. The setting will be remembered for future visits.

Despite the phenomenal amount of traffic that passes through Google's homepage every second of every day (which would make it an advertiser's dream billboard), the site's front end remains one of the cleanest and most minimal on the Web.

Other search engines

If Google falls short, try **Yahoo!**. For years its search was driven by other engines (including Google), but it now has its own technology and the results are fairly impressive. The other biggies are **Ask** (previously known as Ask Jeeves) and Microsoft's **Live Search**.

Yahoo! www.yahoo.com
Ask www.ask.com
Live www.live.com

Or, for searching blogs, the best engine is **Technorati**.

Technorati technorati.com

As for the rest, many search engines simply license access to the search technology of one or more of the above, perhaps adding their own special angle. **Dogpile**, for example, combines results from all the major searches and uses all money raised to support animal rescue projects.

Dogpile www.dogpile.com

From time to time, a new and different search engine comes along and makes a splash in techie circles.

Turbo 10, for instance, theoretically lets you search across hundreds of small search engines simultaneously, promising to access bits of the "deep Net" that others can't reach. In truth, though, such newcomers rarely make even the slightest dint in Google's hegemony.

Turbo10 www.turbo10.com

For more info than you could ever possibly want about the murky world of search engines, see:

Search Engine Watch www.searchenginewatch.com
Search Engine World www.searchengineworld.com

These sites keep tabs on all the finer details, such as who owns what and how they tick – useful if you have your own site and want to generate traffic. They also report on technologies that are in the pipeline.

Technorati search the blogosphere...

How to Google (properly)

Google comes up with the goods quickly and easily in many cases. But a few basic tricks can help you quickly hone searches that deliver too many results.

An example search

Suppose we want to search for something on the esteemed author, Angus Kennedy. A few years ago, if you entered angus kennedy into a search engine, you'd get a list of pages that contained the words

Tip: Below the main Google search field are two radio buttons that allow you to search either the entire Web, or just pages from your "local" Google region – a handy way to narrow down your search.

"angus" or "kennedy", or both. Fine, but it meant you'd get loads of pages about Angus cattle and JFK. These days, Google looks for pages containing *both* words. But that doesn't guarantee that the two words will be found next to each other. What we really want is to **treat them as a phrase**. To do this is, enclose the words in quotes:

"angus kennedy"

Now we've captured all instances of angus kennedy as a phrase, but since it's a **name** we should maybe look for kennedy, angus as well. However, we want to see pages that contain either version. We can do this by inserting an upper-case "OR" between the terms:

"angus kennedy" OR "kennedy angus"

By now we should have quite a few relevant results, but they're bound to be mixed up with lots of irrelevant ones. So we should narrow the search down by excluding some of the excess, such as pages that contain a different person with the same name. Our target writes about French literature, so let's get rid of that pesky Rough Guide author. To **exclude** a term, place a minus sign (-) in front of it:

"angus kennedy" OR "kennedy angus" -"rough guide"

Site searches

These days, there's rarely a pressing need to use any search engine other than Google. But you'll regularly need to use the searches built into online stores, encyclopedias, newspaper archives and more. Bear in mind that these won't always work the same way as Google in terms of the way they handle capitals, dashes between words, brackets, wild cards, truncations and Boolean operators* such as AND, OR and NOT.

   Also bear in mind that, if a site's internal search is poor – as is so common – you'll often get better results with a Google search

Tip: Especially if you have a slow connection, don't just click on a search result then hit the Back button if it's no good. Instead, run down the list and open the most promising candidates in new browser windows or tabs (for the keyboard shortcuts to do this, turn back to p.77). It will save you tons of time, as you can read one while the others are loading.

Tip: When Googling a phrase, you don't have to include the quotation marks at the end of the phrase – ie searching for **"flying fish** will produce the same results as **"flying fish"**.

* Boolean operators are words that are used to connect "search terms" to create an almost algebraic "search statement". Their moniker comes from the English mathematician George Boole (1815–64), who first devised the concept. Curiously, though he died over a century before search engines were conceived, his name is an anagram of "Googlee bore".

A rough guide to Google wizardry

Though Google is the world's most popular search engine, the majority of its users don't make the most of its many special commands. So here's a tutorial in the finer points of Google searching. It may just change your life…

BASIC SEARCHES

Googling: **thomas clark**
> finds pages containing both the terms "thomas" and "clark".

Googling: **"thomas clark"**
> finds pages containing the exact phrase "thomas clark".

Googling: **thomas OR clark**
> finds pages containing either "thomas", "clark" or both.

Googling: **thomas -clark**
> finds pages containing "thomas" but not containing "clark".

All these commands can be mixed and doubled up:

Googling: **"thomas clark" OR "tom clark" -economist**
> finds pages containing *either* name but not the word "economist".

FIND A SYNONYM

Use ~ before a word to search for synonyms and related words. For example:

Googling: **~mac**
> will find pages containing "macintosh" and "Apple" as well as "mac".

FIND A DEFINITION

Googling: **define:calabash**
> finds definitions from various sources for the word "calabash". You can also get to a definition

(from www.answers.com) of a search term by clicking the link in the right of the top blue strip on the results page.

FIND A FLEXIBLE PHRASE

Use an asterisk as a substitute for any word in a phrase.

Googling: **"tom * clark"**
> finds "tom frederick clark" as well as just "tom clark".

SEARCH FOR A PAGE THAT NO LONGER EXISTS

Let's say you visit **www.roughguides.com**, a page you looked at the other day so you know it exists, but, to your horror, it doesn't seem to be there. Fear not, Google probably has a copy.

Googling: **cache:www.roughguides.com**
> finds Google's "cached" (saved) snapshot of the page, if it has one. (You can reach the same page by searching for **www.roughguides.com** and then clicking the "cache" link in the relevant result.)

SEARCH WITHIN A SPECIFIC SITE

Use the **site:** command to search within a specific website. This usually gives more, better and more clearly presented results than the site's internal search would (if it has one at all). For example:

Googling: **site:www.guardian.co.uk "thomas clark" OR "tom clark"**
> finds pages containing either version of Thomas Clark's name within the website of *The Guardian* newspaper.

SEARCH URLS (WEB ADDRESSES)

The commands **inurl:** and **allinurl:** let you specify that some or all of your search terms appear within the address

(URL) of the page. This can be very useful if you remember only part of a web address you want to revisit. It's also good for limiting your search to certain types of websites. For example:

Googling: **"arms exports" inurl:gov**

> finds pages containing the phrase "arms exports" in the webpages with the term gov in the address (ie government websites).

SEARCH TITLES

intitle: and **allintitle:** let you specify that one or all of your search terms should appear in the title of a webpage – the text that appears on the top bar of your browser window when viewing a page. This can be useful if you're getting lots of results that mention your terms but don't specifically focus on them. For example:

Googling: **train bristol intitle:timetable**

> will find pages with "timetable" in their titles, and "train" and "bristol" anywhere in the page.

NUMBER & PRICE RANGES

Google lets you search for a range of numbers – which can be especially useful for dates. You can also search for a range of prices, though at the time of writing this only works with the dollars sign.

Googling: **1972..1975 "snooker champions"**

> finds pages containing the term "snooker champions" and any number (or date) in the range 1972–1975. Googling **numrange:1972–1975** has the same effect.

Googling: **$15..$30 "snooker cue"**

> finds pages containing the term "snooker cue" and any price in the range $15–30. Googling **pricerange:15–30** has the same effect.

SEARCH SPECIFIC FILE TYPES

The command **filetype:** lets you specify that your search terms should appear in a specific file, such as pdf format. For example:

Googling: **filetype:pdf climate change statistics**

> would find pdf documents (likely to be more "serious" reports than webpages) containing the terms "climate", "change" and "statistics".

FIND LINKING PAGES

Links are usually one-way: you can see links from a page, but not links *to* a page. In Google, though, you can find out. For example:

Googling: **link:www.guardian.co.uk/environment**

> finds pages which have a link to the Guardian environment homepage.

CALCULATIONS & CONVERSIONS

OK, so it's not exactly searching, but Google can act as an excellent calculator. It can cope with standard mathematical functions – such as * (multiply), / (divide), + (add), - (subtract) and ^ (raise to the power) – as well as hundreds of units of measurement, from Fahrenheit to hectares. For example:

Googling: **3465*34223**

> will give you the answer 118,582,695.

Googling: **(24-9)% of (36^4 - 3)**

> will give you the answer 251,941.95.

Googling: **51 Fahrenheit in Celsius**

> will give you the answer 10.55 degrees Celsius.

Googling: **5 gallons in teaspoons**

> will give you the answer 5 US gallons = 3840 US teaspoons".

limited to the site in question. You can do this via the Advanced Search page, or via a special command. For example, Googling "Jimmy White" site:bbc.co.uk **would bring up pages from** www.bbc.co.uk containing reference to everyone's favourite snooker star.

Google images

Like most major engines, Google offers **image-specific searches**, which can prove very handy. However, they are far less comprehensive than text searches because they rely on image file names and the like. So just because a photo of you doesn't appear when you tap your name into an image search, it doesn't mean you're not adorning a page somewhere. Try running a normal search too, and browse the hits for relevant photos.

Some people consider the image search at Live.com to be superior to the one at Google.

Advanced searches

For a host of additional variables to play with hit the Advanced Search button to the right of the main Google search field. This offers simple access to many of the advanced tricks listed on the previous two pages.

Translations

If your results include pages in certain foreign languages, Google (and others) can translate them, albeit pretty roughly, into English or a different language. Just click the "translate" link on the relevant result.

If you want to search pages that are in a specific language, or from a specific country, hit the "Language Tools" button to the right of the main Google search field.

Tip: Though they're mostly limited to the US, Google can retrieve relevant information if you search for a flight number, an express delivery tracking number, a vehicle ID number and many other such things.

Think logically

To increase your search success and efficiency, think logically about an **exact phrase** that might appear on a target page. This makes finding facts and other specific things incomparably quicker and easier. Making a simple phrase with "is", "was" or another short word will often do the trick.

Let's say you want to find an alternative for the network software NetStumbler but you don't know

of any. Instead of just searching for NetStumbler and browsing through hundreds of mostly useless results, try entering **"NetStumbler or"**. Another example: you've heard a friend talking about a "wiki" but you don't quite understand what a wiki is and you can't find an answer online. Instead of searching for wiki, which will bring up plenty of incomprehensible results, try searching for the phrase **"a wiki is"**.

Googling from your browser

All decent browsers these days – including Firefox or Safari – come with a **Google search box** built into the toolbar at the top of the window. This allows you to quickly search the Web without first heading to Google's homepage; for even speedier access, there's usually a shortcut key for jumping to the search box: in Firefox, for example, press **Ctrl+K** (PC) or **Apple+K** (Mac), or use the Tab key to toggle between the Address bar, Search box and the currently open webpage.

Things are slightly different in Internet Explorer 7. Its search box queries Microsoft's Live Search, but can be configured to use Google instead (see IE's Help for more information). Alternatively, if you want to have all of Google's advanced tools instantly available within IE, you could install the **Google Toolbar**. You can drag text from a webpage straight into the search box, and click from one search result to the next without returning to the list.

Google Toobar toolbar.google.com

Googling

Using either the Toolbar or a built-in search tool, you can employ all the standard tricks described on the previous pages.

Most other search engines – and many other sites – offer a similar toolbar plug-in to Google's. Bear in mind, though, that they all have the potential to make your system more unstable, so only download what you really need – or at least really want. Always check the privacy small print, to be sure you're not installing spyware (see p.168), and never install any add-ons from sites you don't trust.

If you are determined to have lots of search toolbars at your disposal, you could try the **Groowe Toolbar** (www.groowe.com), which combines the capabilities of the Google bar with those of Yahoo!, YouTube, Amazon, Download.com and lots of other major sites. But you'd probably be better off mastering the art of Firefox Address Bar searching…

Firefox searching

One of the best features in Firefox (see p.69) is its customizable search tools. Internet Explorer 7 offers something similar, but's not as user-friendly. Here's how it works in Firefox:

▶ **Pick any site**, or a specific section of a site, where you often use a search box – it might be Amazon's Music Department, Wikipedia, a newspaper, whatever. Let's take the map site MultiMap as an example. First, go to the site and right-click (Ctrl+click on Macs) on the search box in question; from the menu, select "Add a Keyword for this Search".

▶ **Pick a keyword** You'll be prompted to pick a name for the search (this will appear in your Bookmarks) and a keyword. Pick something short and relevant to the site in question. In this example, let's say "map".

▶ **Search from the Address bar** Now, to search MultiMap, you can simply type the keyword and your search terms straight into the Firefox Address bar. To see a map of the postcode W1D 6HR, for example, type: *map W10 6RH*

> **Tip:** Firefox's address bar searching is especially useful if the site in question has a sluggish homepage or you have a slow connection.

map W10 6HR

More from Google

Google Alerts: find new stuff as it's written

Google Alerts offers a free and reliable way to keep track of a particular topic, story or person on the Web. Simply enter your search terms and whenever they appear in a new or updated webpage, you'll receive an email with a link to the page. Other similar services include TracerLock.

Google Alerts www.google.com/alerts
TracerLock www.tracerlock.com

Google Answers

If, even after you've honed your Web search skills, you still can't locate an answer to that burning question, you could always turn to someone else for help. First, try posting a question to a relevant online forum or try AllExperts – where volunteers advise people on their areas of expertise for free. Still no luck? You could try Google's pay-to-use Answers service. For between $2 and $200, an "expert" researcher will do the hard work for you and present you with a detailed response.

AllExperts www.allexperts.com
Google Answers answers.google.com

iGoogle homepage

If you find yourself smitten with all things Google then you might want to consider creating an iGoogle homepage for yourself which can then be set as your browser's "home" (see p.68). The iGoogle homepage is basically your own personally customized version of the main Google page, so as well as the Google search field you get to add so called Google Gadgets – little self-contained apps (applications) that can do everything from display new mail from Gmail to keeping you up to date with news feeds, the weather and much

BetterSearch

If you use Firefox (see p.69), and you want to change the way that Google and other search engines operate, you could install the BetterSearch extension. This allows you to add page thumbnails, Amazon ratings and more to your search results. It slows Google down a tiny bit, but it is useful.

BetterSearch
bettersearch.g-blog.net

Tip: Browsers that feature an Address bar search field allow you to highlight any text on a webpage and drag it straight into the search field.

99

Web directories

It's occasionally more useful to browse a range of sites within a topic or region rather than throw darts at the entire Web. For this you should turn to a **subject directory**. These aren't compiled by machines trawling the Web – they're put together by human beings. Everything is neatly filed under categories, making it easy for you to drill down to what you're after.

The problem with directories is that they're rarely very up to date or comprehensive. But they can still prove useful – both for locating things when Google fails to deliver, and for simply exploring the outer reaches of the Web that you'd never have thought to search.

The biggest general directories are **Yahoo!** and the **Open Directory**. Yahoo! may these days be best known for its search engine, messenger, webmail and mailing lists, but its directory was what established it as one of the most popular sites on the Net – and it's still up there, albeit not as current as it once was.

Yahoo! dir.yahoo.com

The Open Directory, aka **dmoz**, is a more recent project, which aimed to get around the problem of funding by encouraging anyone to become a volunteer editor. The Open Directory can be accessed via the dmoz homepage, but Google hosts a faster (and better organized) version of the same links.

Open Directory www.dmoz.org
Google Directory directory.google.com

Another directory worthy of a mention is **About. com**. Unlike others, its topics are presented by expert guides. This makes it more up to date, and an excellent jumping-off point for a whole host of topics.

About.com www.about.com

There's no shortage of other broad directories, though few are really worth using these days. That said, many sites maintain useful directories of links on specific subjects – though you'll usually find these more easily by doing a Google search. If that fails, you could try a directory of directories and search engines, such as:

Complete Planet www.completeplanet.com

more. In fact, the Google Gadget developer community is so active, that if you can think of something that you'd like a gadget to do, chances are that it's already been built and all you need to do is add it to your page via the "Add stuff" link.

To get started with iGoogle, all you need is a Google account (which is the same as a Gmail account, see p.109). To find out more, visit:

iGoogle www.google.com/ig

And more…

Some of the other wings of the Google empire are covered elsewhere in this book. For example:

▶ **Google Docs** See p.281
▶ **Google Groups** See p.139
▶ **Google Mail** See p.109
▶ **Google Maps** See p.288

But there's much more to the world's most popular website. To see what Google are experimenting with right now, go straight to:

Google Labs labs.google.com

Or for answers about every Google-related question you could ever want to ask, see gpsgfaq.googlepages.com. More Google news, views, gossip, tips, history and the rest can be found at:

Unofficial Google Weblog google.weblogsinc.com

Tip: From your iGoogle homepage, click the "Change theme…" link to access hundreds of custom display settings and backgrounds for your page.

8

RSS feeds

Choose your own news

One of the greatest things to happen to the Web in recent years has been the massive growth of RSS – short for Really Simple Syndication. RSS allows you to view "feeds" or "newsfeeds" from blogs, news services and other websites. Each feed consists of headlines of new or updated articles, along with the full text or a summary or extract. If you see something that you'd like to read, click on the headline to view the full story.

One benefit of RSS is that it saves you regularly visiting your favourite sites to check for new content: if something's been added or changed, you'll always know about it. But the real beauty of the system is that you can use a tool called an **aggregator** or **feed reader** to combine the feeds from all your favourite sites. It's almost like having your own personalized magazine or newspaper.

Picking an aggregator

There are two main ways to view RSS feeds. The first is to use an aggregator application installed on your computer. This might be a stand-alone application, such as…

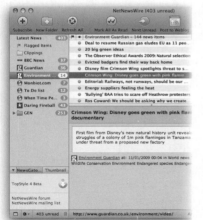

RSS Owl www.rssowl.org
BlogBridge www.blogbridge.com
NetNewsWire www.newsgator.com/INDIVIDUALS/NETNEWSWIRE

… or it might simply be your Web browser. Recent versions of Safari and Internet Explorer have RSS aggregators built right in.

RSS bookmarks in Firefox

At the time of writing, Firefox requires an extension (see p.84) to provide full RSS support. However, it does let you view RSS headlines via "Live Bookmarks". When you go to a site with an RSS feed, Firefox will display a small orange icon at the bottom of the Window. Click this to get the option of subscribing to the feed through the creation of a special RSS bookmark. From then on you can view the headlines for that feed by clicking the relevant entry either in the Bookmarks menu or, even better, the Bookmarks Toolbar. You can also add a Live Bookmark manually – useful if Firefox doesn't find the feed on a page. Click Manage Bookmarks in the Bookmark Menu, press New Bookmarks, and enter the RSS address.

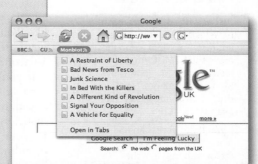

Firefox, meanwhile, offers RSS bookmarks (see box above). For full RSS tools in Firefox or any older browser, grab a plug-in, such as

Lektora www.lektora.com (plug-in for IE and Firefox; PC & Mac)
Wizz RSS www.wizzcomputers.com (plug-in for Firefox; PC & Mac)
Saft haoli.dnsalias.com (plug-in for pre-RSS Safari; Mac)

The second option is to sign up with a Web-based aggregator. This way, you access all your feeds via your own customized webpage. The main advantage of this option is that you can access the page from any computer connected to the Internet – at home, at work and abroad, say. The main online aggregators include:

Bloglines www.bloglines.com
Google Reader reader.google.com
My Yahoo! my.yahoo.com
Waggr www.waggr.com

For links to lots more aggregators, both online and computer-based see: en.wikipedia.org/wiki/Aggregator

The RSS bunny

If you have wireless at home and fancy having a selection of RSS feeds spoken out loud by a plastic rabbit at preprogrammed times each day – and who wouldn't, after all – **check out** nabaztag.com.

Finding and viewing feeds

Most news aggregators offer a list of popular feeds to get you started. But you can delete those – if you like – and add any feed you like. You'll find links to feeds all over the Web. Visit any popular news site or blog and look for a link labelled RSS or XML (see box). Very often the link will be orange.

If you're using a browser with RSS capability, when you click on a link to a feed, it should display properly automatically. Also try dragging the address to your bookmarks bar to reveal a dropdown list of headlines in Firefox. To find out how to combine multiple feeds, search the "help" files in your browser.

If you're using a Web-based aggregator, on the other hand, click on the link to the feed and then copy its Web address. Then visit your aggregator, find the new feed option and paste in the copied address.

Note that some sites have many feeds. The BBC, for example, has a feed for each major section of its news site: World, Politics, Technology, etc.

Podcasts

Though the acronym "RSS" is commonly associated with the distribution of text-based "news", it can also deliver many other types of files: music, video and more. Though many people will not have heard of RSS, they will have undoubtedly heard of **Podcasting** (see p.283), which is essentially online radio delivered, via an RSS feed, as files ready to be played on a computer, iPod or MP3 player (see p.193).

Communication

Email

Like regular mail – only better

9

Email is a remarkable thing: a form of communication that can be as considered as letter-writing but with the convenience of the telephone. A form of communication that, though still relatively young, carries more business correspondence than any other. And a form of communication that cuts through geographical, financial and practical boundaries.

Email is also very simple to get to grips with. However, many users don't get the best out of their account or their mail program, so their email experience is less enjoyable and less efficient than it might be. This chapter may help. It starts at the beginning, looking at the different types of email account that are available, and goes on to look at setting up an email program; organizing messages; collecting mail on the move; staying private; and avoiding junk mail, or spam as it's usually known.

Choosing an account & address

Email accounts and email addresses are very easy to find. However, before you grab the first one that comes your way, determine which type would suit you best. There are three main choices: an account from your ISP, an account from a stand-alone service such as Yahoo! or Gmail, or an address based on your own domain name. Let's look at the pros and cons of each in turn.

Email from your ISP

Most ISPs provide at least one email address as part of any Internet access package. These are usually decent enough in terms of reliability, but most are weak when it comes to online storage space for your messages and the feature set available for checking your mail online. Even more importantly, if you ever switch ISP, you'll lose the address, which can be a real pain. Of course, you can email your regular correspondents and tell them that you're changing address but you're bound to still miss a few messages – especially if you've ever given out your old address on business cards or other stationery. For that reason alone, you'd be far better using a stand-alone email service such as Gmail.

Email jargon: Web access, POP & IMAP

When someone sends you a message, it is delivered to your email provider's server (a special computer connected to the Internet). You can view all your messages that are currently stored on the server by going to the relevant website (eg yahoo.com) and logging into your mail account. You can do this from any computer. It's known as Web access.

Many people only use Web access to send and receive their emails. However, there are various benefits to using a special email application such as Outlook, Mail or whatever tool is built into your mobile phone. For example, this way, all your messages and attachments will be available on your laptop or phone even when you're on a bus or plane and can't get online.

There are two common ways in which an account can be set up to work with a mail application. Some accounts – such as Gmail – offer both. Others may offer only one or the other. The two ways are POP3 and IMAP:

▶ With **POP3**, each time you check for new mail in your mail program, the messages are downloaded from the provider's server onto your computer. It's a bit like a real-world postal service (and, indeed, POP stands for Post Office Protocol). Usually, messages are deleted from the server once this has happened, which, annoyingly, means you won't be able to see them if you check your mail from a different computer. It is possible to avoid this happening (see p.116) but the best solution is to use IMAP.

▶ With **IMAP** the master copy of all messages are based on the server and your mail program simply synchronizes to display the same messages on your computer. This way, if you delete a message on your phone or at work, say, then that message will immediately be deleted on the server and then from your home computer. Likewise, your Sent folder will contain emails sent from home, work or anywhere else.

Gmail and other free email providers

Stand-alone email providers don't tie you to your ISP. Additionally, the best free services – such as Gmail, known as Google Mail in some countries – provide so much online storage for your messages that you can leave all your emails permanently online, allowing you to access them from anywhere. In addition, they also offer POP3 and IMAP access, enabling you to easily access your account with a regular email program or Internet phone.

Gmail also has a great Web interface, allowing you to search through all your messages in seconds, and it automatically organizes your messages into conversations, keeping everything neat and tidy. It features great junk-mail filters and, best of all, it even allows you to import other email accounts so that you can see everything in one place – great if you have an old Hotmail or Yahoo! account that you hardly ever check.

Gmail (Google Mail) www.gmail.com

We'll come back to Gmail later in this chapter. Of course, there are scores of other free email providers on the Web, though none is quite as good as Gmail. That said, many people still swear by the main competitor, Yahoo! Mail:

Yahoo! www.yahoo.com

As for the rest, they're very unlikely to be as good, so unless you have some specific need, you're probably best sticking with the above two services. If you do look elsewhere, the main things to think about are the amount of storage space (don't accept anything less than a gigabyte); the "freezing" period (you don't want an account that deletes all your messages if you don't check your mail for a while); and the degree to which you trust the company in question to stay in business. For thousands of services, see:

Free Email Provider Guide www.fepg.net
Free Email Address Directory www.emailaddresses.com

Hot or not mail?

Microsoft's webmail service, Hotmail, is hugely popular, but compared with Gmail, Yahoo! and other such services, it's pretty crumby. The free version offers a comparatively tiny amount of storage space for messages, and if you don't use your account for just a few weeks it will be "frozen" – your messages will be deleted and you'll have to log in to "reactivate" the account.

Tip: By default, Gmail shows "Web Clips" – ads and bits of news, etc – above your inbox. If this annoys you, you can turn it off in Settings > Web Clips.

Tip: Webmail and ISP email addresses carry **zero prestige**, so if possible avoid using one as a business address. Instead, register your own domain name.

Making the most of Gmail

To give a sense of why Gmail is almost certainly the best email system currently on offer, and to help you get the most from it if you've already signed up, here's a quick look at some of its best features.

Threaded emails

Gmail keeps your email organized automatically by combining all messages with the same subject line into "conversations". This makes it dramatically easier to stay on top of everything.

Archive and search

Once you've finished with an email or conversation, simply press the Archive button and the messages will be removed from your inbox to keep everything tidy. You can still access all your old messages via the excellent search tool or by clicking "All Mail".

Import and send email from other accounts

If you're switching from another email system such as Yahoo! or Hotmail, or from an ISP account, you can automatically pick up new messages from your old account, along with any messages stored on the server, by clicking Settings > Accounts > Get mail from other accounts.

One of the best and most unusual features of Gmail is that it allows you not only to pick up email from other accounts, but also to send from other accounts. This means you can log in to one website to check and send from all your home, work and other email accounts. To set this up, click Settings > Accounts and specify the account you want to be able to send from. Once you've confirmed that you actually own that account by clicking a link in a confirmation email you can then choose which account to send from each time you start a new message.

Ads are optional

Many online email services oblige you to look at ads. With Gmail, however, all you see is a mix of small text ads and mixed news headlines above your inbox. If you don't like these, you can simply turn them off by clicking Settings > Web Clips.

Huge amount of storage space

At the time of writing, Gmail offers around seven gigabytes of storage space for each account, and this rises over time. You can see at a glance how much space you've used up at the bottom of the screen.

Google Docs and Calendars

Once you've logged into Gmail, you're only a click away from a bunch of other online tools such as Google Documents (see p.281) and Calendars. Documents is basically a pared back version of Word and Excel, except your documents are saved in your Google account rather than on your hard drive. That means you can access them from anywhere and easily invite others to view or collaborate on them.

Labs

Click Settings > Labs to reveal a huge range of extra features that are currently being developed either by Google themselves or other programmers. You'll find lots of useful things in there. At the time of writing, the best picks on offer include a Task list for keeping track of things you need to do, and an option for automatically archiving emails as you reply to them – really handy for keeping your inbox tidy.

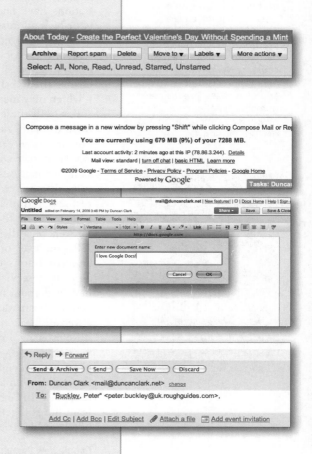

Email via your own domain name

The likes of Gmail and Yahoo! are all well and good, but both options have one built-in problem: you can't completely design your own address. Even in the unlikely event that you can get the address you want – such as john.smith@gmail.com – you're still stuck with the ISP or email provider's name after the @. Also, there's always the possibility – however unlikely – that the provider will change the website or conditions of service in a way you don't like – which may mean changing your email address.

For both these reasons, it's worth considering **registering your own domain name** (web address). Let's say you resigter the domain www.johnsmith.com. You could then use the email addresses mail@johnsmith.com, john@johnsmith.com and/or anything else in the same format. Besides the fact that this kind of address is unquestionably cool, you can also rest assured that you'll be able to keep the addresses forever, regardless of which ISP you use, or the terms and conditions of any specific mail service. You also have a domain registered in case you ever want to put up a website.

Registering a domain isn't very expensive – around $10 per year – though some registrars will charge you extra for a fully functioning email service. The best option is to register your domain with Google, in which case you'll get the email address you want but still get to use Gmail's features and tools. This is the best of all worlds. To sign up, visit:

Google New Domain www.google.com/a/cpanel/domain/new

For more on registering a domain, see p.220.

Email programs

Services such as Gmail offer such good website-based email that many people no longer bother using an **email program** (also known as an email **application** or **client**). However, email programs offer some advantages. They're still slicker and more feature-rich than websites, and they respond to your commands faster – especially if you have a slow Internet connection. In addition, they allow you access to your mail even when you're not connected to the Internet. This can be handy when travelling with a laptop, or if you have a slow or unreliable connection at home.

Which mail program?

If you do decide you want to use a mail program, the first question is which one to use. The most obvious choice is the one already installed on your computer. Modern PCs and Macs both come with a program simply called **Mail**. These share the same name but are completely unrelated. Both are pretty good, with all the features required by the typical email user. But there are various others available to buy or download for free online. These offer some different features, and, in the case of PC users, they may leave you more prone to security risks than the alternatives – simply because Windows Mail is so ubiquitous.

The most popular free email client is **Thunderbird**, a powerful open-source application built by programmers around the world. Thunderbird, the sister application to the Firefox Web browser, is definitely worth trying out – especially for PC users. Mac users may also prefer it, though it doesn't integrate with other elements of the OS X operating system quite as well as Apple Mail.

Another freebie is **Opera Mail**. Like the rest of the Opera browser suite, it was the first to introduce many useful features that have subsequently turned up in its competitors. Its most unique quality, however, is that it's viewed in the same window you use to browse the Web. This is handy for anyone who uses Opera as a Web browser,

Tools & plug-ins

If you want to stick with your current email program, but there's a particular feature that it lacks, it's worth searching around for a plug-in or script that will add the tool you're after. For Windows Mail and Outlook Express extras, browse the software archives list on p.183. Or for dozens of AppleScripts for adding functionality to mail clients on Macs, see:

www.apple.com/downloads/macosx/email_chat

but pretty well rules out the mail program for anyone else.

Thunderbird www.mozilla.org/products/thunderbird
Opera www.opera.com

Mail programs that you have to pay for are typically aimed primarily at business users, and offer advanced contacts, calendar and task-management tools. You can safely get by without all this extra bulk but, if it sounds like your cup of tea, there are various options out there. By far the most widely used is **Outlook,** which ships as part of Microsoft Office for PC. The Mac version is called **Entourage,** but it's roughly the same program. It's certainly worth giving Outlook or Entourage a try if you have Office, but otherwise they're not worth shelling out for. Outside the Microsoft camp, a few people still recommend **Eudora.**

Outlook www.microsoft.com/outlook
Entourage www.mactopia.com
Eudora www.eudora.com

Setting up a mail program

Before you can start sending and receiving messages using an email program, you'll need to set up your account(s). Sometimes this process will be automated, but it's worth taking some time to understand what's going on – to generally demystify how email works, and so you can easily enter your email profile on other machines. You might also like to change a few of the default settings, as they're not always the best for everyone.

First, you need to get your account details from whoever is supplying your email account. That might be your ISP or an online service such as Gmail (in whch case log in, click Settings and enable IMAP access to get things going).

Most mail programs will prompt you to enter your details the first time you run the program. Otherwise, or if you're adding a second account, you need to find the option to add a new account – usually within **Accounts** (in the Tools menu on a PC) or Preferences (in the application menu on a Mac).

Whichever program you're using, the details you'll need to enter will be the same, as listed below. Let's say your name is Anton Lavin and your email address is anton@leisureprince.com:

▶ **Name or Display Name** Who or what will appear as the sender of your mail. In this example, Anton Lavin (or anything else you choose).

▶ **Email Address** Where mail you send will appear to come from. In this case, anton@leisureprince.com

▶ **Return Address** Where replies to your mail will go. Most users opt for their regular email address (anton@leisureprince.com), but you could divert it to another account – a work email account, for instance.

▶ **Outgoing Mail Server (SMTP)** The computer that handles your outgoing mail. You'll need to get its address from your ISP or mail provider, though very often it's the same as the second half of your address, but with mail. or smtp. in front of it. For example: smtp.leisureprince.com

▶ **Incoming Mail Server** The computer that handles arriving messages. You'll need to get its address from your ISP, though it will usually be the same as the last part of your email address with pop. or mail. added at the start. For example: mail. leisureprince.com

▶ **Username** Usually the first part of your email address – in this example "anton". However, in some cases it could be your entire email address or even part of the second half of your address (the account name might be "prince" if the address was anton@prince.leisureprince.com).

Email

One account, two computers

If you regularly use an email program on two or more computers – a desktop and a laptop, say – you can easily set up the same mail account on both. However, if your account is POP3 (see p.108), then any messages you download to one machine will typically no longer be available to download to the other, so you'll end up with your mail archive spread across two computers. One workaround is to tell the mail program on one machine to leave a copy of the messages on the server after downloading – a preference available in with the other settings for the account in question. On the other machine also choose to delete the server copy after, say, a month. That way, as long as you use both computers every month, you'll always have your complete and up-to-date mail archive on both machines. Alternatively, use an IMAP account (see p.108) or stick to accessing you mail via the Web on one or both of your computers.

▶ **Password** Could be either the same as your connection password or separate, depending on your provider.

You may also be asked for a "**description**" or **account name**: simply pick a name to help you distinguish this account from any others.

Adding a second account
With any modern email program, you can collect and send from as many separate accounts as you like. This is useful whether you want to use multiple addresses from one provider, to deal with mail from more than one ISP, or to just set up a new version of your main account with a different return address. It's exactly the same procedure as adding the first account.

Tweaking the settings
If you leave your email program with the default settings, a couple of features might annoy you. Even if they don't, it's worth going through the various options and deciding what you'd prefer: you'll inevitably discover lots of things you didn't know about. For example, you might want to leave copies of recent messages on the server, so you can access them when checking your messages via the Web (see box). To scan the various options, select "Options" from the Tools menu in Windows Mail or Preferences in the Mail menu in Apple Mail.

116

How to use email: the basics

Using email is so simple that we won't waste space here with a detailed, step-by-send guide. But for the small minority of people who have never sent or received an electronic message, here's the least you need to know:

Sending and receiving

▶ **Send an email** Open your mail. Click New or Compose. Enter the recipient's email address in the "**To:**" field. Next, add a **Subject** – essentially just a title for the message so the recipient knows what it's about and can easily find the message in the future. Enter your message text in the main body of the email window and, when you're done, click **Send.**

▶ **Receiving mail** Your mail system should check for new messages every few minutes, but you can force it to check at any moment b hitting refresh (on a web browser) or the **Send/Receive** or **Check Mail** button (on a mail program). Incoming mail arrives in the **Inbox**, unless you set "filters" to dump it elsewhere; see p.123. If you use a mail program, you easily **can change the new-mail alert sound:** on a PC, look under Sounds in the Control Panel; on a Mac, open Apple Mail, click Preferences in the Mail menu, and look under General.

▶ **Unread messages** Messages that haven't been read yet will be marked in bold and/or have a closed envelope symbol next to them. And each mail folder will display a number telling you how many unread messages it contains (if any). If you click on a message and it becomes "read" without you actually reading it, or you just want to remind yourself to return to it later, right-clicking will give you the option of marking it as unread again.

▶ **To, Cc, Bcc – sending to more than one person** If you want to send the same message to multiple people, you have two options. When you don't mind the recipients knowing who else is receiving it – or you want the recipients to be able to reply to them all – use the "**To:**" field and "**Cc:**" fields. These are basically the same, the distinction being that they allow you to let people know whether they are the primary recipient or just being "copied in". If, however, there are names that you want to be masked from the other recipients, put these addresses in the "**Bcc:**" (**blind carbon copy**) field. Everyone, including those you Bcc, will be able to see who the message was addressed and copied to, but no one will be able to see who was in the "Bcc:" field. If you want to send a bulk mail without disclosing anyone in the list, put yourself in the "To:" field and Bcc everyone else. If you don't see a Bcc option, you may need to click a link or turn it on via the View menu.

▶ **Replying** To reply to a message, click **Reply** or – if you want to send to everyone who received the original – **"Reply all"**. Typically, the original message will appear in your reply, differentiated by colours, lines or tags (>). You can keep parts or the entire original message or delete the lot – so when someone asks you a question or raises a point, you're able to include that section and answer it directly underneath. This saves them having to refer back and forth between their message and your answer. You can normally tell if a message is a reply because the subject will start with "Re:".

▶ **Forwarding a message** If you'd like to share an email with someone, just click Forward. You can tell if a message has been forwarded to you because the subject line will start with "Fwd:" or "Fw:".

Bouncing back

If you send an email to a badly constructed or nonexistent address, your message should "bounce back" to you with an error message saying what went wrong. This tends to happen within a matter of minutes. Sometimes, however, mail bounces back after a few days. This usually indicates a physical problem in delivering the mail rather than an addressing error. When it occurs, just send it again. To do this, find the message in your sent items folder, select all the text and click Copy in the Edit menu. Then click "Reply All" and paste the message back into the body of the email. Remove yourself from the list of recipients and click send. This way your resent message won't be styled as a reply, and you don't have to enter the recipients manually.

Signatures

All mail programs let you set up a **signature**. This appears automatically on the bottom of a new email, a bit like headed notepaper. It's common practice to put your address, phone number, title (obviously only put in things that you don't mind everyone in the world seeing), sometimes rounded off with a recycled witticism. To create and manage your signatures, look for settings or preferences option on your online email system or mail program.

The Address Book

PCs, Macs and online email systems all offer a place for storing email addresses and other contact details. The advantages of an online system are that your contacts are available from any computer, anytime, and everything is safely backed up on the Web. That said, it is perfectly possible to back up the contacts stored on your PC or Mac (see p.169).

On a PC, the contacts tool is Address Book, and you can open it from the Start menu (it's under Programs, within Accessories) or by pressing the book icon in Outlook Express or Mail. On a Mac, look within Applications or on the Dock at the bottom of your screen.

Whatever contacts system you use, you can add a new person either by opening your contacts list and pressing "new" or "add", or by right-clicking an email and choosing "Add sender to Address Book".

Once someone's in your Address Book, you can type the first few letters of their email address, name or "nickname" (if you've assigned them one) into the To: field of a blank message, and the full version should automatically pop up. Alternatively, select one or more people in your Address Book and click the "send mail to" option.

If you want to migrate from one contacts system to another, there's almost always a way to do it. First, explore the export options of your existing address book to see whether you can save all your contact information into a file that can be imported into the new system. If this doesn't seem to be possible, try Googling and you'll usually be able to find a downloadable tool that will make the switch for you.

vCards

A **vCard** is an address-book entry with as many contact details as you care to disclose. You might like to attach a copy to your mail so your recipients can add it to their address books. To set it up in Windows Mail or Outlook Express, edit the "Business card" section under the Compose tab in Options.

Tip: In email programs, like any others, the fonts on offer depend on the font files installed on your computer. Not everyone has the same fonts, so if you use a fancy gothic script in an email, the person receiving it may see something completely different. The only fonts you can be absolutely certain that everyone will have are Arial, Times New Roman and Courier.

Return receipts

If you'd like to know if your mail has been opened you could try requesting a "**read receipt**". These notify you that your message has been opened by the recipient, but only if their mail program supports the **Message Disposition Notification** (MDN) standard. Not only that: even if their mail program supports it, when they receive your message a box will pop up asking whether they'd like to acknowledge receipt. If they say no, you'll get no receipt. In other words, it's not a reliable system and really **not worth the bother**.

Still, if you feel like experimenting with it, you can either request a receipt for individual messages (on the Tools menu in Outlook Express or Mail) or turn them on for all messages (within Options in the Tools menu). If you're serious about confirmation, however, ask your recipient to reply, send a follow-up or simply make a phone call.

HTML & rich text

Originally, email was a strictly plain-text affair. Microsoft Exchange introduced formatting, but it didn't really make an impact until Netscape introduced **HTML mail** as a new standard. This immediately blurred the distinction between email and the World Wide Web, bringing webpages right into emails.

Using email's HTML capabilities, Web publishers, particularly magazines and news broadcasters, can send you regular bulletins formatted as webpages complete with links to further information. It also means you can easily send webpages by email. In Windows, either drag and drop them into a message or choose Send Page from under the File menu of Internet Explorer. On a Mac, choose Mail Contents of This Page from the File menu in Safari.

HTML also lies behind the options for styling the text in your emails with different fonts, sizes and colours, or adding background colours, pictures or sounds. In this context it's usually referred to as Rich Text format, and your mail system will let you choose whether to compose messages in Plain Text (no formatting) or Rich Text.

These days all widely used mail programs and online systems can handle HTML, but the function is partially disabled in many big offices for security reasons. In this case, the recipient will get a weird-looking plain-text email with all the formatting as a useless and time-wasting attachment. For this reason – and because too much fancy formatting can detract from one of email's strongest features, simplicity – don't spend too much time worrying about the appearance of your email. Just get the words right.

Attachments

You can attach photos, documents and any other files to an email message as attachments. Just start a message, click the paperclip icon and locate the file you want to send. Or, if you're using a mail program, simply drag and drop the file or files into the message window.

Unless you know your recipient won't mind, it's bad practice to send attachments of more than a few megabytes. Larger attachments may bounce back and can take ages to download, getting in the way of the recipient's other messages.

For large files, a better option is to use a free file transfer website such MailBigFile or YouSendIt. Simply plug in your address and the recipients address, enter a message, point the website to the file in question and press send. The site will upload the file to the Internet and email the recipient a link to the file.

MailBigFile www.mailbigfile.com
YouSendIt www.yousendit.com

Zipping files

If you're **sending lots of files** – either in an email or via a website such as USentIt – you may want to bundle them all into a single compressed file or "archive". This is more convenient to send and will have the added advantage of shrinking the file size, thereby speeding up the sending and receiving process.

Receiving faxes and voicemail through email

Although thanks to email the days of fax are numbered, not everyone is quite up to speed. Fear not. It's usually possible to set up your PC or Mac to send and receive faxes. First connect a telephone cable to your computer's modem (even if you're using broadband for Internet access). Then:

▶ In Windows XP, open the Control Panel, click Add or Remove Programs, choose Add/Remove Windows Components, check the Fax Services box and click Next.

▶ In Windows Vista Business or Ultimate editions, open Windows Fax & Scan from All Programs.

▶ On a Mac, set things up via the Print and Fax section of System Preferences.

Receiving faxes on your PC or Mac is fine for home use, but what if your computer is in Houston and you're in Hochow? Or you want a US fax number, say, for use in Britain? For a small subscription charge, services such as **Efax** (www.efax.com) and **J2** (www.j2.com) will allocate you a phone number in the US or UK, or in hundreds or cities worldwide.

Faxes sent to these numbers are converted to email attachments, redirected to your email address or online mailbox, perhaps even with the faxed type converted into copyable, editable text. Callers can also leave voice messages, which will be forwarded as compressed audio files. Sending faxes from your Desktop is also a breeze, and the whole thing can even integrate with your Internet phone.

The most common compressed format is **zip** (.zip), which pretty-well everyone should be able to open these days. To create a zip file on any recent computer, simply select the folder or files you want to compress and then look in the File menu. On a PC, click **Send To Compressed Folder**; on a Mac, select **Compress** or **Create Archive Of**. If you have an older computer, you may need to download a compression program to do this (see p.182).

Note that the degree to which the files will shrink when zipped depends on the type of files you're sending. Compressed formats such as JPEG, GIF and MP3 won't get any smaller. See p.216 for more on compressing images.

Folders and labels

Just as it's a good idea to keep your work desk tidy and deal with paperwork as it arrives, try to keep your email in some kind of order. All email systems let you organize your correspondence into **folders or mailboxes**. It's good practice to use several such folders, dividing your mail into general topics – "family" and "work", for instance – or more specific things such as individual conversation topics. Once you've dealt with a message in your Inbox, either delete it or put it into a topic-specific folder.

You'll find an option for creating a new folder in the File menu of your mail program, or as a link on the main page of your online mail system. Things work slightly differently in Gmail, which encourages you to simply "Archive" messages once you've done with them. When you press archive, the email goes into your "All Mail" folder. If you also want to mark it as "family", "work" or whatever, you apply a "label" rather than dropping it into a folder. This way, you can apply more than one category to each message.

Filtering – message rules

You can set up your email system to **filter** incoming mail as it arrives. You might, for example, want all email from a particular person, or containing certain key phrases, to bypass the inbox and be sent straight to a particular folder or be deleted. This can be useful for general housekeeping as well as dealing with mailing lists (see p.129) and junk email (see p.124).

Filters also come into their own if you're sharing a mail program with other people. Simply set your mail program to automatically put all incoming messages into separate folders according to who they're addressed to (Apple Mail does this anyway).

To get started with filters, look for the "rules" or "filters" option – either on the main page of your online mail system or, if you use a mail program, in the Tools menu or Preferences panel.

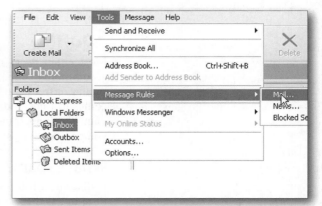

Tracking replies

It's a good idea to transfer each message out of your inbox and into a folder as you reply to it (or ignore it). That way you'll know that anything left in your inbox is still to be dealt with and you won't accidentally lose important messages under piles of junk. Or you might prefer to move anything that needs attention into a special folder until it's dealt with, so you never forget to reply to or act upon an email.

Another option is to "**flag**" messages for attention. On a PC, clicking in the flag column to the left of the sender in the mail folder will toggle a red flag on and off. Click on the top of the flag column to sort the folder and you can instantly see what's outstanding. In Apple Mail, select an email and choose **Mark>Flag** from the **Message** menu.

Backing up your mail

People sometimes forget when backing up essential files on their computer to do the same for their email archive and address book, though losing this data can be catastrophic. For more information on how to do this, see p.169.

Spam

Most email users receive a certain amount of unsolicited mail – commonly called **spam**. The odd junk email offering you easy money or free porn is not much hassle to delete, but when the spam comes in thick and fast, as it has a habit of doing, it can be a real pain. There are, however, steps you can take to reduce the amount you get – or at least the amount you see in your inbox.

What's spam?

Unlike most Internet slang, "**spam**" isn't an acronym or abbreviation, nor is there any logical relationship between junk email and canned meat. According to Net folklore, the word probably came from a Monty Python sketch. Whatever its origins, "to spam" means to send bulk email to a list gathered by unscrupulous means (or to post commercial messages inappropriately across multiple newsgroups. The messages themselves are also called "spam".

✉ xd4amU1qy@excite.com	Free Loan Quotations.....Lower your Rate!
✉ corn3161@elvisisthebomb.com	New Internet Casino $10 free on signup!!!!!
✉ marketpicks@taurus.prover.com.br	STOCK EXPECTED TO SOAR!!
✉ TheCellularDirectory@excite.com	Are you in the Cell411 Directory?..................
✉ 73E3w9SPS@mail.com	DISCOUNT FLORIDA DISNEY VACATION
✉ jamses098@usa.net	Rates DROPPED! Need Money? Aggressive le
✉ WorldWideInternic.com	RE: change your email address
✉ c379sg72@caramail.com	**Beautiful, Custom Websites $389 Complete!!
✉ DomainRegistryInternational.com	RE: change your email address
✉ wehret@usa.net	Order Your Viagra On Line Today !!
✉ wendolin17@aol.com	$69.95 a month lets you talk all you want
✉ TjG11QaB6@oceanfree.net	Cash In Hand and Lower Your Rate!
✉ newsletter@mydomain.com	You may have a 6:30am appointment
✉ marketpicks@taurus.prover.com.br	STOCK EXPECTED TO SOAR!!
✉ dessert@xgd123.com	Re: I'll tell you why!
freefromdebt@my-map-of-tasmania.com	Erase_Your_Debt_Today Guaranteed!!!!

What's not spam?

Although some of the mail you receive might be delivered in bulk or seem irrelevant to you, it's not spam if you've granted permission for someone to mail you. For example, you might have given your email address when you registered with a website and checked the box to keep you informed of special deals, or given the OK for them to pass your details on to their partners. This is known as **opt-in** or **permission-based** email. The difference between this and spam is that you should be able to get off the list by "**unsubscribing**".

If there isn't an unsubscribe instruction within the email, contact the site's support address and demand to get off the list. With genuine spam, however, you can't get off the list, and the return addresses are almost always bogus.

Stop them getting your address

The first thing you can do is try to prevent spammers from getting your address in the first place. **Guessing** is surprisingly common. They simply take a dictionary of names, append it to a list of domain names, run a test mailing and perhaps cull any that bounce back to them. So if your email address is john@hotmail.com or jane@a-major-ISP.net, there's not much you can do to stop them. You can,

How spammers get your address

The main ways spammers can get your address are: guessing it; harvesting it from the Web; tricking you into giving it to them through a website; or buying it from a mailing list merchant. Once they have your address, you can be sure they'll try to sell it to someone else. That means once you start receiving the junk, it's not likely to stop. In fact, it will probably get worse.

however, reduce the chance of them finding your email online by avoiding posting it anywhere on the Web, if possible. If you do want to post it – on your website, for example – consider putting an image of your email address, rather than writing it onto the webpage as text. This will avoid any malicious software recognizing it as an email address.

It's also perhaps worth setting up a secondary email address for registering with forums, competitions and the like. Only give your main address to a website when you're making a credit card purchase or you're sure they're reputable. If you do give your main address, ask not to be sent any offers from the site's "associates".

Spam solutions

Spammers know they're detested, but that doesn't bother them. It's a numbers game. They know there'll always be someone stupid enough to send them money. There's no point replying or asking to be taken off their list. They rarely use a valid email address and if they do it's normally shut down almost instantly. However, there are some things you can do to improve things.

Modern email systems have decent spam filters built in and turned on by default. Gmail's are particularly good, so one option is to send and receive via your existing address, but through a Gmail account (see p.110). Alternatively, you could try a free third-party plug-in for your mail program, such as:

MailWasher www.mailwasher.net

In **Apple Mail** and various other programs, you "train" the program to recognise spam by selecting each unsolicited message and clicking the Junk button. As time goes by, the program will get better and better at spotting spam and eventually you may trust it to divert any message it suspects directly into a spam folder. You may first have to turn the junk filters on in Preferences.

In **Windows Mail**, by contrast, the filter should be effective straight away, as the program downloads information about what is likely to be spam from the Internet.

If you can't beat the spam, a more comprehensive option is to sign up with Spam Arrest. You have to pay a small monthly fee (around £2/$3) but it will cut out 100 percent of spam. Once signed up, you set up a list of approved email addresses (or entire domains) – for example by uploading your address book. When someone who isn't on this approved list emails you, they are automatically sent a reply to verify that they're a real person.

Once they've done that (which involves typing a word into a box), the original email is sent to you and the sender is added to the approved list.

Spam Arrest www.spamarrest.com

Privacy

As email becomes ever-more intrinsic to all aspects of life, it's increasingly important to know that your messages are private. One threat to your email privacy is in the workplace. Indeed, when using a work account, your boss probably has the power to read your mail – in some companies it's standard practice. So don't use your work mail for correspondence that could land you in hot water. Instead, use a personal account that can be checked via the Web.

However, with any email account it's possible that someone could snoop on your messages as they journey across the Internet to or from your Inbox. Whoever provides your email account could – if they wanted – read your messages before they even got to you. A determined hacker may be able to do the same. In truth, neither possibility is very likely, but if you're concerned, you may want to consider using encryption. However, it's a bit of a pain.

Encryption

Encryption allows you to **scramble a message** so only the intended recipient can read it. There are various types of encryption, all of which involve using a mathematical algorithm to turn your text into what looks like meaningless junk, until the recipient uses the correct "code" or "key" to unscramble it.

One encryption option involves using a **digital certificate service** (see box opposite). Another is to use **PGP**, which stands for **Pretty Good Privacy** but is actually a military-strength technique. With PGP, you generate a public and a private key from a passphrase. You distribute the public key (by sending it to people or publishing it on your website) and keep the private key secure. When someone wants to send you a private message, they scramble it using your public key. You then use the private key, or your secret passphrase, to decode it. As you probably already twigged, it's only worth it if you're really concerned about your privacy.

For more about PGP and other security add-ons, see:

International PGP Home Page www.pgpi.org
Message Security Tools www.slipstick.com/addins/security.htm

Digital signing

Digital signing is a way to prove that an email was written by the person it claims to have come from. Here's how to get your signature. First, fetch a personal certificate from **Thawte** (www.thawte.com) or **Verisign** (www.verisign.com). Once it's installed, open your mail security settings (within Options or Preferences) and see that the certificate is activated. You may choose to sign all your messages digitally by default, or individually. Then send a secure message to all your regular email partners, telling them to install your certificate. Those with compatible mail programs can add your certificate against your entry in their address books. Then they'll be able to verify that mail that says it's from you is indeed from you. Don't use it flippantly, though, because it's a pain for your recipients.

Tip: HushMail and Mute-Mail offer privacy-focused email accounts with secure storage, encrypted messaging between users, and other such features:

HushMail www.hushmail.com
MuteMail mutemail.com

Sending email anonymously

Occasionally, when sending mail or joining a discussion, you might prefer to **conceal your identity** – to avoid embarrassment in health issues, for example. There are two main ways to send mail anonymously. The first is to sign up for an email account under a false name – or with a privacy specialist (see box, opposite).

The second involves **changing your configuration** so that it looks like your mail is coming from somebody else, either real or fictitious. If anyone tries to reply, their mail will attempt to go to that alias, and not to you. But be warned: it's possible to trace the header details back to your server if someone's eager – and, if you're up to no good, your national law enforcement agency might do exactly that.

Mailing lists

If you want email by the bucketload, join some mailing lists. This involves giving your email address to someone and receiving whatever they send until you beg them to stop. Mailing lists fall into two distinct categories.

The first are simple **one-way** newsletters, set up by a company or organization to keep you informed of news or changes: anything from hourly weather updates to six-monthly reports from a charity. Most busy sites publish newsletters these days. The other category is **two-way discussion lists**, in which the messages are written by the subscribers. A popular example is Freecycle (see p.154).

Discussion lists: how they work

Discussion-style mailing lists usually have two addresses: the **mailing address** used to contact its members, and the **administrative address** used to send commands to the server or administrator of the list. Don't mix them up or everyone else on the list will think you're a dill.

Start your own discussion list

Discussion lists are free to set up and simple to manage via the Web. If you'd like to create your own, see:

Coollist www.coollist.com
Topica www.topica.com
Google groups.google.com
Yahoo! groups.yahoo.com

WELCOME TO COOLLIST
the free mailing list

Many lists are **unmoderated**, meaning they relay messages immediately. Messages on **moderated** lists, however, get screened first. This can amount to censorship, but more often it's welcome, as it can improve the quality of discussion and keep it on topic by pruning irrelevant and repetitive messages. It all depends on the moderator, who's rarely paid for the service.

If you'd rather receive your mail in large batches than have it trickle through, request a **digest** where available. These are normally sent daily or weekly, depending on the traffic.

Climbing aboard a list

Joining should be simple. In most cases, you **subscribe** by email or through a form on a webpage. It depends who's running the list. Once you're on an open list, you'll receive all the messages sent to the list's address, and everyone else on the list will receive whatever you send. Your first message will either welcome you to the list, or ask you to confirm your email address (to stop prank subscriptions). **Keep the welcome message**, as it might also tell you how to **unsubscribe**, and set other parameters such as ordering it in **digest format**. You'll need to follow the instructions to the letter.

Coping with the volume

Before you set off subscribing to every list that takes your fancy, consider using **separate email addresses** for mailing lists and personal mail. Apart from the obvious benefits in managing traffic and filtering, it protects your main account from spammers (p.126). If you do set up an extra address, remember when posting to select whichever account you want to use before hitting Send.

Even if you only use one address, it pays to **filter** your list messages (p.123), so your high-priority mail doesn't get buried amongst the endless tide.

How to find an email address

Probably the best way to find out someone's email address is to simply **ring up and ask**. Don't know their phone number? Try an online phone directory (see overleaf). Alternatively, if you know where they work, look up their company's website. Still no joy? If they fall into the long-lost category, it might be possible to trace them though the Web. Start by **searching Google** for leads (remember to search for their name as a phrase; see p.92). You might find their name mentioned somewhere on the Web, and perhaps even their personal website. If not, try social networking sites such as Facebook (see p.238) or a find-your-schoolmates site such as:

Friends Reunited www.friendsreunited.com
Class Mates www.classmates.com

With Friends Reunited, you won't get the person's email address straight off, but if they are registered, you'll be able to pay a fee to contact them.

People finders

Your email address should be private unless you instruct someone to list it in a directory or make it public in some other way. Unlike the telephone networks, there are no official public email registries. There are, however, a few independent **people-search services** that boast huge email address databases – sometimes combined with street addresses and phone numbers. Unfortunately, you'll find most of the email addresses are out of date. Still, if you're trying every angle to locate a long-lost childhood sweetheart, they might be worth a look as a last resort.

Internet Address Finder www.iaf.net
WhoWhere www.whowhere.com
Yahoo! People Search people.yahoo.com

Look in the phone book

Another way to track someone down is via directory enquiries or a phone book, most of which have a presence online on sites such as:

192.com www.192.com (UK)
Anywho www.anywho.com (US)
BT Directory Enquiries www.bt.com/directory-enquiries (UK)
CitySearch www.citysearch.com (US)
SuperPages.com www.superpages.com (US)
White Pages www.whitepages.com.au (Aus)
Yellow Pages www.yellowpages.com.au (Aus)
Yellow Pages www.yell.co.uk (UK)

Chat & calls

10

Instant messaging, video conferencing and Internet phone calls

Back in the Internet days of old, "chat" referred to geeky Internet Relay Chat, complete with its obscure commands, confusing channels and free-for-all chat rooms, which were mainly used by frustrated teenagers (plus the occasional pervert) to flirt with each other. Thankfully, things have moved on. Today, "chat" programs let you exchange real-time typed messages with friends and family – and also to make voice and video calls. Such programs offer a fun way to communicate and can save you money, too.

Assuming you have broadband, you can make computer-to-computer calls – with or without video – to anywhere in the world for free. You can also call regular and mobile phones. This can be very useful if your home phone is often in use, effectively providing a second line without any standing charge. Potentially, it can also slash your phone bills, especially if you regularly call long distance. Prices are as low as 2¢/1p per minute to landlines and mobiles in most of Europe, North America and Australasia (note that UK mobiles are more like 15p per minute).

Even if you don't have broadband, you can still use instant messaging, whereby you exchange typed messages with your contacts in real time.

The basics

To get started with messaging or calls between computers, you first need to download and install a **"messenger" or "chat" program**. There are various options out there, most of which offer calls to real phones in addition to typed messaging and voice and video calls between computers. If you don't like the idea of using your computer to make calls, but you still want to save money on your phone bill, you might prefer to investigate an Internet-phone subscription service – see p.137.

Skype, AIM, Yahoo!, Live…

One problem with the various chat programs is that they can't all communicate with each other. So in order to chat with or call a particular person's computer, you'll need to have that person install the same or a compatible program. Here are the most popular choices.

AIM www.aim.com (PC & Mac)
AIM, short for AOL Instant Messenger, offers messaging, voice and video calls to anyone using AIM, iChat and ICQ. There's also an optional AIMPhoneLine service for calling and receiving calls from regular phones.

iChat www.apple.com/ichat (Mac only)
iChat comes pre-installed on recent Macs and is available to buy for older Macs. You get free text, voice and video to other iChat users plus PC users running AOL messenger. The audio and video quality is great, and you can include up to ten people in a single conversation. However, you can't call regular phones.

Tip: The technology that allows computers to connect to normal phonelines is called **VoIP** (Voice over Internet Protocol), though terms such as **"Internet telephony"** or **"broadband phone"** are also used.

Calling from your computer: what you'll need

To make decent-quality computer-to-computer voice calls, you'll need an audio headset or handset. It is possible to get by with a regular microphone and speakers (including those built into most laptops), but these tend to lead to annoying feedback and echoes because the sound from the speakers get picked up by the microphone.

When one or preferably both parties are using a headset or handset, the audio quality usually sounds far better – more like a regular phone call. The least expensive option is a call-centre-style headset that will plug into your computer's mic and speaker sockets. A neater-looking alternative is a USB handset (pictured, bottom; also see p.16), but these cost a little more and are best for desktop computers where they remain permanently plugged in (on a laptop you might have to mess around with settings each time you plug and unplug the handset).

For video calls, you'll also need a webcam. These come built in to some modern computers (including most Macs), but are also available to buy separately. They're not expensive, though it's worth avoiding the very cheapest as the quality varies widely. Read reviews or see the thing in action before buying. If you need a webcam for a Mac that doesn't have one built-in, be sure to check its compatibility, as most are PC-only.

Finally, for decent-quality voice or video calls, both parties will need broadband. Dial-up connections can be used, but the sound will be awful and the video will be more like an inch-wide slideshow, updating every second or so – worth it, perhaps, for a quick glimpse of a loved one at the other side of the world, but not as a real means of communication.

Skype www.skype.com (PC & Mac)
Chat for free with other Skype users in messages, voice and video. Optional paid-for service ("SkypeOut") for calls to regular phones.

Windows Live Messenger get.live.com/messenger (PC only)
Previously called MSN Messenger. Enables messaging, voice and video calls with anyone using Windows Live Messenger or Yahoo! Messenger. Optional "Live Call" service lets you call regular phones.

Yahoo! Messenger messenger.yahoo.com (PC & Mac)
Messaging, voice and video calls with anyone using Windows Live Messenger or Yahoo! Messenger. Optional "Yahoo! Voice" service for calling regular phones.

Others you may come across include **ICQ**, which is mainly focused on typed instant messaging, **Jabber**, which is a powerful, open-source system accessible via various programs but mainly used by techie types and companies.

ICQ www.icq.com
Jabber www.jabber.org

If your friends are split across numerous systems, you can install more than one program. Or you could use a single program that can tap into various systems. There are many of these, but the most widely used is **Trillian**, which offers access to AIM, ICQ, MSN and Yahoo!.

Trillian www.trillian.cc

Getting started

Once you've got a messenger installed, you'll need to set up a username and password. The exact method depends on the program, but it's usually self-explanatory. Then you're ready to log-in and add some contacts.

If your friends are already set up, email them and ask for their usernames – it will often be their email address, but not necessarily – which you can then add to your buddy list. Refer to Help within your program of choice for specific instructions. From that point on, it's hard to go wrong. You'll be able to see when your contacts are online, and vice versa, and start a typed, voice or video conversation at the touch of a button.

To call a regular phone, first buy some credit on the website of your messenger. Then you should be able to simply enter a phone number (with a "+" and the international dialling code) and press call.

Exploring the options

Once you've got everything up and running, take the time to browse through the program's Options (on a PC) or Preferences (on a Mac). For example, you can choose whether you'd like the program to start up whenever you turn on your computer, when you connect to the Internet or simply when you ask it to.

Also check out the options for appearing like you're offline, busy, etc – sometimes you might want to be able to see which of your friends are available, but not necessarily want them all to be able to see you. However, if you simply have someone on your buddy list who you'd rather hide from permanently, add them to your Block List (look in Options or Preferences).

Using a regular phone

As we've seen, one option for making PC-to-Phone calls is to use a program such as Skype or Yahoo! Messenger, which allow you to call landlines and mobiles directly from your computer. An alternative is a **broadband phone** service which allows you to attach a regular phone handset to your broadband modem. This can be

Tip: One disadvantage of broadband phone services is that they don't work if there's a powercut. Also, because calls aren't routed via your local exchange, VoIP can't always substitute a standard or mobile phone if you need to make a call to the emergency services.

more convenient, since it saves you being tied to your PC or Mac, and still offers massive discounts on call charges.

Some broadband-phone services are designed to completely replace your current phone service, but others are designed to run in parallel. Note that in many cases you'll need to keep your existing phone service running for incoming calls and/or to keep your ADSL broadband connection functioning. Many broadband phone

Old-school discussions: IRC, chat rooms & newsgroups

Back in the days before the likes of Skype and Yahoo! Messenger, the term "chat" referred to two rather different forms of online communication: IRC and chat rooms. Both are still around … just about.

IRC, which stands for **Internet Relay Chat**, is similar to instant messaging in that it takes place via a special chat program. However, it's a rather geeky system, requiring you to know various special codes to make the most of it. As such, those still inhabiting the system are mainly techie types who got to know it years ago. If you fancy exploring this old corner of the Internet, download an IRC program such as…

Ircle www.ircle.com (Mac)
mIRC www.mirc.co.uk (PC)

…enter a nickname and (fake) email address and choose a chat server address from the list. You'll probably soon be confused, so pick up some tips here:

IRC Help www.irchelp.org/irchelp/networks
IRC-Chat.org www.irc-chat.org

Like almost every other aspect of the old-world Internet, chat moved onto the Web, taking the form of **chat rooms** – special webpages where people can quickly and easily join in a discussion. Chat rooms were very

popular for a while, but their numbers reduced massively after instant messaging evolved. Many were also closed down due to allegations that paedophiles were using them to "groom" children. There are still a few chat rooms out there, but you'll struggle to find anyone you actually want to chat with. These days, most feature little more than unrelated streams of comments, often

services charge a subscription that includes unlimited national calls, with a small surcharge for long distance. Some of the most popular services include:

Broadvoice www.broadvoice.com (US)
BT Broadband Talk www.bt.com/broadbandtalk (UK)
VoicePulse www.voicepulse.com (US)
Vonage www.vonage.com (US & UK)

of the type "Any sexy girlz wanna get with me??!!". If that sounds like your bag, test the water at:

ChatAvenue www.chat-avenue.com
Excite chat.excite.com
JustChat www.justchat.co.uk
TalkCity www.talkcity.com

An even more venerable form of online communication is **Usenet** – a discussion system that's been up and running for nearly thirty years. It's heyday has been and gone, due to the advent of such new-fangled technologies as the World Wide Web, but it's still a remarkable phenomenon, used by many people. And you can't really say you've experienced the Net until you've given it a go.

Usenet takes the form of thousands of so-called **newsgroups**, each of which is like a public notice board focusing on a specific topic. When you send – "post" – a message to a newsgroup, everyone who subscribes to that group will receive it. They can then contribute to the discussion publicly by posting a reply and/or contacting you individually by email.

Traditionally, you read and post to newsgroups with a program called a **newsreader**, which may be combined with an email program (in the case of Outlook Express or Windows Mail). But these days you can also access newsgroups via the Web at **Google Groups**, which has

amazing archives of discussions going back decades in addition to a useable-enough way to contribute to current discussions.

Google Groups groups.google.com

For more information on Usenet and newsgroups, or for help using a proper newsreader, see:

Slyck www.slyck.com/ng.php
News Readers www.newsreaders.info

Acronyms & emoticons

An Internet phrasebook

Before the Internet became a public thoroughfare, it was overrun with academics. These greasy geek types could be found chatting and swapping shareware on the bulletin-board networks. As the Internet was popularized this culture collided with the less digitally versed general public. While the old-school types are now in the minority, their culture still kicks on – as witnessed by the continued use of their abbreviated expressions.

Low transfer speed, poor typing skills and the need for quick responses were among the pioneers' justifications for keeping things brief. But using Net lingo was also a way of showing you were in the know. These days, it's not so prevalent, though you're sure to encounter acronyms occasionally on forums and elsewhere.

Chat is a snappy medium, messages are short, and responses are fast. Unlike with CB radio, people won't ask your "20" to find out where you're from but they might ask your **a/s/l** – age/sex/location. Acronyms and abbreviations are mixed in with normal speech and range from the innocuous (BTW = by the way) to a whole panoply of blue phrases. But don't be ashamed to stick with plain English, Urdu or whatever. After all, you'll stand a better chance of being understood.

Net acronyms include:

AFAIK As far as I know
AOLer AOL member (rarely a compliment)
A/S/L Age/Sex/Location
BBL Be back later
BD or BFD Big deal
BFN or B4N Bye for now
BOHICA Bend over here it comes again
BRB Be right back
BTW By the way
CUL8R or L8R See you later
CYA See ya
F2F (S2S) Face to face (skin to skin)
FWIW For what it's worth
g Grin
GR8 Great
HTH Hope this helps
IAE In any event
IM(H)O In my (humble or honest) opinion

IOW In other words
IYSWIM If you see what I mean
LOL Laughing out loud
MOTD Message of the day
NRN No reply necessary
NW or NFW No way
OIC Oh I see
OTOH On the other hand
POV Point of view
RO(T)FL (MAO) Roll on the floor laughing (my ass off)
RTM or RTFM Read the manual
SOL Sooner or later
TIA Thanks in advance
TTYL Talk to you later
WRT With respect to
WTH? or WTF? What the hell?
YMMV Your mileage may vary

Smileys & emoticons

Back in the old days, potentially contentious remarks could be tempered by tacking <grins> on the end in much the same way that a dog wags its tail to show it's harmless. But that wasn't enough for the E-generation, whose trademark smiley icon became the 1980s peace sign. The same honed minds who discovered that 71077345, when inverted, spells "Shell Oil" developed the ASCII smiley. This time, instead of turning it upside down, you had to look at it sideways to see a smiling face – an expression that words, supposedly, fail to convey. At least in such limited space. Inevitably this grew into a whole family of **emoticons** – emotional icons.

The odd smiley might have its use in defusing barbs, but whether you'd want to use any of the others is up to your perception of the line between cute and dorky. The nose is optional.

Acronyms & emoticons

Anime-style

A few others, some Japanese anime-derived, work the right way up:

(_)] Beer
@^_^@ Blushing
*^_^* Dazzling grin
\o/ Hallelujah
^_^; Sweating
T_T Crying

For more…

If you come across an abbreviation you don't understand, ask its author. Don't worry about appearing stupid – these expressions aren't exactly common knowledge. Alternatively, consult one of the many online references, such as:

Acronym Finder
www.acronymfinder.com
Emoticon Universe
emoticonuniverse.com
Microsoft lexicon
cinepad.com/mslex.htm
NetLingo www.netlingo.com

:-)	Smiling	$-)	Greedy
:-D	Laughing	X-)	I see nothing
:-o	Shock	:-X	I'll say nothing
:-@	Screaming	:-L~~	Drooling
:-(	Frowning	:-P	Sticking out tongue
:'-(	Crying	(hmm)Ooo.. :-)	Happy thoughts
;-)	Winking	(hmm)Ooo.. :-(	Sad thoughts
:-I	Indifferent	0:-)	Angel
X=	Fingers crossed	}:>	Devil
: =)	Little Hitler	:8	Pig
{}	Hugging	@}-`–,––	Rose
:*	Kissing	8:)3)=	Happy girl

Emphasis

You could also express actions or emotions by adding commentary within < and > signs. For example:

<flushed> I've just escaped the clutches of frenzied train spotters
<removes conductor's cap, wipes brow>

Or by using asterisks to *emphasize* words. Simply *wrap* the appropriate word:

Hey, everyone, look at *me*.

el33t h4x0r duD3!

When your mouse misleads you into young, impressionable and nerdy realms you might encounter what looks like randomly garbelled text. But look carefully and there might be a message. l00k 4t ME. I'M @n eL33t h4x0r dUD3 translates as "look at me, I'm an elite hacker dude". But don't look too hard. This kind of so-called **leetspeak** is usually a good indicator that it's time to get out of there.

Buying & selling

Shopping

Have your credit card handy

It's not ideal for every type of product, but in many cases online shopping is incomparably better than the real-world alternative. In no market, mall or arcade will you find so much choice or, just as importantly, advice and information. You can sift large inventories in seconds, read reviews, get details of the latest products or receive recommendations based on your tastes.

If you're shopping for music, for example, you could plough through a performer's entire back catalogue, listening to samples as you read what other customers have to say about each album. You can order obscure items from a specialist on the other side of the world, or send a search engine to forage for the best prices or availability across hundreds of shops simultaneously. And, despite the concerns of many Internet newbies, online shopping isn't a security risk. Follow the advice in this chapter and you'll be fine…

How it works

Shopping's the same the world over: you choose your booty, head to the checkout, fix the bill and carry it home. That's also how it works online – except you don't have to do the carrying. On most sites you kick off by either browsing or searching, and then add items to a virtual **shopping basket**. You can usually click on a basket icon at any time to see what you've added so far and remove things you've decided you don't want.

When you're ready to **check out**, you'll be prompted to create a new account (if you haven't shopped there before) and enter your personal and payment details. As with mail order, there are usually check boxes asking whether you'd like to receive mail from the seller or their "associated" parties. Unless you really trust the site and genuinely want to hear about new products and special offers, say no.

Once you've shopped at a site, you'll probably only have to enter your username and password next time you return. Your name, address and perhaps also your credit card details will pop up automatically; you might even be able to make "one-click" purchases to save you going through the delivery and confirmation stages.

Almost all shops send you an instant email confirming your order after you've passed through the checkout. Keep all these confirmation emails together in a folder so you can refer to them later if something goes amiss or you want to track your order.

Shop safe

Shopping online is now a standard part of life for millions, but some people still worry about the risk of fraud and rip-off merchants. With talk of organized online crime and identity theft on the rise, the concern is understandable. But as long as you use legitimate sites and follow the basic rules laid out below, you're very unlikely to have any problems. Indeed, using your credit card online should be no riskier than using it on the high street, where every part-time waiter and shop assistant has direct access to your card details.

▶ **Use your common sense** If anything at all seems fishy about a site, don't shop there. Avoid sites that haven't gone to the effort of registering their own domain name (merchants using free servers like Geocities should be regarded as classified ads rather than shops).

▶ **Look for a street address and phone number** If you can't find out how to get in touch with a real person at a real address, then tread carefully. An email

Are you covered?

Paying by credit cards online is actually usually safer than sending a cheque in the post, since most cards offer some degree of protection against fraud, businesses going bankrupt before you receive your goods, and so on. Read the fine print on your agreement for specifics, but normally you're only liable for a set amount. You might also be able to pay a yearly surcharge to fully protect your card against fraud, though this is usually bad value unless you think you're more at risk than others. If you suspect you've been wrongly charged, ask your bank what to do, but also contact the site in question – even some auctions sites will pick up the bill if you've been conned.

address isn't enough; and a free email address, like Hotmail, spells trouble. Mind you, failure to display a phone number doesn't make them instantly suspect. It's an all-too-common omission on even the best-known sites.

▶ **Only enter card details on secure webpages** When a webpage is secure, the beginning of the address reads https:// rather than http:// and a little closed lock symbol appears on your browser window. If you're concerned about a site's security, shop elsewhere or phone through your order.

▶ **Never send your credit card details by email** It's asking for trouble.

▶ **Don't give extra information** To make an online purchase you should only need to provide your name, billing address, delivery address, credit card number, account name, expiry date and, sometimes, the three-digit security code on the signature strip. You should never need any other form of identification such as your social security, health insurance, driving licence or passport number.

▶ **Don't let browsers "remember" your passwords** Even if you only shop from a home computer, always choose the "Not now" or "Never" option if prompted when entering store login and password details. This is even more paramount when using machines in public spaces such as libraries and cafés.

▶ **Don't believe everything you read** As much as the Net is the greatest source of consumer advice, it's also a great source of misinformation. Seek out a second opinion before you buy on the basis of a recommendation.

For more on avoiding online scams, see p.175. Or, for more about safe shopping, see: www.safeshopping.org

Tip: Don't use your banking username and password when signing up for an online store. Also don't use your email or dial-up connection details and, for extra security, don't use the same username and password on different shopping sites.

Tip: Regardless of whether you use a card online, you should always check your statement each month and immediately report any discrepancies to your issuer.

Know your product

Whether you're buying online or off, the Net is an invaluable mine of consumer advice. Naturally, consumer-written reviews can often be more anecdotal than scientific, and they're somewhat prone to rigging. But while you can't take it all at face value, the more you know, the better your chance of a happy purchase.

For buying guides, customer opinions, ratings and product reviews, try these:

Amazon www.amazon.com
Consumer Guide www.howstuffworks.com/consumer-guide.htm
Consumer Reports www.consumerreports.org
Consumer Review www.consumerreview.com
Consumer Search www.consumersearch.com
Dealcatcher www.dealcatcher.com
Dooyoo www.dooyoo.co.uk
Epinions www.epinions.com
Review Board www.reviewboard.com

You could also use Google to locate sites that specialize in your desired product category. Such as:

CNet www.cnet.com (Computers)
Digital Photography Review www.dpreview.com (Digital Cameras)
The Gadgeteer www.the-gadgeteer.com (Gadgets)
Audio Review www.audioreview.com (Hi-Fi)

And if you have a specific question you want answered, again, search Google (see p.91), including Google Groups, as you'll often find that someone has already answered the exact same question:

Google Groups groups.google.com

Then there's always consumer organizations, such as:

Which? www.which.net (UK)
Consumers Int. www.consumersinternational.org (INT)
Choice www.choice.com.au (Aus)

Among other things, these can alert you to problem products and recalls. Alternatively, go straight to the following, but don't expect a pleasant read – the sheer number of recalls will make you realize how many dodgy items you must have consumed without ever realizing it:

UKRecallNotice www.ukrecallnotice.co.uk (UK)
Consumer Product Safety Commission www.cpsc.gov (US)
Product Recalls www.recalls.gov.au (Aus)

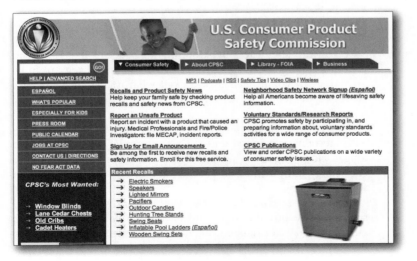

Buying foreign

With the Net at your fingertips, you're ready to shop the entire world. Placing an order with a foreign store should be no harder than doing it locally, especially if you pay by credit card. But it does require a little more effort on the vendor's part, and certain products aren't suitable for export – the result being that many stores won't accept foreign orders. You can usually find this out fairly quickly by locating the site's shipping and handling section.

Before you leap on a foreign bargain, **ensure that it will work at home**. Phone or power plugs can be adapted quickly, but if the conversion involves something complex like replacing a power transformer, ask if it's worth the effort.

Finally, when applicable, ask if items are covered by **international warranties**, whether spares are available locally, where you'd have to send it for repairs and who would be responsible for shipping. This can vary between individual products: some computer firms, for example, offer international warranties on their laptops, but not on their desktop machines.

Is it really a steal?

Sure you can spend less by shopping abroad, but if saving cash is your primary motive you'll need to do your figures carefully. To start with you'll need to work out what it costs in your own currency, which of course you can do on the Web (see box opposite).

Next, balance the shipping costs against transit time. Heavy items will naturally cost more, and cheaper shipping options will take longer. How long can you wait? If you need it pronto, you'd better check they have it in stock – which is best done by phone if you want to be sure.

Finally, of course, there's the **sticky issue of tax**. The ideal scenario is to buy duty-free and have it arrive untaxed by local customs. That can happen, but it will depend on the countries

Converting units and currencies

If you're buying from abroad, units and currencies can both be confusing, but fear not – there's plenty of help to be found online.

For units, Google (www.google.com) is your first ally. Let's say you're a European and you're trying to figure out whether a 12" object you've seen on eBay US is going to fit through your letterbox:

Googling: 12 inches in centimeters
Returns: 12 inches = 30.48 centimeters

This little trick works for all sorts of obscure measurements and weights (see p.95). As long as you use the word "in" and stick to the Americanized spellings of words like "meter", then Google will twig that you are asking for a conversion rather than a search.

As for currency conversions, your best bet is XE:

XE.com www.xe.com

involved, the nature of the product, what it's worth and whether anyone can be bothered to chase it up. The US is the most complex area due to its state taxes. Technically, US residents should be able to buy duty-free between states as long as the shop doesn't have an office in their home state.

If you need more info on your tax laws, call your local post office or customs helpdesk. Or try unpicking some sense from:

HM Customs & Excise www.hmce.gov.uk
US Customs www.customs.gov
Australian Customs www.customs.gov.au

Seek and find

If you know the exact product you're after, use Google to locate the manufacturer's website, not only to see if they sell directly (or offer a list of approved resellers) but also to check whether a new version of whatever item you're seeking has just come out. This is a particularly good idea with electrical goods, since many of the "bargains" found at online retailers are actually end-of-line models – not necessarily a problem, but you should know before you buy. Before purchasing directly from the manufacturer or an approved dealer, however, you might want to search around to see if you can find the item cheaper elsewhere...

Finding the best deal

If you're after a specific product that various online stores have on offer, you can use **comparison engines** (also called **shopping bots** or **bargain finders**) to do the leg work. You simply enter a product or keyword and they return a list of prices and availability across a range of retailers. This sounds great – and it can be – but few comparison engines seem capable of keeping their databases current, and some only show results from certain "partners", which entirely defeats the point. Furthermore, the bots can be deeply annoying when you're using a search engine to try and find a product on sale – they come top of the list of results but with a page that offers no useful information.

Still, despite their shortcomings, the bots that specialize in one product group do a good job, particularly if they scan a lot of shops. And if you're after a book or piece of computer equipment, they're almost always the best place to start, not least as some of them factor in shopping costs, which online

Tip: Thousands of independent traders and small businesses have made their home on eBay, making it an excellent place to compare up-to-date prices on an enormous range of products. And with "Buy It Now" options and new eBay Express, you can shop there and then rather than having to hang around for the end of an auction. For more on eBay, see p.155.

AddALL Book Search and Price Comparison
Be smart: don't buy any book without comparing the price.
Save your TIME and MONEY with AddALL.com in your book shopping.

In Print Books | Used & Out of Print Books | Magazine | Music | Movie | Credit Card | Help

| FAQ/About us | Recommend us | Browse | Memo | Book Reviews | Random Quotes |

HELP Topics
- new books
- used books
- use a coupon
- Memo
- Printer friendly
- Customized search result
- No cookie option
- Match this title
- Refine it
- Search books at eBay
- Slow link
- Tips & Tricks
- Frequently asked questions
- Glossary
- Useful links

Multiple Title

Looking for a book? Want a deal?
No problem AddALL!
Search and Compare among 40+ sites, 20,000 sellers, millions of books!

Find it

Search by: TITLE
Shipping Destination: Select One
U.S. State: Select One
(for sales tax)
Display in: US$

Find it   Start Over

Searching for Out of Print Books? [Click Here]

Other Comparison Sites
- Out of Print Books
- Magazine
- Music CD/Tape
- Movie DVD/VHS

stores sometimes make difficult to find until you've already entered your card details.

For books, try:

AddAll www.addall.com (worldwide)

And for computer stuff, begin at:

PriceWatch www.pricewatch.com (US)
Shopper.com shopper.cnet.com (US)

For anything else, try **Google Products**:

Google Products froogle.google.com (UK/US)

… followed by:

Buy.co.uk www.buy.co.uk (UK utilities & banking)
Deal Time www.dealtime.com (US, UK)
Kelkoo www.kelkoo.co.uk (UK)
My Simon www.mysimon.com (US, UK)
Shopping.com www.shopping.com (US, UK)
Yahoo! Australia shopping.yahoo.com.au (Aus)

If these don't do the trick, try comparing prices manually, which will mean tracking down lots of relevant online stores. A search on Google will often do the trick, though avoid including "shop", "shops", "shopping" or "cheap" in your search terms, or you'll get lots of duff results. If a search doesn't deliver, you could alternatively try the Open Directory shopping section, as served by Google.

Open Directory Shopping directory.google.com/Top/Shopping (US)

If you're outside the US, try locating the shopping area of your country's own section of the Open Directory, by drilling down from:

Open Directory directory.google.com/Top/Regional

Tip: If using Google or any other search engine to locate an item for sale, try including…

-shopping -cheap

…at the end of your search. This will help get rid of the scores of annoying price comparison sites that specialize in making the useless pages that so often dominate search results.

Tip: Shop.com offers convenient access to various stores via a single check out.

www.shop.com (US)
www.shop-com.co.uk (UK)

As a last resort, you could try some **shopping directories**, of which there are many online. But they're rarely very comprehensive, and they often make browsing hard work. For example:

Aussie Shopping www.aussie-shopping.com (Aus)
British Shopping www.british-shopping.com (UK)
Buyersguide www.buyersguide.to (US)
Store Zone storezone.co.uk (UK)

Prefer it on paper?

If you can't bear to leave the world of shopping catalogues behind, fear not: you can order nearly any catalogue online via the company's homepage (find it using Google), and, if you're in the US, you'll find many of them scanned and searchable at The Online Catalogues website:

Online Catalogs www.onlinecatalogs.com (US)

And more...

You'll find short guides to buying music, cars, books, travel, financial services, groceries and more in *Things to do online*, which starts on p.249. Or if you fancy buying something with one or more previous owners, read on.

eBay

13

Tips for buying and selling

Whether it's new or used, collectable or disposable, common or obscure, you can bet it's up for grabs on eBay – either in an auction awaiting your bids or available to "buy now", just like in an online store. eBay isn't all about buying stuff, of course – it also makes it quick and easy to sell stuff. Whether you want to shift some junk from the loft or pack in your day job and start an online store, eBay is the place to do it. It's amazing what gets sold, and indeed purchased, on there:

BizarreBids.com www.bizarrebids.com
Who Would Buy That? www.whowouldbuythat.com

eBay is huge, with hundreds of millions of users (including tens of thousands of full-time traders) in more than thirty countries. Sometimes described as the fastest-growing company in history, the site was born in 1995 and today is a bigger economy than many nations. Once you drop into your local branch and get started, it's not hard to see how it's become so successful. eBaying (yes … it's a verb too) is not only useful but also thoroughly addictive.

Tip: When setting up your eBay account, use a unique password – not the same one you use for email, Internet connection or other online stores.

eBay Australia www.ebay.com.au
eBay UK www.ebay.co.uk
eBay US www.ebay.com

You can browse eBay without registering, but to begin buying or selling you'll need to set up an account. Look for the "resigter" link near the top of the page. Once that's done, you can monitor all your transactions from the "My eBay" link.

Buying on eBay

The really great thing about eBay is that it places hundreds of sellers alongside each other, making it incredibly easy for buyers to compare prices and products with the minimum of effort. But, of course, you need to know how to find what you are looking for.

Browsing and searching

As with most online stores, these are the two main ways to drill your way down into eBay – you can search, or you can browse

Search here

Browse here

by category. Searching is more common, but browsing a category can help you stumble upon things that you might not have thought to search for.

Some top tips for searching eBay:

▶ Look out for eBay's suggested alternative search terms. For example, when you search "70s chair", small links may appear under the search box for, say, "retro chair" or "egg chair".

▶ As with Google (see p.91), there are numerous commands you can use to fine tune your results: for example, if you are after something nice to hang from the ceiling in the nursery, searching "mobile -phone" will return results for mobiles, excluding any pages that also contain the word "phone". For a full list of search commands, see: pages.ebay.com/help/find/search_commands.html

▶ Make use of the "Categories" dropdown menu or "Advanced search" link on the eBay homepage. For example, you could choose to limit your "mobile" search to items listed within the "Baby" category.

▶ Once you have a list of results, explore the "Sort by" options (at the head of the list). Price, distance from you and time remaining are all on offer.

▶ If you don't get any results, try clicking the "Search in Titles & Descriptions" box. This broadens the search to include pages that include your search term anywhere in the item description.

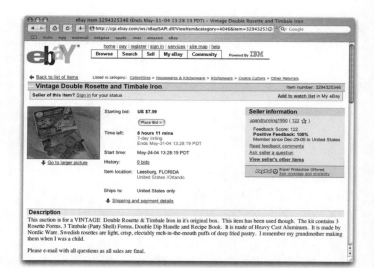

Auction-style listings

Though there have been, and still are, dozens of online auction sites, eBay has unequivocally established itself as the leader of the pack, with millions of goods in thousands of categories being bid on, bought or sold, every day.

So, how does it work? Well, you know how real-world auctions work: the sale goes to the highest bidder, so long as it's above the reserve price. It's the same on eBay, but less stressful. Most obviously, you don't have to drive across town to get to the auction house and place your bid.

Bidding on an eBay auction generally works like this: when you have found something you want, you submit a **maximum bid** that is higher than the current bid or any minimum bid the seller may have set. The auction site will then bid incrementally on your behalf, gradually raising your bid as necessary – up to your specified maximum – to fend off other bidders. If your bid is the highest when the auction's clock stops ticking, the deal is struck.

Tip: Some categories, such as clothes and cars, include a "Refine search" panel to the left of the main listings, which allows you to filter your results even further. For example, when searching clothes you can specify sizes, brands, colours, etc.

Fixed-price listings

As well as auction-style sales, eBay also allows people to sell things via a fixed-price, "buy it now" model. This option is popular with eBay traders selling brand-new goods, partly because it allows sellers to offer multiple items for sale. The buyer simply clicks "buy it now" and, if offered, specifies how many of the item are desired.

When viewing eBay listings you can use the yellow tabs near the top of the page to toggle between viewing these "Buy it now" items alone, just the "Auctions", or "All items".

eBay buyer tips & tools

▶ **Bid sensibly** When bidding on an auction, decide on a maximum price and stick to it – don't succumb to the thrill of the chase. Entering an auction at the very last minute with a clinching bid can be a good way to score a bargain.

▶ **Check the feedback** Buyers and sellers on eBay are rated by other users. Some sellers decline to accept bids from punters without a certain score; likewise, you should always glance at the rating of a seller before committing yourself to a bid. If you're asked to leave feedback by a seller, do so, and make sure they return the compliment. These ratings can also be a useful means of sizing up your opponents during an auction.

▶ **Check the postage** Postage and packing costs should always be checked before you commit to a purchase. Some sellers' "Buy it now" prices may seem like a snip, but when P&P is added you find yourself paying over the odds.

▶ **Use the tools at your disposal** Email or Skype (see p.136) a seller if the details of an item don't tell you

what you want to know; "watch" items you are interested in without actually bidding; and view an auction's "bid history" to get a feel for the competition.

There are also loads of downloadable tools on offer that promise to improve your eBay experience – or to help you get a better deal. For example, "sniping" tools, such as Esnipe or BidNapper, can sometimes get you a better price at eBay by waiting until the last seconds to up your bid.

BidNapper www.bidnapper.com
Esnipe www.esnipe.com

Or, if you use Firefox as your Web browser, try installing the Ebay Negs! Extension (via the Tools menu), which allows you to see at a glance any negative feedback that an eBay trader has received.

For more tools and plug-ins, search for "auction" at any major software archive (see p.183).

eSnipe — Place your eBay™ bids in the last few seconds of the auction – automatically!

Best offers

A relatively new addition to eBay is the "Submit best offer" option. When this is offered, the buyer can submit a price offer and the seller has 48 hours to either accept or decline it.

Selling on eBay

Selling on eBay can range from submitting a simple product listing to creating a bells-and-whistles shop complete with interactive product descriptions and the like. To get started with a simple listing, log into eBay, click the "Sell" button and fill in the on-screen form. Some pointers to help you get it right:

▶ **Title** This is the most important field, as it determines the search terms that will result in people finding your listing. Make every one of those 55 characters work for you, and don't waste them on words like "brilliant", which nobody is going to search for anyway.

▶ **Description** This is the field where you make your pitch, so keep it clear and informative, and think what *you* might want to know if buying that specific item on eBay. You can either work in "Standard" mode, using the text editing tools provided, or, if you want to do something more elaborate,

Tip: A new way to attract trade is the "Get It Fast" badge, which declares that you will ship goods overnight within one day of receiving payment. This feature is enabled within the "Postage" section of the selling form, under "Domestic options".

Tip: Don't post poor-quality images of your items! Photos that are blurred, out of focus or misrepresent colours will turn many potentially bidders away. For advice on taking photos for eBay use, see: pages.ebay.com/help/sell/photo_tutorial.html

work in the "HTML" mode. You can then, for example, create a background image for your listing description, add scrolling text, or create table layouts. See the box, below, for more details.

▶ **Pictures** Click "Add pictures" to reveal a new window where you can choose either "Basic" mode, and upload your images straight to eBay, or "Self-hosting" mode, for when the images are already online in your own Web space or elsewhere. With self-hosting, you simply enter the URLs of the images, and you don't have to pay eBay for their image hosting. Note that you can also add pics within the item description when using HTML mode – just add an <img> tag with the URL of the relevant image (see p.212).

▶ **Listing designer** For a small charge you can use this feature to apply a pre-existing "theme" to your listing. They are not especially inspiring, but do spice things up with very little effort on your part.

▶ **Postage** There are loads of options here, so be careful to review it all properly, as you may end up offering certain services or insurance options accidentally. If you are selling many items, check out the "Combined postage discount" options.

eBay & HTML

If you want to use the HTML mode to enter your item description, you'll need to use standard HTML tags such as <b> and <table>. For an intro to HTML, turn to p.212. Or to grab loads of ready-made eBay-friendly HTML, try these websites:

Online Auction Trader www.onlineauctiontrader.com/htmlguide.htm
Copy & Paste HTML for eBay eobcards.com/tutorial3.htm

Also check out the eBay Community pages, where you'll find Discussion Boards and Groups dedicated to the subject:

eBay Community hub.ebay.com/community

Note that HTML code won't work in any part of the selling form other than the "Description" field.

Seller fees

When you first create a listing, you will be required to supply credit card and bank details for security checks. You don't actually have to pay anything, however, until you start selling. At that point each item you list incurs:

▶ **An insertion fee**, along with fees for any listings features that you sign up for. These fees are pretty minimal, but can stack up – especially if you sell a lot of low-value items.

▶ **A proportion of the sale price**, assuming that the item sells. The standard rate is 5.25%.

These fees are totted up on a monthly basis and can be honoured automatically by authorizing eBay to debit the money from either

---

eBay seller tips & tools

A few selling tips that should give you a head start:

▶ **Update your listing during an auction** Use the options in the "Selling" section of "My eBay" to update your listing during the auction. Change the images perhaps, and if interest seems sluggish, consider lowering your reserve price (though this can't be done during the last 12 hours of the auction).

▶ **Include the brand name in your auction title.** Where relevant, this can help a lot, as brand names are among the most commonly searched terms.

▶ **Research items before you list them** If, for example, there are already dozens of identical products listed that are attracting few bids, you can set your start price to undercut, or simply choose not to bother.

▶ **Use the "added value" options** Having your item listed with a "gallery image", "bolding" or as a "featured item" can make a world of difference. It costs a little more, but is usually worth the investment.

▶ **Choose the right end time** Many people bid at the last minute, so it pays to set up your auction so that it ends at a time when your potential buyers are likely to be logged into eBay. Perhaps the best model is a 10-day auction, listed on a Thursday: your auction will be live over two weekends and finish on a Sunday – the most popular day for bidding.

If you get to the point where you're selling a significant volume of items on eBay, investigate the various tools that will help speed up the process and improve the look of your listings. The obvious candidate is eBay's own Turbo Lister II. It's free to download, easy to use, and – for bulk listings – infinitely faster than the regular eBay listing form.

Turbo Lister II pages.ebay.com/turbo_lister

your bank, a credit card or your PayPal account (see below). Alternatively, you can choose to cough up by sending a cheque in the post.

On top of the actual eBay fees, sellers who use PayPal (see below) will pay a small fee for each payment that goes into their PayPal account…

Paying up and being paid

Once an auction or sale has ended, it's up to the buyer and seller to arrange delivery and payment. Most buyers choose – and most sellers prefer – to settle transactions using **PayPal**. This online payment system has been popular among eBay users for years – and especially since 2002, when eBay purchased PayPal for $1.5 billion.

You can get by without PayPal, but to make the most of eBay it's definitely worth signing up for an account. It lets you make payments to other PayPal users at the click of a button – no waiting around for cheques to clear; and no need to give out your bank details. The money goes directly from the buyer's PayPal account into the seller's PayPal account.

In order to make a payment with PayPal, you either need to place funds into your PayPal account or authorize PayPal to debit your bank account or credit card directly. If you receive a payment, the money arrives in your PayPal account and you can either transfer the funds to your bank or leave them where they are for future PayPal purchases.

PayPal is generally safe and easy. It's free for buyers, inexpensive for sellers, and offers generous protection against fraud for eBay customers. Moreover, PayPal is quickly becoming a standard way of paying for inexpensive items not just on eBay, but on the rest of the Web too. For the full story or to sign up, visit:

PayPal www.paypal.com (INT)

There are other similar services out there, some of which, such as the UK's NoChex service, are safe and reliable. But think carefully before signing up with any obscure payment system – it's more secure (and useful) to stick with PayPal.

NoChex www.nochex.com (UK)

eBay woes

eBay auctions are essentially based on trust and, understandably, many new users feel uneasy about sending money to a vendor before any goods have been received (it almost always happens this way around). But you're unlikely to run into trouble – especially if you stick to sellers with good feedback ratings. An estimated 98 percent of eBay transactions go through with no problems. Moreover, eBay will refund you up to around £100/$150 if you're unlucky enough to get ripped off, and you can't resolve the problem by communicating directly with the seller.

Perhaps the most common dodgy dealings to be carried out via eBay is the selling of counterfeit and stolen goods. The best advice here is just be careful: read listings thoroughly, and if you are at all unsure about what you are buying, ask the seller to agree a returns policy before you bid. If they don't respond to your request, or you don't trust their reply, bid elsewhere.

Another type of foul play is "shill bidding" – the process whereby a seller forces up the price of something they themselves are selling, either by asking a friend to bid or by bidding on their own item under a false account. This isn't as prevalent as you might think, since it's risky for the seller – if someone ends up as the highest bidder on his or her own item, then he or she will lose their real bidder and still have to pay the eBay commission. Moreover, eBay prohibits shill bidding, and there have even been cases that have led to prosecution. For tips on how to spot a shill bidder, see:

UK Auction Help www.ukauctionhelp.co.uk/shill.php

For more advice and help with a range of security issues, visit your local eBay Safety Centre. In the UK and US visit:

eBay UK Safety Centre pages.ebay.co.uk/safetycentre
eBay US Security Center pages.ebay.com/securitycenter

Or, for the full eBay story, pick up *The Rough Guide To eBay*.

Other auction sites

You won't find anywhere near the volume of product that you will in eBay auctions anywhere else, and many of the remaining competitors are little more than "ghost towns" frequented by a few diehard users. Even big players such as Amazon and Yahoo! have now drawn a line under their auction activities.

In the US, however, try Property Room, run by the police, where you can bid on unclaimed stolen items:

Property Room www.propertybureau.com

But you might conclude that for some objects, such as art and antiques, there's no substitute for bidding in person, in which case use the following site to find upcoming auctions in your area:

Internet Auction List www.internetauctionlist.com

The Internet is also home to various twists on the bidding game, and other ways to shop. At Priceline, for example, you can state how much you'd like to pay for travel products (hotels, flights, etc) and see if an agent bites; and uBid hosts auctions by businesses rather than punters, making it a good place to snap up clearance items.

Ventures like these attract publicity, so watch the Internet sections of your newspaper for further leads. But be warned: although they promise the world, users often you end up with a so-so deal.

Priceline www.priceline.com
uBid www.ubid.com

Security & software

Security

14

Viruses, hackers, scams & other headaches

The Internet may be the greatest wonder of the modern world, but it does come with certain downsides. Increased access to information is great, but not if the information being accessed is yours – and private. Of course, there are threats to privacy and security in the real world, but on the Internet things are rather different, not least because the wrongdoer may take the form of a piece of software, entirely invisible to the victim: a virus that damages your files, say, or a keylogger that keeps a record of the usernames and passwords you type into webpages and then sends them to someone on the other side of the world. All of this is rather unsavoury, to say the least, but worry not: if you follow the advice in this chapter, you – and your data – should be fine.

The bad guys

The villains that threaten your files and privacy fall into two categories: bad software, known as **malware,** and bad humans, known as **hackers**. Here's a quick look at each, followed by some tips for keeping them at bay.

Malware

"Malware" is short for "malicious software", which pretty well sums up what it is: computer code written with the express purpose of doing something harmful or shady. Though people often use the word "virus" to refer to all of them, there are actually a number of different types of malware out there…

▶ **Viruses** are programs that infect other program files so that they can spread from machine to machine. In order to catch a virus you must run an infected program (or, less likely these day, boot your machine with an infected floppy disk inserted in the drive). There are thousands of strains, most of which are no more than a nuisance, but some are capable of setting off a time bomb that could destroy the contents of your hard drive. A "macro virus" spreads by infecting Microsoft Word or Excel documents. So always opt to disable macros when opening an emailed document.

▶ **Worms**, like viruses, are designed to spread. But rather than wait for an earthling to transfer the infected file or disk, they actively replicate themselves over a network such as the Internet. They might send themselves to all the contacts in your email address book, for example. That means worms can spread much faster than viruses. The "email viruses" that have made world news in recent years have, strictly speaking, been worms.

▶ **Trojans** (short for Trojan horses) are programs with a hidden agenda. When you run the program it will do something unexpected, often without your knowledge. While viruses are designed to spread, Trojans are usually, though not always, designed to deliver a one-off payload. And a custom-built Trojan can be bound to any program, so that when you install it the Trojan will also install in the background. There are dozens of known Trojans circulating the Internet, most with the express purpose of opening a back door to your computer to allow hackers in.

▶ **Spyware**, which may arrive via a Trojan, is software designed to snoop on your computing activity. Most commonly it's planted by some kind of marketeer, who wants to find out about your online surfing and spending habits – usually to sell to someone else. But in theory it might also be installed by someone with physical access to your computer who wants to keep an eye on you or even record the keystrokes when you log in to an Internet banking site.

▶ **Adware** is any software designed to display advertisements. Some of it is perfectly legitimate – you accept a program with an ad banner, say, in return for getting it for free – but others may be installed without your consent and have the sole purpose of bombarding you with pop-ups.

Backing up mail, bookmarks, etc

What with viruses, hardware crashes, computer thefts and other potential risks to the data on computers, it's worth backing up everything fairly regularly onto some kind of removable media such as an external hard drive (manufacturers include Lacie and Western Digital), iPod or pen drive. And this doesn't just mean copying your documents across: your Internet-related things such as email, bookmarks and address book can also be a real pain to lose.

Windows features a Backup Wizard which can help you set up a regular backup schedule to an external hard drive, while recent versions of Mac OS X come with a built-in application called Time Machine. Both can be used to back up all the data on your machine – your address book, bookmarks and mail included – though you could choose to handle the process manually by seeking out the specific files:

▸ **Bookmarks** Nearly all Web browsers offer an export option for bookmarks in the File menu.

▸ **Email** On a PC, open Outlook Express or Mail and choose Options in the Tools menu. Click on the "Store folder" button and move this entire folder. While you're at it, save your **mail account settings** with the export option under Accounts (in the Tools menu). On a Mac, simply copy the folder Library/Mail within your home folder.

▸ **Address book** On a PC, open Outlook Express or Mail, click Export in the File menu and follow the prompts. On a Mac, copy AddressBook from Home/Library/Application Support.

The other alternative is to either mirror or keep the data online – in the "cloud", to use the Internet jargon (see p.281). With a web-based email set-up such as Gmail (see p.110), your mail archive and address book resides online and is accessible from anywhere. Similarly, Apple's MobileMe subscription service and Microsoft's Windows Live services can be used to sync emails, bookmarks and contacts between your computers and your online account.

MobileMe www.apple.com/mobileme
Windows Live home.live.com

"Hackers"

The term "**hacker**" is somewhat fuzzy, as its original meaning – still in use among the computerati – is a legitimate computer programmer (see en.wikipedia.org/wiki/Hacker). But it's the popular definition that concerns us here: someone who wants to break into, or meddle with, your computer. They may be a professional out to steal your secrets or a "script kiddy" playing with a prefab Trojan. They might be a vandal, a spy, a thief or simply just exploring. As far as you're concerned, it doesn't matter. You don't want them, or their handiwork, inside your computer.

Preventative medicine

That all adds up to a pretty intimidating list, but don't despair – there are various measures you can take to ensure that your data and privacy remain intact.

Rule #1: Keep your system up to date

Many security breaches involve a programmer taking advantage of a security flaw in Windows or a Web browser. So it's critically important to keep your system up-to-speed with the latest security updates. If you don't, simply connecting to the Internet or viewing a webpage could be enough to let in some kind of malware. Keeping up to date also means you'll get new features and fixes for software "bugs" that cause crashes and other annoyances.

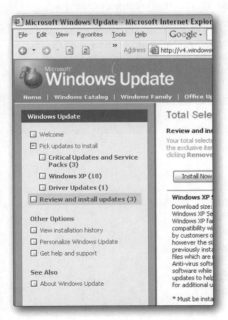

Recent versions of Windows and Mac OS, and Web browsers such as Firefox, will automatically prompt you to download periodic updates. If you have a slow Internet connection, you might want to be selective about which updates you accept, but at a minimum *always* accept anything that mentions security. And tend towards accepting all updates.

On older PCs, you may need to kickstart the updates process manually by selecting Windows Update from the start menu and clicking "**Product Updates**". In particular, if you're running a version of Windows XP from before 2004, and you haven't already done so, make absolutely sure you download and install **Service Pack 2** (SP2). This is a major upgrade to the operating system and includes many essential security repairs as well as useful extras such as pop-up blockers for Internet Explorer. If you have a slow Internet connection, you may struggle to download the full SP2, but at least get the "lite" version – which contains the essential security fixes – and consider ordering a copy of SP2 on CD. Among other things, SP2 allows you to have important updates downloaded automatically in the background – definitely an option worth using.

Rule #2: Don't run dodgy software

This includes steering clear of free downloads from websites which seem in any way untrustworthy, or which you reached via a pop-up or banner ad. It also means thinking carefully before opening suspicious **email attachments**, even from people you know – the message may have been sent by a piece of software without them ever knowing about it.

An up-to-date virus scanner should check attachments as you receive them, but this is not entirely foolproof, so it's worth also learning to spot a potentially dodgy file. This can

be done by looking at the file extension at the end of the file name. Windows and Mac OS X hide many file extensions by default, but you can find out what kind of file something is by right-clicking it and selecting Properties (PC) or selecting it and pressing Apple+I (Mac).

Most file types could theoretically be adapted to include some kind of threat. However, for many of the most commonly emailed file types, the risk is basically nonexistent. You needn't worry about:

Plain text .txt
Images .jpg, .gif, .bmp, .tif, .wmf
Movies .avi, .mpg, .mov, .wmv
Portable documents .pdf
Audio .mp3, .mp4, .wav, .wmf
Internet Shortcuts .url

Webpages (.htm, .html) and attached **emails** (.eml) are also normally safe, though they can potentially include scripts so tread carefully. The following file types are **highly suspect and should never be opened** unless you're certain they're safe: .bat, .com, .exe, .inf, .js, .jse, .pif, .reg, .scr, .shs, .vbe, .vbs, .wsf and .wsh

Tip: Never install free browser or mouse cursor enhancements – including so-called "Web accelerators". They very often contain adware or spyware.

Don't be fooled by fake extensions

Before you click on that attachment that appears to be a safe music, movie, image or document file, **check its icon**. Is it the right one for that type of file? If not, you might find a long series of spaces inserted between a fake extension and a real one, for example: Me_nude.AVI　　　.pif (the real extension is .pif). Always double-check.

Rule #3: Hide behind a firewall

A **firewall** serves to prevent anyone from even being able to detect your computer on the Internet, let alone invade it. Recent versions of Windows come with a basic firewall built in, which will be activated by default. You can check by opening Security Center from the Control Panel.

If you have Windows XP from 2004 or before, however, and for some reason you haven't installed Service Pack 2 (see p.170), you'll need to activate the Firewall manually. In the Control Panel select Network and Internet Connections, followed by Network Connections. Right-click the icon for your Internet connection and select Properties from the menu. Under the Advanced tab you'll see a box that can be checked to activate your firewall protection.

While the Windows firewall is much better than nothing, it's a long way from being totally impenetrable. For more protection, try the free version of **ZoneAlarm** – especially if you use Windows XP. There are other options, such as **Norton's Personal Firewall**, but they're not free and they don't offer much extra for the typical home user:

ZoneAlarm www.zonealarm.com
Norton Firewall www.symantec.com

Both the above come as stand alone programs or as part of comprehensive security suites complete with virus and spyware scanners. For more on choosing and installing a firewall, see:

Home PC Firewall Guide www.firewallguide.com

As for Macs, OS X comes with a pretty decent firewall installed; to check its status, or define what traffic it will or won't allow through, open System Preferences and look for the Firewall tab within the Sharing panel. There are various other products out there, but it's certainly not imperative that you use one of them.

NAT routers

If you use a router for wireless Internet or to share your connection between multiple computers, it will probably be using NAT (Network Address Translation), a system by which the router communicates one IP address to the Internet while concealing the IP address of the computers on your network. This adds an extra level of protection, and makes you immune to certain virus woes. You may want to check whether NAT is enabled by checking your router configuration settings.

Tip: Firewalls occasionally stop legitimate Internet programs – peer-to-peer file-sharing applications for example – from working properly. If you have any such problems after installing or activating a firewall, refer to the help file to work out how to set "exceptions" and make other configuration changes.

Security

Rule #4: Scan

Virus scanning software keeps track of your computer activity to protect you from viruses, Trojans, worms and other such evils. No scanning software is 100 percent effective, but they do add an extra layer of security to your PC. (There are also scanners available for Macs, but for now risks seem too low to make them worth paying for.) In order to be effective, virus scanners need to keep themselves up to date by downloading information about the most recent threats from the Internet. As such, they are often sold as a subscription service.

Many PCs come with a year of free coverage from one of the major commercial scanning systems, such as:

TrendMicro www.trendmicro.com
McAfee www.mcafee.com
Norton www.symantec.com

Once that expires, you'll need to pay to add another year's protection. However, you could instead opt for the free, but perfectly good, scanner offered by AVG.

AVG Free free.grisoft.com

Virus scaners can be activated as and when you like, or set to protect your system in "real time", scanning emails as they arrive, disks as they are attached, and so on. (The latter is safer, of course, though it can get annoying, as it all takes time).

Whichever scanner you use, you may also want to download and run **SpyBot Search & Destroy**, a free program for identifying and removing spyware.

SpyBot Search & Destroy www.safer-networking.org

Online virus scans

If you don't have any anti-virus software (or the package you do have is out of date or not working) and you think you may have contracted something nasty, you could try a free online scan at the following websites:

TrendMicro HouseCall
housecall.trendmicro.com
McAfee FreeScan
freescan.mcafee.com
Symantec Security Check
security.symantec.com

Tip: Most virus scanners put an icon in the System Tray, next to the Windows clock. Clicking it will bring up a panel of options for configuring your scanner.

Virus warnings

Most people with an email account have at some stage received an email about a terrible new virus or other online threat. Even if it's from someone you know, don't forward it on – or act on any instruction within it – without first checking its legitimacy, since most are hoaxes. Most hoax warnings are harmless, but others may instruct you to delete a "dangerous" file that turns out to be a part of your operating system. For legitimate information about current viruses, see:

CA www.cai.com/virusinfo
Virus Bulletin www.virusbtn.com
Symantec www.symantec.com/
security_response

Rule #5: Enable wireless security

If you have a wireless router at home, be sure to implement a few basic security measures. First, add a WPA password, as described on p.50, to make sure your connection is only used by the people you want to use it. If you currently use a WEP password, switch to WPA if your router offers it – it's *much* more secure.

Next, make sure you set your own username and password for accessing your router settings (a separate setting from the password needed to connect to the router and use the Internet). Otherwise, anyone within range could log-in, mess-up your settings and even turn off your password.

All these settings are most commonly configured via a Web browser (as shown), but the exact details vary from router to router, so refer to your manual for more information.

Rule #6: Consider switching browser & mail program

Many of the "virus" crises and other problems that have caused grief for Internet users in recent years have relied on the fact that the majority of people use Microsoft's default Web browser (Internet Explorer) and email client (Mail or Outlook Express). You're likely to be less at risk if you switch to alternatives, the obvious choices being **Firefox** as a browser (see p.69) and **the web-based** Gmail (see p.110) for email. This isn't something that Mac users need to worry about so much.

Don't get scammed

As well as looking after your data and privacy, it's worth protecting your wallet. That's not difficult if you use your common sense and follow these pointers:

▶ **Don't respond to spam** (unsolicited email; see p.125). Those "get paid to surf", "stock tips", "work from home", "recruit new members", "clear your credit rating" and various network-marketing schemes *are* too good to be true. It should go without saying that ringing a number to claim a prize will only cost you money. If you get one of the notorious messages inviting you to take part in an African money-laundering scam, beat them at their own game: www.flooble.com/fun/reply.php

▶ **Beware the phishermen** "Phishing" is a cunning form of online scam in which someone pretends to be from your bank, ISP or any other such body, and asks you to hand over your personal information either directly or via a webpage. The classic example is a scammer sending out a mass email claiming to be from a bank, with a link pointing to a webpage purportedly on a real bank's website. In fact, all the details are slightly incorrect (for example, the page might be at www.hsbc-banking.com instead of www.hsbc.com) but the recipient doesn't notice, assumes the email is legitimate and follows the instructions to "confirm" their online banking details on the fake site – in the process giving them to a criminal, who can then empty their account. The moral of the story: never respond to emails – or instant messages – requesting private information, however legitimate they seem. Windows Vista comes with a phishing filter built in, but it still pays to be vigilant.

▶ **Think before pressing OK** If you're browsing the Web and a box pops up offering a program or ActiveX control, never accept it unless you actually want what's on offer and you're absolutely positive it's from a reputable firm. If you just press OK to dismiss an annoying box you might inadvertently install something dodgy such as a dialler program that will call an extra-premium-rate number, somewhere abroad, from your computer.

▶ **Be careful of "adult" sites** It is often said that the majority of online scams involve porn sites, not least because the victims are often too embarrassed to report the problem. Don't pass over your credit card details to adult sites unless you're prepared to be stung. And, whatever you do, don't download any connection software, picture viewers or browser add-ons from such sites.

▶ **Don't trust investment advice** found online, whether on the Web or through a newsletter.

▶ **Consider giving money to charity** rather than using an online casino.

▶ **Beware free trials and subscription services** that require your credit details. You might find it harder to cancel than you anticipated. Or they might charge you whether you use the service or not. Check your bill carefully each month for discrepancies, and make sure the subscription doesn't renew itself automatically.

▶ **Shop sensibly** See p.146.

Read all about it

For more advice and information on online fraud, see:

CyberCrime www.cybercrime.gov
Cyber Criminals www.ccmostwanted.com
OnGuardOnline www.onguardonline.gov
Scambusters www.scambusters.com
Wikipedia en.wikipedia.org/wiki/Internet_fraud

Software downloads

So many programs, so little time

Whether you're after a new Web browser, a free word processor, or some obscure CD-mastering software, the Internet is the first place to look. There are all kinds of things on offer – freebies, trial versions, pay-to-download applications and upgrades for the programs you already have. There's also a huge amount of contraband – "cracked" versions of commercial packages illegally made available for free. This chapter explains all.

The basics

Free and almost free

The software available on the Internet ranges from the completely free to the temporarily free, and from the completely legal to the entirely illegal. Here's a breakdown of the various categories of downloads you might come across…

▶ **Freeware** is any software that the author distributes for unlimited free use; however, there may be restrictions on you distributing or altering the program.

Software downloads

▶ **Adware** is free software that includes advertising banners or pop-ups as a way for the developers to make some money from their handiwork.

▶ **Shareware** is software that can be downloaded for free, though if you use of the program you're requested to make a contribution to the developers.

▶ **Donationware** is similar to shareware: you are expected to make a contribution to the developer (or sometimes a third party, such as a charity) based upon how useful you have found the software to be.

▶ **Beta versions** are basically "works in progress" that developers distribute for free in order to get feedback, so that they can improve the final version. They will often only work for a limited period and will, by definition, be imperfect. But you may get some perfectly functional software for free. To see what's currently in the Beta stage, see: www.betanews.com

▶ **Demo versions** If you're interested in buying a particular package, check out the manufacturer's website to see if they offer a downloadable trial version. These usually either stop working after a couple of weeks, or they'll work forever but be crippled in some way (not allowing you to save files, for example). Also check to see if the company offers a freeware version.

Warez

Just because you can find a program on the Internet doesn't mean it's legal – the Internet is rife with **warez**, also called **pirated** or **cracked** software. This is commercial software distributed illegally, either with its original serial number or with the need for a serial knocked out by some clever programming. These days, most illegal software downloads take place via the file-sharing networks discussed in chapter 17, but there's still a lot of warez on the Web, too. Though it's pretty unlikely that anything will happen to you, if you download and install any warez software you will be **breaking the law**. Furthermore, cracked software is sometimes unstable and may even present security risks.

Be careful

As the previous chapter should have made clear, dodgy software is one of the biggest threats to your data and privacy. So while it might be tempting to install every piece of free software you come across online, it's worth exercising a degree of caution if you want to avoid viruses and the like. A few rules to bear in mind:

▶ **Use your common sense** Avoid any software from a developer (programmer) whose website seems in any way untrustworthy.

▶ **Read reviews** Favour programs that have favourable independent reviews.

▶ **Go to the source** Download directly from the developer's site or a respected software archive.

▶ **Scan** Check downloaded software with a virus scanner (see p.173) before installing (see p.181).

▶ **Avoid "enhancers"** Be suspicious of any program that offers to "accelerate your browser", "optimize your modem", "enhance your mouse cursor", or the like.

A download lowdown...

Whether you're seeking out a specific program or just browsing a software site, downloading a program is usually very simple – click on a link, wait for a file to download and double-click it to start the installation. That said, things can be a bit more confusing, so read on to arm yourself against the likes of mirror sites and decompression issues.

Mirror sites

Often when you click a link to download a file or program you will be offered several alternative, or "**mirror**", sites from which

Scareware

Also worth keeping half an eye open for is so-called scareware – software that is pretty worthless, but which the sellers try to scare unsuspecting Internet users into buying with horror stories about often nonexistent viruses or other threats. If you stick with the brands of anti-virus software discussed on p.173 then you should feel safe in the knowledge that you are doing everything you should and thus not feel compelled to download anything from potential scareware peddlers.

to download. This serves two main purposes: to make the download faster (by avoiding too many people accessing a single server simultaneously, and by offering servers in different geographical locations around the world), and to avoid small developers having to pay for enough bandwidth to serve a big file thousands of times per day. Generally, pick the mirror that's geographically closest to you, though don't worry too much – these days it usually doesn't make a huge difference to the speed.

Starting a download

When you click on a link to a program, or any other type of file that can't be displayed as by your Web browser, your browser will begin the download process. If you use Internet Explorer, that means offering whether you want to **Open or Save** the file. Open is useful is you want to play or display the file as it downloads (if you're downloading a movie or sound file over a high bandwidth connection, for example), but for programs you're better pressing Save and choosing a default location (such as the Desktop).

Firefox, by contrast, offers you a choice between saving it to the Desktop or opening it with a specific program, while Safari simply downloads the file to your Desktop.

There's no reason to down tools while you wait for a download to finish. You can continue to browse the Web, and even start more downloads. Don't be surprised, however, if webpages take longer to appear with a download going on in the background.

Managing downloads

Though Internet Explorer still insists on showing the progress of each download in its own window, other browsers, such as Firefox and Safari, let you see all current and previous downloads in one convenient download window. This may pop up when you kick

Downloads window showing:
- _40193103_nuclear22_disko24may_vi.ram — 0.2 KB
- KathWilliamsSCR1.zip — 253 of 892 KB — stopped
- 1159paper.sit — 130 KB
- Ticker Installer (PPC) — 487 KB
- Y5160e00.pdf — 179 KB
- Y5160e01.pdf — 558 KB
- Clear — 18 Downloads

FTP or HTTP – huh?

You don't need to understand the protocols used for transferring files on the Internet, but you're likely to bump into the terminology at some stage, so it doesn't hurt to have an idea of what it's all about.

In computing, a protocol, roughly speaking, is simply a set of rules relating to the way in which two bits of "end points" (computers, bits within a computer, or bits of software) communicate in the carrying out of a specific task. When it comes to downloading files from the Net, the two most commonly used protocols are **HTTP** (HyperText Transfer Protocol, also used for webpages) and **FTP** (File Transfer Protocol, only used for file transfers).

These days most files are downloaded via HTTP, but some still come via FTP. This doesn't make much

difference to you, as you can enter an ftp address (eg ftp://ftp.fish.com/work/jane.doc) directly into your browser just like a Web address, and the file will start downloading in just the same way. But if you explore the ftp server by going "up" a level or two (for example to ftp://ftp.fish.com), all you'll see is a list of files and folders rather than any webpages. If, as occasionally happens, you're offered a choice of downloading a particular file via FTP or HTTP, flip a coin.

Today, the only time most users will have to deal consciously with FTP is for uploading files to a remote server – for example, when creating your own website. For this, you'll want a stand-alone FTP program, many of which are available for free at the big software download sites (see p.183).

start a download, but you can also open it at any time, from the Tools menu (Firefox) or the Window menu (Safari).

If you download a lot of big files over a slow connection, you might want to try out a special **download manager** program. These can speed things up, let you pause and resume downloads, and do various other clever things such as search for alternative mirror locations and tell you which one will be quickest. For example, try **Download Accelerator Plus** or shareware **Mass Downloader:**

Download Accelerator Plus www.speedbit.com
Mass Downloader www.metaproducts.com

Installing

Once you've downloaded a program, you'll usually need to install it. With some tiny programs, this isn't necessary, since the downloaded file may literally be the program: double-click the icon to run it.

Usually, however, double-clicking the icon will either automatically start the installation or will **decompress** the file, "unzipping" its contents to reveal either an installation file or a folder (see box).

If you get a folder, look inside for installation instructions – perhaps in the form of a "readme" file. On a PC, you'll generally have to find and double-click a file called "install.exe" or "setup.exe". On a Mac, you typically just have to simply drag a single file into your Applications folder.

Once a program has been installed, you can delete the original download file and any unzipped folders left lying around on your Desktop. Simply drag them to the Trash.

Decompressing files

Files available for downloading are very often **compressed.** There are two reasons for this: compressed files are "smaller", and hence quicker to transfer; and with compression you can bundle a selection of files into a single convenient "archive" file.

Recent PCs and Macs contain all the tools necessary to automatically extract common compressed formats such as **zip**. Simply double-click the compressed file. On a PC, Windows will display the files contained inside (it's best to drag them out onto the Desktop rather than installing a program from this preview). On a Mac, an uncompressed version will simply appear next to the original.

If you have an old PC or Mac, or you're downloading a more obscure type of compressed file, you may need some extra tools to get the decompression to work.

PC users, for example, would need the free **Stuffit Expander** to open Stuffit files (recognized by their .sit extension), which are still occasionally created by Mac users. Most other compressed formats – such as **rar** – can be opened with a free decompression utility such as **7Zip**.

Stuffit Expander www.allume.com
7Zip www.7-zip.org

If you come across a file type that even the above won't open, look up the file extension (the suffix in the file name after the dot at:

Wikipedia en.wikipedia.org/wiki/List_of_file_formats

Recent versions of both Windows and the Mac OS can also create zip archives: on a PC right-click the file or folder in question and choose "Send to compressed file". In OS X, right-click the file or folder and select "Compress…".

Uninstalling

If a program doesn't float your boat, **uninstall** it from your hard drive so you don't clog up your system with rubbish. In Windows, that means deleting it from within Add/**Remove Programs** in the Control Panel. If the program isn't listed here, look for an uninstall icon in its folder in the Start menu. If neither exists, it will be safe to delete the file directly from its folder (usually in Program Files on your C: drive).

On a Mac uninstalling a program usually involves simply removing it from the Applications folder, but if the program came with uninstallation instructions, follow them. Alternatively, use the free application AppCleaner to do the job:

AppCleaner www.freemacsoft.net/AppCleaner

Tip: If you're on a Mac, some programs will download as DMG files, which when double-clicked create a virtual hard drive on the Desktop containing the program file, perhaps plus instructions. Once the installation is complete, "eject" the virtual drive by dragging it to the Trash.

Software archives

Most individuals or companies that produce software offer downloads direct from their websites. But there are also sites designed to help you find what you're looking for, listing, reviewing and rating programs and sorting them into various categories. Some of the best include:

Download.com www.download.com
ZDNet Downloads www.hotfiles.com
Rocket www.rocketdownload.com
Tucows www.tucows.com
VersionTracker www.versiontracker.com
Winfiles www.winfiles.com

Software downloads

Program numbers

You can judge how up to date a program is by its number. Taking Internet Explorer as an example, you might come across IE5.01, IE6.1 and IE7.0, among others. The number before the decimal point tells you the **series**, in this case 5, 6 or 7. The number after the decimal point tells you if it is the original release (.0) or an **interim upgrade** (0.1, 0.01, 0.2, etc) within the series. The various versions of the same series are often collectively referred to with an "x". So, "IE5.x" refers to any series 5 release.

Interim upgrades generally fix problems and add on minor features. In doing so they render the previous release obsolete. A new series usually heralds major changes and bug fixes, but also often adds extra system demands. Thus, if your computer resources are low, you may find an earlier series more suitable.

To make matters a bit more confusing, developers sometimes release a new "build" of the same program. So you and a friend may both have IE5.5 – but if you downloaded it later, you might have a later build that's fixed a few minor bugs. To see a program's build number, choose the "About" option from the Help menu (PC), or the menu bearing the program's name (Mac OS X).

Mac specialists

Of all the Mac sites, the obvious port of call is the Apple OS X download site: it's well laid out and offers not only software for every occasion, but a ton of free Widgets to use on the OS X Dashboard. When you're done there, check out the others.

Apple Downloads www.apple.com/downloads
I Use This osx.iusethis.com
Mac Orchard www.macorchard.com
Pure Mac www.pure-mac.com

Freeware specialists

Freeware www.freewarehome.com
Freeware Guide www.freeware-guide.com
No Nags www.nonags.com

Hardware drivers

PC Drivers HeadQuarters www.drivershq.com
WinDrivers www.windrivers.com

Tip: If you still can't find what you're after, you could also consider trying a file-sharing network (see p.202).

Music
& video

Music, video & TV

Stream it live or download it for later

In the early days, when the Web was thoroughly geeky, listing your entire music collection on your website was deemed cooler than posting your résumé. Back then, it wasn't practical to put actual audio online – let alone video – as the large size of the files made it too time-consuming to download. But file compression technology has advanced, Internet connections have got faster, and music and video have become a major part of the online world.

Dealing with high-quality online music, and especially video, is still very frustrating if you have a dial-up connection. However, with broadband there's no end to what you can enjoy – from music tracks and countless radio stations to YouTube clips and movie-on-demand services.

The basics

Music as it's stored on CD is too bulky to be very useful online. A minute of sound needs roughly 10MB of disk space, which means a four-minute track would take around two hours to download with a 56K modem, and ten minutes via an average broadband connection. Video is even bigger – much bigger, in fact. A single DVD can hold more than ten gigabytes, which would take a painfully long time to download and would fill a sizeable chunk of your hard drive.

Thankfully, some clever technology allows music and video files to be "compressed" into space-efficient formats such as MP3 and MPEG, which are far quicker to transfer. They work by stripping out elements of the sound or picture information that are unimportant to your ears or eyes. Music and video files can be compressed to a greater or lesser extent: greater compression means worse sound or picture quality but faster download times.

Music and video files can be made available over the Internet in two ways. They can be "**streamed**" – played straight off the Web in real time – or **downloaded** to your computer, where you can keep them for as long as you like and listen and watch at your leisure.

Streaming it...

Streaming audio and video is usually highly compressed and therefore also not great in terms of quality (especially when it comes to video). Its main use is for online radio – see p.282 – and "webcasts" of concerts or other events. But it's also used for previewing CDs at online music stores such as Amazon, for video clips on sites such as YouTube and for radio and TV shows made available online.

Some streamed content is only available at a particular time – just as with "real" TV and radio – but the rest is available on demand, permanently left online for you to stream whenever you like. One thing you can't usually do with streamed media (at least not without special software) is save it to your hard drive.

Among the most common file formats employed for streaming audio and video is **RealMedia**. To watch or hear anything in this format, you'll need to download the free version of RealPlayer from:

RealPlayer www.real.com

Mac users should also grab **Windows Media Player** (PC users will usually have it already), for playing back streaming content in the Windows Media Format.

Windows Media Player www.windowsmedia.com/download

Likewise, PC users should grab the Apple equivalent:

QuickTime www.apple.com/quicktime

Digital rights management

There's nothing the record and movie industries fear more than the uncontrolled distribution of their copyrighted material. It's increasingly hard to see how the companies will ever be able to stop people sharing files that they have ripped from their own CDs or DVDs, even if they succeed in killing off file-sharing networks like KaZaA (see p.203).

One strategy for stopping people freely distributing the music or video they have purchased and downloaded from legitimate online sources is called **DRM** – digital rights management – and it involves embedding special code into music files to impose certain restrictions on what you can do with them. For example, tracks downloaded from Apple's iTunes Store historically had DRM that stopped you making the file available on more than a certain number of computers or using it with any non-Apple MP3 player. The reincarnated Napster, meanwhile, has used DRM to ensure that the files you download via their "unlimited" subscription service will only be played back for as long as you remain a subscriber.

If you're determined, it is usually possible to circumvent DRM limitations. For example, if the DRM on a downloaded music file doesn't stop you burning it to CD, you could try doing just that and then ripping the track from the CD back into your computer. You may also find software online that can strip the DRM away, leaving a file you can do anything with. Even if these approaches fail, there's always the option of playing back the file while rerecording it with an audio editor.

In early 2009, the iTunes Store, the largest player in the legal music download market, announced it was to become completely DRM-free, a move that could mark the beginning of the end for digital rights management. Yet DRM remains a hotly debated issue in relation to everything fom movie downloads to eBooks. Advocates of the free distribution of media see DRM as an infringement of their rights, while others see it as a legitimate way for copyright holders to safeguard their products from piracy. But whatever your view, be sure to check what limitations will be imposed on any media you pay to access.

…downloading it

Streaming straight off the Web is fine for taste-testing CDs at Amazon, listening to otherwise-unavailable radio stations or watching "viral" video clips that a friend has emailed you a link to. But when you have the opportunity to download a track or video to your hard drive, the quality can be incomparably better – because they don't need to be so compressed. And once you have the file on your own computer, you can play it again and again without going online, and even move it to a portable device (see p.193).

The most common formats for downloadable music are **MP3**, **AAC** and **WMA** though there are plenty of others (see box opposite). The compression level of these kinds of files is expressed as a **bitrate**, which tells you the average number of zeros and ones used to store each second of audio data. The higher the figure, the better the quality, but the longer the download time.

Most music files available online are encoded at a bitrate of **128Kbps** (128,000 bits per second). This isn't far off CD quality – you probably won't be able to tell the difference over your computer's speakers, but you might if you play it through a decent home stereo. A four-minute track turned into a 128Kbps MP3 will be around 3.8MB. With a 56K modem, this should take less than fifteen minutes to download; with a 1Mb broadband connection, it will be finished in less than one.

The most common formats for downloadable video are **MPG** and **AVI**. Confusingly, however, each of these can contain video created using various different "codecs" (see p.200).

Music

Choose your jukebox

A "jukebox" is a program for organizing and playing your virtual music collection. That includes tracks that you've downloaded from the Net, and those that you've "ripped" from your own CD collection. Jukeboxes are also used for transferring tracks onto portable MP3 players (such as iPods), creating playlists and burning CD compilations. There are many jukeboxes out there, but the most popular by far are iTunes and Windows Media Player:

▶ **iTunes** Probably the best jukebox around. Built into all recent Macs and available as a free download for PCs, it's also the only jukebox that will work with an iPod (see p.193). iTunes plays back AAC, MP3, Apple Lossless and various other file formats, but not DRM-protected WMA files of the sort that are available from many of the commercial download services

Common online music formats

MP3 [Moving Pictures Experts Group-1/2 Audio Layer 3]
The most common format for online music.
File name ends: .mp3
Pros: works with any computer or player. Lets you make MP3 CDs with more than ten hours of music for use on special MP3 CD players.
Cons: doesn't sound as good as AAC or Ogg Vorbis at the same bitrate.

WMA [Windows Media Audio]
Microsoft's own audio format.
File name ends: .wma
Pros: good sound for the file size.
Cons: can only be played back on certain hardware and software if the file has DRM copy protection (see p.189).

AAC [Advanced Audio Coding]
A relatively new encoding format that is being pushed by Apple and which, by general consensus, sounds noticeably better than MP3.
File name ends: .m4a (standard), **.m4p** (with DRM).
Pros: excellent sound for the file size.
Cons: only works with certain software and hardware (including Apple's iTunes and iPod).

Ogg Vorbis
A relatively new open-source audio format that's set to give MP3 a run for its money. For more visit www.vorbis.com
File name ends: .ogm
Pros: encoding audio files and streaming audio.
Cons: currently incompatible with much software and hardware.

AIFF & WAV [Advanced Interchange File Format & Wave]
Uncompressed music formats. AIFF is traditionally associated with Macs, and WAV with PCs, though they both work on each platform.
File name ends: .aif, **.wav**
Pros: perfect sound quality.
Cons: massive files (around ten times bigger than most MP3 or AAC).

Audible
A special format for spoken-word recordings.
See www.audible.com
File name ends: .aa

(see p.194). However, iTunes does give you access to the iTunes Music Store, which has millions of tracks on offer for $1 or 79p per pop. To get the latest version of iTunes, visit www.itunes.com and for the full story check out *The Rough Guide to iPods & iTunes*.

▶ **Songbird** Like the Firefox Web browser, Songbird is an open-source application from the Mozilla stable. It's a relatively young but very high-quality program, and benefits from a wide range of downloadable enhancements and plug-ins made available by the developer community. Best of all, you can use Songbird in conjunction with iTunes, allowing you to swap between the two players while only having to maintain one "library" of music. Download Songbird for free, for Mac or PC, from: www.getsongbird.com

▶ **Windows Media Player** is built into all recent copies of Windows and is a bit like an ugly, badly designed version of iTunes. As a jukebox, it's only available for PCs; the Mac version is just for playing back files, not for organizing and managing your music. If you want to use a non-iPod MP3 player, or to buy tracks from many of the services listed on p.194, you may be stuck with it, though it's worth trying Yahoo! Music Jukebox and Winamp instead (see below). You can get the latest version through Windows Update (see p.70) or by visiting www.windowsmedia.com/download

There are various other decent jukebox programs out there, with Winamp (www.winamp.com) being among the best. You'll find hundreds more at the software sites listed on p.183.

Where to find the music

Unless you're after something obscure, you're unlikely to have many problems finding music on the Internet. But whether it will be legal or illegal to actually download it is another matter.

Move your music & video

Once you've downloaded half the music ever recorded, there's no need to play it back via your tinny computer speakers. One option is to **connect your PC or Mac to your hi-fi**. Assuming your computer has a headphone or line-out socket, and your hi-fi has a line-in socket, this is easily done with an inexpensive mini-jack to RCA cable. If you use iTunes (on either a Mac or PC), you could also stream your music wirelessly from your computer to your stereo via an AirPort Express unit (see www.apple.com/airportexpress), or even to your TV or home cinema rig using Apple TV (see www.apple.com/appletv).

Alternatively, depending on any DRM limitations embedded in your downloaded files, you could play your music on:

▶ **MP3 players** These Walkman-like devices can store some or all of your favourite tracks (not just in MP3 format) and play them back when you're on the move. The smaller, less expensive devices hold only a few hours of music on flash memory; the more expensive models, such as Apple iPod Classic (pictured), feature their own integral **hard drive** and can hold thousands of hours of music, and video too.

When buying any kind of MP3 player, consider its capacity, weight, battery life, available accessories and the formats it can play back. For more information on

iPods, the world of the MP3, and "ripping" DVDs into an iPod-friendly format, see *The Rough Guide to iPods & iTunes*.

▶ **Mobile phones** MP3 phones are becoming increasingly popular. When buying, the two most important considerations are the formats they will play and their capacity. Some have several gigabytes of memory built in, while others feature an expansion slot that will take additional memory cards. Many service providers now offer MP3 download services direct to your phone.

▶ **CDs** Most jukebox programs – and lots of stand-alone burning applications – will let you write your music files to CD, for playing back on a standard hi-fi system. You could also burn special **MP3 CDs**, which allow you to squeeze more than ten hours of music onto a single disc – but it will only play back on a CD player that supports MP3 CDs. For more see:

CDR FAQ www.cdrfaq.org
CDR Labs www.cdrlabs.com

▶ **DVDs** When it comes to **video**, you have an extra motivation for burning your downloads to disc: they'll quickly fill up your hard drive if you don't. Many of the movies available via file-sharing networks are compressed, which is fine for watching them on your computer, but, if the quality is worth it, you may want to burn them to DVD and watch them on your TV. Obviously, you'll need a DVD-burning drive on your computer. There are also now video equivalents of MP3 CD players – DVD players that can read MPEG and DivX. See, for example:

Kiss-Technology www.kiss-technology.com

On the **legal** front, download-quality music falls into a few main categories: music you can **pay to download** on a song-by-song or album-by-album basis; subscription services, which charge a monthly fee to access their archives; and authorized previews or freebies from record companies and artists. These are all discussed below. You may also come across recordings that are so old they are no longer in copyright – though this is esoteric stuff.

On the **illegal** front, these days the majority of pirated music and video is exchanged via peer-2-peer (P2P) file-sharing applications. These make it easy and quick to get hold of just about anything you want without paying a penny – but if you use them to download copyrighted material, you will be breaking the law. For more on file sharing, see p.202.

Following is an alphabetical summary of the main legal music sites and services. Nearly all these services are compatible with any MP3 player hardware or jukebox, but there are a few with specific quirks or limitations, so read the small print carfully before signing up.

Amazon www.amazon.com
Launched in 2007, Amazon was the first store to offer exclusively DRM-free music in the MP3 format. There are millions of tracks, all of which can be downloaded directly to your iTunes or Windows Media library.

Russian MP3 sites

In between the legit and the illegit, there are MP3 websites that are, well, kind of legal. MP3million, for example, is the latest of a string of Russian sites that use a loophole in their country's broadcast law to openly offer a huge download archive without permission from the labels. It's left up to you to ensure you don't break the law of your own country when downloading. Other sites that have come and gone operating in the same way include ALLOFMP3.com and MP3Sparks.com.

MP3million www.mp3million.com

AudioLunchbox www.audiolunchbox.com
A top-class selection from independent labels. Most tracks are 99¢, though there are freebies to be had too.

Bleep www.bleep.com
Electronica and indie, including everything from the Warp Records catalogue and loads more. You can preview whole tracks before buying, at which point expect to pay 99p per song or £6.99 for an album.

Download.com Music
music.download.com
Free music by amateur or up-and-coming artists. It's the archive that used to live at MP3.com – now a site that lets you compare (and search for tracks across) the major music services.

eMusic www.emusic.com
Aside from Amazon, perhaps the main competitor to iTunes, this brilliant service offers 4 million songs from indie labels. For the $9.99 per month basic package you get 30 tracks – which works out at only 33¢ per track.

IntoMusic www.intomusic.co.uk
Indie and alternative stuff for 60p per track. There are subscription and buy-in-bulk payment options for keen users.

iTunes Store www.itunes.com
Controlling over eighty percent of the global music download market, iTunes is head and shoulders above of the competition. It offers a pay-per-track model, with around ten million audio tracks available via the iTunes jukebox software (see p.191). Most selections are priced at 99¢/79p and all downloads are DRM-free; however, at the time of writing, each downloaded file has the email address of the downloader "stamped" into it. This means that if your iTunes tracks did ever end up on a file-sharing site, they could be traced back to you. iTunes Store tracks are downloaded in Apple's own AAC file format (see box, p.191), which will play on all iPods and some non-Apple MP3 music players.

Music & video

Mondomix mp3.mondomix.com
A one-stop shop for World Music MP3s from around the globe.

MySpace.com music.myspace.com
Literally tens-of-thousands of bands and artists representing every genre of music under the sun. Most offer, at the very least, a few songs to be streamed from their page, while others make their tracks available as either free or pay-for MP3 downloads.

Tip: When signing up for any subscription service, such as Napster's, be sure to read the small print to find out exactly what you're getting for your money. With many "unlimited access" services, for example, you'll find that your downloaded music ceases to play the moment you cancel your subscription. With others, the DRM will impose annoying restrictions – such as stopping you burning tracks to CD.

Napster www.napster.co.uk (UK)
Napster www.napster.com (US)
Having inherited its name from the renowned illegal music sharing system that was shut down in 2002, the current Napster service offers "permanent" downloads at 99¢/79p per song or unlimited access to millions of tracks in return for a monthly fee. Napster does not officially work with iTunes, iPods or Macs. But PC users might be interested to check out the service, perhaps even to use alongside iTunes.

Nervous Records www.nervous.co.uk/download.htm
MP3s from the rockabilly label (not to be confused with its NYC name-sake), at 99¢ a shot.

Rhapsody www.real.com/rhapsody
Unlimited access to more than three million songs for $13 per month (computer only) or $15 per month (if you want to use an MP3 player). "Permanent" downloads are separate, at 79–99¢ per track. This service is available for both Mac and PC users, but not outside the US.

Trax2Burn www.trax2burn.com
House music galore, at 99p per track.

We7 www.we7.com
Not the greatest collection of tunes as yet, but We7 offers an interesting twist on the MP3 download model. All the MP3s are free to download, but each one contains an audio advertisement that is heard every time you play the track. After living with the ad for a four-week period, you can choose to keep the music, minus the advert. The money that We7 accumulate from ad sales is then used to pay the artists, so it works a little like commercial radio.

Supermarket sites

The supermarket chains are doing their best to take a slice of the music download market. While they may not carry the millions of tracks found on iTunes, both Tesco in the UK and Walmart in the US offer among the most competitive prices for mainstream artist selections.

Tesco www.tescodigital.com
Walmart mp3.walmart.com

Online radio

The other main source of online audio is Internet radio. There are thousands of stations playing every minute of every day, and the quality isn't too bad. See p.282 for more information.

Video & TV

Video is an ever-growing part of the Internet – from comic clips and full-length movies to webcasts of concerts and watch-on-demand TV catch-up services.

TV on demand

The most exciting recent development in online video is that many television channels and production companies are making their recently aired shows available online for free. The BBC got things going with its **iPlayer**, which offers everything broadcast on BBC television and radio stations over the last seven days. Fairly soon, ITV, Channel 4 and Five followed suit with similar services. (At the time of writing some of these sites are PC-only, though they may work on Macs by the time you read this.)

BBC www.iplayer.com
ITV itv.com/ITVPlayer
Channel 4 channel4.com/4od
Channel 5 demand.five.tv

For a relatively small subscription charge, you can also access Sky TV channels via the Web:

Sky TV skyplayer.sky.com

In the US, some channels and production companies make recent shows available but others prefer to make their content available via TV-on-demand sites such as **Joost** and **Hulu**. These both offer a good mix of popular TV seasons, documentaries and music videos, but currently work only in the US.

Hulu www.hulu.com
Joost www.joost.com

Downloadable movies & TV shows

The **iTunes Store**, available only through iTunes (see p.191) offers an impressive selection of music videos and a decent selection of TV shows and movies (the latter also available for "rental"). These videos are offered at a reasonable though not ideal resolution of 640x480 pixels (though some material is also now available in high definition if downloaded using an Apple TV device).

As for contraband, lots of TV shows and movies are easy to track down – albeit in poor quality streams – via an ever-changing roster of link sites, but expect to be bombarded by pop-ups and casino click-throughs in exchange for your televisual fix. The P2P networks discussed in chapter 17 are rife with much higher-quality versions, but they're mainly illegal and often require you to mess around with video codecs (see box, p.201).

Tip: If you want to download a video from an online stream so that you can watch it on an iPod, say, copy and paste the video's link to www.keepvid.com. but bear in mind that this should not be done with copyrighted streaming material.

Movie trailers

If you're trying to decide what to see at the cinema, or rent from the DVD store, you'll have no problem finding trailers to help you choose. Either search Google for a particular movie title or drop into an archive such as:

Apple Trailers www.apple.com/trailers
Movie List www.movie-list.com
Movies www.movie.com

Tip: Still not sure what to rent? Get movie recommendations based on your tastes at www.tastekid.com.

Video clips: YouTube, etc

YouTube, which has quickly grown to become one of the most pop-ular sites on the Internet, is a huge archive of video clips uploaded by its users. It's best know for funny video clips – many of them home movies – though it's also home to loads of classic TV and film footage, much to the consternation of the copyright holders.

It's easy to spend countless hours on YouTube. If you're just browsing, to avoid trudging through loads of lame stuff, look at the Featured Clips links on the homepage and try the ones with the highest user rating.

YouTube www.youtube.com

Various other sites have followed suit and offer comparable "swamps" of video clips for you to wade through. MySpace and Google are the pick of the bunch:

Google Video video.google.com
MySpace vids.myspace.com

Video Podcasts

Video Podcasts, aka Vodcasts or vlogs, can be played either on your computer or on a MP3 player. They're mainly free and range from TV news bulletins to Yoga or Photoshop tutorials. You can find video Podcasts via a directory such as MeFeedia (see p.236 for more) or an aggregator with a built-in directory, such as iTunes.

MeFeedia mefeedia.com

Webcasts

A webcast is online video streamed in real time. They're often used for things such as concert broadcasts and news bulletins. But dig around and you'll find all sorts of stuff, from the Science Of Cooking (www.exploratorium.edu/cooking/webcasts) to 24-hour prerecorded United Nations TV programming (www.un.org/webcast).

Video formats & codecs

Two common formats for video downloads are **MPG** (or MPEG) and **AVI**, though each of these can contain video created using various different "codecs" (compression systems), such as DivX.

Most MPG and AVI files can be played in Windows Media Player or QuickTime, though to view films encoded with DivX you'll need to grab the free **DivX Player** (or the relevant plug-in for Windows Media Player) from:

DivX www.divx.com

DivX might not be the only codec that you are missing, so you might want to search the online software archives listed on p.183 for a "codecs pack". Alternatively, grab the free VLC media player, which comes with a comprehensive library of codecs built in – it can deal with almost anything, and is available for both PCs and Macs:

VLC www.videolan.org

Also worth knowing about is GSpot (PC only), which can analyze individual video files and tell you which codec you need. You then drop by the GSpot website to download the ones you need:

GSpot headbands.com/gspot

P2P file sharing

Legalities & practicalities

The commercial online music services described in the previous chapter may be competing with each other, but collectively their main competitor is P2P file sharing, a technology that allows computer users all over the world to "share" each other's files – including music files – via the Internet. Even if you've never heard of P2P ("peer-to-peer") you've probably heard of some of the programs that have made this kind of file sharing possible, such as KaZaA and, historically speaking, Napster. And you've probably also heard people debating the legal and moral ins and outs of the free-for-all that file-sharing programs facilitate. If not, don't worry – the next few pages will bring you up to speed.

A peer-to-peer primer

On a home or office network, it's standard for users of each computer to have some degree of access to the files stored on the other computers. P2P file-sharing programs apply this idea to the whole of the Internet – which is, of course, simply a giant network of computers. In short, anyone who installs a P2P program can access the "shared folder" of anyone else running a similar program. And these shared folders are mostly filled with music and video files.

With literally millions of file sharers online at any one time, an unthinkably large quantity of content is up there. And it's not just music and video: any file can be made available, from images to software and documents. So, whether you're after a drum'n'bass track, a Web-design application, a Chomsky speech or an episode of *Friends*, you're almost certain to find it. But that doesn't mean that it's legal. If you download or make available any copyright-protected material, you are breaking the law and, while it's still currently unlikely, you could in theory be prosecuted.

The legal battle

Continuous legal action saw Napster – the first major P2P system – bludgeoned into submission (it has now resurfaced as one of the larger legitimate online music providers; see p.197). A similar fate befell Scour, this time because of movie rather than audio sharing. But these casualties just paved the way for the many alternatives, of which the most popular has proved to be KaZaA, which now stands by some margin as the most downloaded program in the history of the Internet.

So far, despite their not inconsiderable efforts, the music, film and software companies have failed to put an end to this new-generation file sharing. Mainly this is because, unlike the old programs, the new ones create a genuinely decentralized network. In other words, they don't rely on a central system to keep tabs on which files are where. This means that, even though the programs are mostly used for the illegal distribution of copyrighted material, the companies producing them can't easily be implicated in this breach of the law – just as a gun manufacturer couldn't easily be sued for a shooting involving their product.

This immunity wasn't to last, however. In 2005, the Recording Industry Association of America (RIAA) and the Motion Picture Industry (MPI) were successful in closing down the company behind the Grokster P2P program. It remains to be seen how long the others will survive.

In the meantime, the music industry, led by RIAA, has instead gone after the people who clearly *are* breaking the law: individual file sharers downloading or making available copyrighted material. Quite a few individuals have now been prosecuted, but with many millions of people using file sharing each day, it seem very unlikely that the record companies could go after every one of them. Even if they could, that approach might be useless against the next generation of P2P programs, which will use encryption to make it difficult to track who is downloading and uploading what.

Whether or not it's ethical to use P2P to download copyrighted material for free is another question. Some people justify it on the grounds that they use file sharing as a way to listen to new music they're considering buying on CD; others claim they refuse to support a music industry that, in their view, is doing more harm than good; others still only download noncontroversial material, such as recordings of speeches, or music that they already own on CD or vinyl and can't be bothered to rip or record manually.

It's a heated debate – as is the question of whether file sharing has damaged legal music sales, something the industry insists upon, but which many experts claim is questionable.

Networks and programs

Though all P2P file sharing takes place via the Internet, there are various discrete "networks", the main ones being **BitTorrent**, **eDonkey2000**, **FastTrack** and **Gnutella**. Each is huge and accessible via various different programs, many of which are very sophisticated, with built-in media players or even the ability to import downloaded tracks directly into a playlist in iTunes.

Note that some file-sharing programs come with unwelcome extras such as spyware and adware – something long associated with KaZaA, for example. So proceed with care. At a minimum, PC owners should run a virus scanner and SpyBot S&D (see p.173). Mac users are much less at risk.

Below is a list of major networks and some of the most popular programs for accessing them. All of these can be downloaded and used for free, though some nag users to make a donation to the developer or pay for a more fully featured, ad-free version. Note that new P2P programs come out all the time and some programs can access more than one network.

Gnutella

Gnutella is a very popular network accessible via a wide range of user-friendly programs such as:

LimeWire www.limewire.com (PC & Mac)
Morpheus www.morpheus.com (PC)
Acquisition www.acquisitionx.com (Mac)
Shareaza sourceforge.net/projects/shareaza (PC)

Torrents

With most P2P systems, users search for the files they are after within the P2P program itself and then download them directly to other users. An exception to this rule is BitTorrent. WIth this system, users first search the Web for so-called **torrent files** of the music or video they're after. These small files are quickly downloaded and opened with a BitTorrent applica- tion, which then downloads – or at least tries to download – the music or video from a variety of other users. The more people who are using a particular torrent, the faster the data flows and the quicker each person's download arrives.

BitTorrent is hugely popular for large files – espe- cially albums, movies and television shows. Indeed, according to some estimates, it sometimes accounts for as much as a quarter of Internet traffic. As with the other networks, however, using torrents to download copyrighted ma- terial is against the law.

To get started with BitTorrent, you first have to download a suitable application (or "client"). There are numerous options out there, including several of the P2P programs listed in this chapter. But the most popular dedicated torrent clients are BitTorrent and Vuze. The latter is particularly slick and, as well as the inevitable contraband, offers access to an extensive network of non-copyrighted material, including hundreds of intriguing if not necessarily entertaining "fan-made" sci-fi movies.

BitTorrent www.bittorrent.com
Vuze www.vuze.com (PC & Mac)

FastTrack

Thanks to the success of KaZaA, this extremely well-stocked network has been the focus of much of the legal battle. Applications for accessing the network include:

KaZaA www.kazaa.com (PC)
Poisoned www.gottsilla.net (Mac)

Since 2004, iMesh has offered a legal option for accessing the FastTrack network from the US and Canada. Now recognized by the record labels' association, the site charges a monthly subscription fee to tap into the shared library of millions of songs.

iMesh www.imesh.com (PC)

And more...

There are many other programs and networks out there. **Soulseek**, for example, is popular for underground and alternative music, and allows users to download whole folders at once.

SoulSeek www.slsknet.org (PC & Mac)
SolarSeek www.solarseek.net (Mac)

For more information, including reviews of all the available programs, see:

Slyck www.slyck.com (PC & Mac)
ZeroPaid www.zeropaid.com (PC & Mac)

Stake your claim

Your own website

18

Not as hard as you'd think

You don't need to be anyone particularly important or a company with something to sell – if you have something to say or display, there's plenty of room for you on the Web. As long as it's not against the law, you can publish whatever you like, from instructions for building a psychotronic mind-control deflecting beenie (zapatopi.net/afdb.html) to an illustrated archive of your navel fluff collection (feargod.net/fluff.html). And, while the finer points of Web design are hard to master, it's really not very difficult to create a simple site.

The first questions you need to ask yourself are what you want to use the website for, and whether you really want to start from scratch. If you just want an easy way to put your thoughts or pictures online, with minimum technical fuss, then you might consider starting off with a **blogging** or **photo-sharing service**. This way, you can be up and running in minutes, without any technical know-how, though you won't have total control over how your site looks. For more on blogging see p.230, and for photo-sharing see p.260.

If you want a little more control, but you still don't want to do anything technical, you could opt for an automatic **website builder**. The result might look a bit prefabricated, but you can create a

site through a step-by-step wizard, or by simply filling in a set of templates. Most domain registries and hosting services offer such tools (see p.222), or you could try a special service such as the very well-regarded Mr Site:

Mr Site www.mrsite.co.uk

If, however, you want complete control over your website, the best option is to create and publish your own webpages from scratch. It's not too hard to get started, and the whole process helps demystify how the World Wide Web functions. Read on…

The least you need to know

This chapter will walk you through the basic process of creating a website and getting it online. But it pays to clear up a few basic facts at the outset about what exactly a webpage is:

▶ **Each webpage** consists of an HTML file (which itself contains just text) plus separate files for any pictures, videos or sounds used within the page. The HTML file specifies how each extra files fit into the page.

▶ **These files** – including the HTML and images, etc – reside on a computer that is permanently connected to the Web. This computer is known as a server, and it is said to "host" the pages.

▶ **When a reader** types the address of the webpage into their Web browser, the HTML file and associated images are temporarily downloaded from the server to the reader's computer and displayed as a whole.

With this in mind, publishing a single webpage involves the following key steps, each of which is discussed in this chapter:

▶ **Create an HTML document** using a text-editing or HTML application.

▶ **Prepare any image files** to appear in the page.

▶ **Choose your address** If you want a specific Web address – such as www.yourname.com – you'll need to register the relevant domain name (see p.222). Otherwise, you might use the address provided free with some webspace from your ISP.

▶ **Park your page** Using a so-called FTP program, upload your HTML and image files onto a server. It might be a server that you pay to use or some free webspace provided by your ISP.

Good design, bad design

Because there's more than enough room on the World Wide Web for everyone who wants to publish a site, and absolutely no means of quality control, the Internet has become a haven for bad design and content that's impossible to digest – dayglo pink text against a bright green background, for example, complete with distracting flashing images and fancy mouse cursors. So, before you even get near to any site-building tool, think about how you want your pages to look and who your audience is, and try not to make the same mistakes that others have made:

Bad Design Features www.ratz.com/featuresbad.html
Web Pages That Suck www.webpagesthatsuck.com
Worst Of The Web www.worstoftheweb.com

Vincent Flanders'
Web Pages That Suck
On our 13th year of sucking

If the point of your website is to convey some message about you, make sure it's not a bad one. The first step in that direction is to present your site in a way that's **easy to navigate**, and your pages so they're **easy to read**. Almost all successful sites stick to a similar minimal structure. The buzzword for this is "usability". You can read all about it here:

Usable Web www.usableweb.com
WebWord Usability Weblog www.webword.com

If, after all that, you're still considering a patterned background, at least spare a thought for the colour-blind:

Vischeck www.vischeck.com

Some common tags

▸ **Bold** <b></b>

▸ **Italics** <i></i>

▸ **Underline** <u></u>

▸ **New paragraph** <p>

▸ **Line break**

▸ **Horizontal rule** <hr>

▸ **Text size**
<font size=4></font>

▸ **Text colour**
<font color=red></font>

▸ **Add an image** <img
src="http://www.myserver.
com/dog.jpg">

▸ **Indented text**
<blockquote></blockquote>

▸ **Web link**
<a href="www.roughguides
.com">Rough Guides</a>

▸ **Email link** <a href="mailto:
youraddress@hotmail
.com">Email Me</a>

▸ **Align left or right** <div
align="left"></div>

▸ **Centered** <center>your
text</center>

Stage #1: Starting out with HTML

Once you've worked out what to say on your site and how you want it to look, the next thing to decide is how to convert your thoughts into **HTML – HyperText Markup Language** – which, despite its intimidating name, is actually not too hard to get to grips with.

In short, HTML is the code used to style and position the text, images and other components within a webpage. A Web browser reads the code and works out from that how to display the contents of the page. These days you don't have to learn HTML to make a webpage, as various special programs will do the techie bit for you (more on these later). However, at some point you'll probably need to go in and tweak the raw code, so it's worth knowing at least the basics.

HTML basics

HTML is much simpler than computer programming in general, and it only takes a few hours to learn the basics. Next time you're online, examine the raw HTML code that makes up any webpage – choose to view the "Source" from your browser's View menu. The first thing you'll notice is that the text is surrounded with comments enclosed between less-than and greater-than symbols, like this:

<BOLD>My head hurts</BOLD>

These comments are known as **tags**. In the example above, the tags would make the text "My head hurts" appear bold. **Most tags come in pairs** and apply to the text they enclose. A tag featuring a forward slash signals the end of a pair of tags' relevance, as in: </BOLD>

Making a simple webpage is basically just a matter of putting the page's title, text and weblinks within the necessary tags. If you want to include any pictures, video, sounds, etc, you need to put the relevant file in a folder with the HTML file and "point to them" within the HTML by enclosing their file names in yet more tags.

Creating HTML

Since HTML is just plain-old text, it's possible to create a webpage using any simple **text editor** – such as Notepad (PC) or Text Edit (Mac). The box below shows you how it's done. The problem with this technique, however, it that it's time consuming and a bit boring. Hence most people choose to use a special HTML **editing program**, which will take care of some or all of the tagging automatically. Some of the tools are relatively simple – you still look at the raw code, but the program automates much of the tagging, saving

Write a page – right now

Let's dive straight in and make a simple page. Open a text editor like **Notepad** or **SimpleText**, and then type in the following:

```
<HTML>
<HEAD><TITLE>My First Page</TITLE></HEAD>
<BODY>I am a genius</BODY>
</HTML>
```

The paired <HTML> and </HTML> tags signify that the document is (yes, you guessed it) an **HTML file**, and that it has a beginning and an end.

And with that, bravo – you've finished! Save the page onto your Desktop with the name index.html, and then open it in your Web browser (if double-clicking doesn't work, drag the file into a browser window).

You'll see your page has two parts: a **head** and a **body**. The head contains the title, which is displayed in the top bar of your browser. The body defines what appears within the browser window.

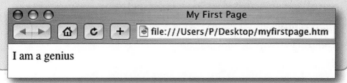

How to link

The Web is all about hyperlinks between pages. In HTML, to create a link, you use "a" tags to enclose the text (or image) that you'd like to appear on the page, and specify the link address within the first tag in the following format:

<a href="www.cats.com"> My favourite feline resource<a>

In this example, the text "My favourite feline resource" would appear in the webpage. When clicked, it would take you to www.cats.com.

You can link to another page within your own site in the same way. If the page you want to link to is in the same folder as the page you're linking from, you can just specify the file name instead of the full web address.

Your own website

Tip: If you find a page you like, view the Source (via your Web browser's View menu) and try and work out what's going on. Sometimes it will be impenetrably complicated, but it can be a great way to learn. Best of all, you can copy and paste sections of code into your own pages, and then replace the text and images with your own.

Fonts and webpages

HTML editors allow you to specify fonts for your text. Bear in mind, however, that not every computer has the same fonts installed, so it's safest to stick with the few almost universal fonts, which include: Geneva, Verdana, Arial, Times New Roman and Courier New.

There are ways around these limitations, however. One option – suitable for headings – is to save your text as images in a program such as Photoshop. Another is to investigate the dark art of embedding fonts within webpages (see http://tinyurl.com/af6rm).

you some legwork. Popular examples include the following free or inexpensive options:

AceHTML www.visicommedia.com
Arachnophilia www.arachnoid.com/arachnophilia
HTML Kit www.chami.com/html-kit

More popular, however, are so-called **WYSIWYG** ("what you see is what you get") HTML editors. These allow you to create the pages without looking at the HTML at all. However, they also let you edit the raw code – which is essential, since no WYSIWYG process creates perfect HTML. This way of doing things isn't just restricted to the dedicated site editors: office programs such as **Microsoft Word** can save your documents as HTML ready for shipment onto the Web (just create the document and press Save As Webpage from the File menu). Nonetheless, a dedicated website editor will do a better job.

Anyone who has purchased a Mac in recent years will already have an excellent WYSIWYG editor called **iWeb**, which can also be purchased as part of the iLife suite of applications.

iWeb www.apple.com/ilife/iweb

Otherwise, you could explore a freebie…

Site Studio sitestudio.psoft.net (Mac)
XStandard www.xstandard.com (PC & Mac)

…or investigate the more feature-packed commercial products. **Microsoft Expression Web** makes the transition from familiar products like Word relatively painless. But the industry standard is **DreamWeaver**. Download the free trials from:

Expression Web www.microsoft.com/expression
Macromedia www.macromedia.com

For many more options, see:

Tucows www.tucows.com/Windows/DevelopmentWebAuthoring
Wikipedia.com en.wikipedia.org/wiki/List_of_HTML_editors

Take a tutorial

Many of the programs mentioned above come with some sort of HTML tutorial (look in the Help menu). But to learn more about working with HTML, look online. You'll find just about everything you need to know via the following:

About.com html.about.com
HTML Goodies www.htmlgoodies.com
WebMonkey www.webmonkey.com
W3 www.w3schools.com

Saving your pages

On most sites, when you call up the homepage by entering the relevant domain into your browser (eg www.mysite.com), the page that appears is actually an HTML file called index.html or index.htm. It's the same end result as entering www.mysite.com/index.html, but to make things look neater, the last bit of the address isn't usually displayed. So, when you save the front page to your site you should call it index.html – all in lower case. Then people only have to enter the general address for your site in order to get to your homepage.

The rest of your pages should also use the same file extension (.html or .htm) and be given not-too-long names that relate to their contents. Unless you have a very good reason, save all your file names in lower case, as it's less likely to cause confusion. Finally, **don't use names containing spaces** (use hyphens or underscores instead) or non-English language characters.

Stage #2: Prepare your images

Placing and preparing graphics is half of the art of Web design. First, there's the issue of getting photos and other "artwork" to look right and download quickly. Second, there's the skill of creating images that are integral to the design of the page. If you look online you'll find that lots of "text" actually consists of images – as this allows designers to use any font and special effect.

Reducing an image's file size

Before you post a digital image on the Web (or attach it to an email, for that matter; see p.120), you'll probably need to reduce its size in bytes, otherwise it will take an age to download. You can do this in two ways – both of which will need some kind of image-editing software (see box opposite).

▶ **Reduce the dimensions** of the image in pixels, making the picture itself smaller. For example, if it measures 1024x768 pixels, you could reduce it to, say, 800x600. You could also crop the image, chopping off excess from the edges. These techniques will change the size and shape of the image, but not otherwise affect the quality.

▶ **Compress the image** Compressed image formats such as JPEG and GIF allow an image to be made much smaller in terms of file size. If you compress too much, the reduced file size will come at the cost of image quality – things might start to look blocky or blurred. Done right, however, the compressed version will look identical to the naked eye but will be much smaller in terms of file size. When you save or resave a compressed image in a graphics program (see box opposite), you can select from various different compression levels, allowing you to try various options and strike a good balance between image quality and file size.

Creating images

There are three ways to produce a digital image. First, by taking a photo with a **digital camera** (or a still from a **digital video camera**) and importing it into your computer. Second, by using a **scanner** to import a virtual copy of an existing photograph, drawing or just about anything else two-dimensional. These days, decent-enough digital cameras and scanners can be picked up inexpensively.

The third technique is to create images from scratch on your computer using a **drawing program**. You'll find many such tools for free via the various download sites (p.183), but they pall in comparison with professional-level products such as:

Illustrator
www.adobe.com/illustrator
CorelDraw
www.corel.com
Fireworks
www.adobe.com/fireworks

Image-processing software

Unless you have a really old computer, your system will probably already be able to open most types of image file. But to create, resize or compress pictures for your website, you'll need some image-editing software.

If you already have a program for managing your digital photographs, then you might find that this has all the editing and re-saving tools that you need. iPhoto on Macs for example has decent editing tools and easy export options (select the image you want to re-save and press Export in the File menu).

But there are also many free image editors available to download, from open-source-powerhouse GIMP to the user-friendly PhotoPlus. You'll find more through the software sites listed on p.183.

GIMP www.gimp.org
PhotoPlus www.freeserifsoftware.com

Also worth investigating are free online browser-based photo-editing tools, such as the completely brilliant Pixlr (pictured) and Adobe's US-only Photoshop Express:

Pixlr www.pixlr.com/editor
Photoshop Express www.photoshop.com/express

As for commercial packages, the professional's choice is the full version of Adobe Photoshop, which is great if you can afford it. But there are also many less expensive tools that do nearly as much – Paint Shop Pro being one example.

Photoshop www.adobe.com
Paint Shop Pro corel.com/paintshop

For help using them, try:

PhotoshopCAFE
photoshopcafe.com (Photoshop)
Pinoy7 pinoy7.com (for Paint Shop Pro)

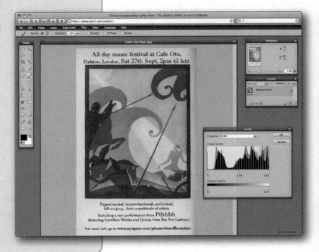

Image tips

▸ Plan the layout of your webpages so you know what sizes of images you'll need. Keep in mind the average size of computer screens when you're laying plans – the last thing you want is for your images to appear either too small or overblown in a browser.

▸ Whenever you compress a file, you run the risk of losing quality. So, rather than make incremental changes to the compressed image, complete any touch-ups and cropping in the original format, and then export images with different levels of compression from that master version. But be sure to keep a copy of your original image.

▸ Remember: the fewer images you use on your webpage and the smaller they are in bytes, the quicker your page will load. So if you plan to display a large number of high-quality photos, consider linking the actual images from **thumbnails** (small, reduced-quality versions). Many HTML editors can do this automatically.

GIF or JPEG?

The two most popular image formats on the Web are **JPEG** (.jpg) and **GIF** (.gif). They both lend themselves to online use because of their small file sizes, though their uses and characteristics are quite different. GIFs can only display 256 colours, while JPEGs can display millions. JPEGs also permit a greater degree of compression for detailed images. For these two reasons, most photographs are best saved as JPEGs.

GIFs have their uses, though. If an image contains a relatively small number of colours or has large expanses of the same colour, a GIF allows a much smaller file size with little loss of quality. GIFs can also be animated like a slideshow, and can have transparent backgrounds. Consequently, they're often used for bars, icons, banners and backgrounds.

Stage #3: Getting fancy

There's almost nothing that you can't do with a webpage. As you move up the levels of sophistication, you might start to move out of the basic HTML and image domain into more complex areas such as **Flash, Shockwave, JavaScript, Java, PERL, CGI** and **Visual Basic**. All of these add powerful tools to a web designer's palette, but bear in mind when employing them that, unless they're actually doing something useful, most of your visitors would probably rather you didn't bother.

Flash

When you see something moving on a website, it may be an animated GIF file (see above), but more likely it's an animation created in **Flash**, a package that allows you to create colourful interactive animations in very small files – a ten-second clip might only take up 10KB, for example. It's widely used online for everything from tiny details to complete websites.

Flash is a serious piece of software, and the price tag and learning curve reflect this. But once you've mastered the basics, it's relatively easy to generate some very nice-looking results.

But beware – the greatest design crime online is the use of flatulent Flash animations to welcome you to a site. It's about as likely to impress your visitors as making them walk across broken glass to read your mission statement. For examples of more appropriate uses of Flash animation, or to download a trial version of Flash Professional, visit:

Flash Pro www.adobe.com/flash

For tips, tools and more, see:

Flash Kit www.flashkit.com
W3 Schools www.w3schools.com/Flash

Java & Javascript

Java isn't a mark-up code like HTML, but a serious programming language designed to be interpreted by any computer. That makes it perfect for the Web as you can place an **applet** (Java program) on your site and make it accessible via your webpage. Most browsers have in-built Java interpreters, so visitors don't need any extra software to view it. Some useful online calculators, translators and interactive quizzes are powered by Java, but then so are countless useless applications that slow your browsing for no good reason. As for writing applets yourself, if you think C++ is a chuckle it's probably right up your alley. Good luck. For some amazing demos, follow the links from:

Java java.sun.com

JavaScript extends the Java concept to HTML and is much easier to work with. Because it sits entirely within the HTML of the webpage, you can pinch the code from other pages, just like with regular HTML. It can add all sorts of things, from displaying clocks, or personalized messages for each visitor to your site, to spawning pop-up windows. Grab code from:

JavaScript.com www.javascript.com
JavaScript Source javascript.internet.com

Any old file

If you want to make any other non-HTML file available on your site – such as a PDF, Word document or MP3 file – just put the file in the same folder as your webpages and link to it in your HTML. A link to a sound file, for example, might look like this:

```
<a href="mysong.mp3">My great new song<a>
```

When the reader clicks the link, the file will either open in their browser or download to their computer, depending on the type of file in question and the browser that they're using.

Stage #4: Get a host & domain

Once your webpages and images are ready to go live, you'll need to get them online, which means putting them on a server computer – a "host" – with an address where people can find them. If your budget is tight, you could simply plant the files in some free space (see box), such as that thrown in by your ISP as part of your Internet connection package.

The problem with using your ISP's space, or any of the other free options, is that you'll end up with a Web address such as:

webspace.myisp.com/peter_buckley

Free Web space

If you don't want to spend any money, you could simply drop your pages onto the Web space that probably comes free with your Internet connection. Ask your ISP if you're not sure whether your subscription includes any space.

One problem with this is, if you switch ISPs, you stand to lose not only the space, but the address. Instead, you could try a free Web space provider. Hundreds of sites will give you all the space you need, plus home-building tools to ease the process of editing and uploading pages, though you rarely get something for nothing, so expect banners or pop-ups on your pages. The big names include:

Tripod www.tripod.com
Yahoo! Geocities geocities.yahoo.com

For more, including links, reviews and recommendations try:

FreeWebSpace.net www.freewebspace.net

Or, to read how to remove pop-up ads from your free space (you shouldn't really, and in theory you might get kicked off), check out:

cexx.org www.cexx.org/diepop.htm

This is fine if you're just putting a page up for fun, but if you're in any way serious about your online presence, you'll really want something more like:

www.peterbuckley.com

You've now reached the point where you have to worry about registering the "domain name", which can be done via a **domain registrar** for a small fee and gives you exclusive use of the domain address for a set period (normally one or two years initially). Of course, if someone else has already taken your ideal name, you'll have to think of another, such as:

www.peter-buckley.com
www.peterbuckley.net
www.peterbuckley.info

There are many possibilities, so you should be able to find something half decent. Any domain registry will instantly confirm what's available, and register an address for you within a matter of minutes. Major domain registrars include:

Domain Direct www.domaindirect.com
DomainMonger www.domainmonger.com
Register.com www.register.com

If you want to associate yourself with a specific country, consider a regional domain ending in a country code, for example:

www.peterbuckley.co.uk

Many of the big registries allow some country-specific registration, but for a full list of available codes and relevant registrars, see the list at:

Uninett www.uninett.no/navn/domreg.html

This will lead to region-specific registrars, such as **123-reg** and **TheName** in the UK, and **NetRegistry** in Australia:

123-reg www.123-reg.co.uk (UK)
NetRegistry www.netregistry.com.au (Aus)
TheName www.thename.co.uk (UK)

Almost your own domain

If your address of choice is gone, you could try **Netidentity**, which will rent you a personalized Web/email address based on one of their countless domains. If they owned www.buckley.com, for example, you might be able to get peter.buckley.com.

Netidentity www.netidentity.com

Or, if you don't want to part with a penny but still want a short, memorable Web address, you could use some free Web space and register with a free forwarding service. For example, you could go to **Beam.To** and register beam.to/peterbuckley. Anyone who visits that address will then be forwarded to your free Web space.

Beam.To beam.to
isCool www.iscool.net

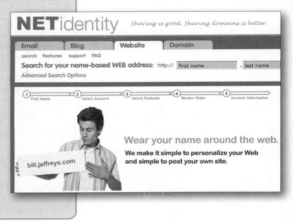

Choose a host

When you register a name, the registrar will probably try and sell you a package that includes a **hosting service** – ie some Web space for your pages to live in. Getting a domain and hosting from the same company is usually the most convenient choice – and usually the best value, too.

A second option, usually offered for free or nearly free with your domain-name registration, is to set up **Web forwarding**. This way you put your pages on some free space from your ISP or another provider (see p.40) and use your newly registered address just as a front door: people can get to your site by entering, say, www. peterbuckley.com, which will forward them to webspace.myisp. com/peter_buckley. Note, though, that some registrars will display – unless you pay a small surcharge – an ad banner at the top of your site to anyone who reached it via the new address.

Using your own computer as a Web server

Most people store their webpages on a server belonging to their ISP or a dedicated Web-hosting service. However, once your computer's connected to the Internet, it can also act as a server just by running the right software.

Besides this software, you'll ideally want three things to run your machine as a server. First, a relatively stable and **secure operating system**, such as Windows 7, XP or 2000, Mac OS X or Linux. Second, an always-on **broadband** connection.

Third, a **static IP address**. When you use your computer as a server, you have the domain registrar point your domain name to your computer's numerical IP address (see p.21). However, most ISPs offer a dynamic IP address, which means your computer's address changes regularly. There are clever ways around this (see www.dyndns.org and www.no-ip.com) but it's probably simpler just to ask your ISP for a static address. Most offer this service for a small monthly fee. Some offer it as standard.

Server software is very simple to install – it's even built-in and ready to go on recent Macs. If you're installing a server system on a PC, make sure you take the time to set up your security options to allow only appropriate access to appropriate directories. That means things like making your webpages read-only and your FTP incoming write-only. Also, note that some ISPs don't allow you to use your connection as a server – they may even try and charge you a fine if you try – so you may want to check the details of your contract first.

The Apache Software Foundation
http://www.apache.org/

The most popular Web server package (and the one built in to recent versions of Mac OS X) is **Apache**. It's open source and downloadable for free. For more on server software, check out ServerWatch.

Apache www.apache.org
ServerWatch serverwatch.internet.com

The third option is to register the domain name and then instruct the registrar to associate the domain with a separate server. This is done by logging in to the registrar's website and specifying the address of the server's DNS option within the website. The separate server might be your own computer (see box opposite) or it might be a hosting company who offer better value, service or bandwidth than the registrar. Compare prices and services listed below.

Find a Host www.findahost.com
Top Hosts www.tophosts.com
Web Host Magazine www.webhostmagazine.com

A few operations will even host your pages for free, such as:

Freeservers www.freeservers.com
100webspace www.100webspace.com

But there's usually a catch. You might get a banner ad above your site, for example. Or the fees may kick in after one year, or when your site gets popular and you exceed your download limit. Before signing up, read some reviews. Here, for example:

FreeWebSpace www.freewebspace.net

Stage #5: Upload your site

Unless you're using your own computer as a Web server, you'll need to upload your pages, images, etc, to wherever they're going to live on the Net. Whoever is providing your hosting or Web space will give you some log-in details. This will usually include a user ID, password and an **FTP** (File Transfer Protocol) address for your space on the server. Then you'll need to use a special FTP pro-

gram to actually move the files from your machine to the server.

Windows has a simple FTP tool built in, called **Web Publishing Wizard**. To launch it, simply select the files you want to FTP and press "Publish these files to the Web". But this approach isn't half as good as a stand-alone drag-and-drop FTP tool that clearly displays your home computer in one panel and your server space in the other. The most popular free options areSmartFTP (pictured) and Cyberduck:

Cyberduck cyberduck.ch (Mac)
SmartFTP www.smartftp.com (PC)

You might also want to investigate a program such as **Linkrunner**, which will scan your pages for broken links and missing images.

Alert Linkrunner www.alertbookmarks.com/lr

Alternatively, investigate the tools built into your HTML editor. Serious packages such as Dreamweaver have excellent FTP and link-checking tools built in.

Stage #6: Get your site noticed

Once you've published your page and transferred it to your server, the real problems begin. How do you **get people to visit it**? People you know or advertise to might arrive at your site by typing in your address – especially if you include it on your stationery, email signature and business cards. But the rest of the online world will get there by either taking a link from another site or by finding you through a search engine.

To increase the links to your site, contact similar sites and suggest swapping links. This sometimes starts a wonderful relationship – and it will also increase your Google ranking.

Get spotted by search engines

The best publicity machines of all, of course, are the search engines. The biggest services should eventually find your site (at least once some people are linking to it) but there's no need to wait. Visit each engine in turn and look for a link to "submit your site" or similar, and follow the prompts. You could use a service such as **AddMe!** to

add yourself to multiple engines and directories at once. But you may get better results doing it yourself.

AddMe! www.addme.com

Raise your ranking

When you enter keywords into a search engine, it will return a list of results in the order it deems most relevant. The ones that appear near the top of the list are inevitably the ones that get clicked. Different engines work in different ways, so even if two engines find the same sites, they might present the results in a different order. Consequently, if you care about your site's ranking – and you should – go directly to Google and the other major search engines and find out how they work.

> **Tip:** For a little insight into the way people search and statistical information relating to specific searches, drop in at www.google.com/trends

Links, links, links

Google is *the* search engine of the moment, in no small part due to the **PageRank** technology that helps it find the most relevant results. Integral to this is the ability to look at a page in terms of who is linking to it. The more sites that link to yours, the better your Google ranking will be – especially if the sites linking to you are ranked highly themselves. This means that one of the very best ways to increase your ranking is to contact sites (ideally well-established ones) and encourage them to have a look at yours and consider linking to it.

You can keep track of the number of sites linking to yours with a free service such as:

Link Popularity www.linkpopularity.com

Alternatively, go straight to Google and search for link: followed by your domain name. For example: link:www.peterbuckley.com

Page titles and meta tags

You can also improve your search engine rankings by dropping appropriate words and phrases into key places in your HTML code. Most importantly, make sure your page titles and file names are relevant. Less significant these days are **meta tag keywords**, though it doesn't hurt to add them. While, you're at it, add some **meta name descriptions** to your pages – these are used by some search engines to give searchers a description of a site.

For example, if the top of the HTML in your homepage page looked like this…

```
<TITLE>Heavy-Breathing Hamsters do Honolulu</TITLE>
<META NAME="DESCRIPTION" CONTENT="Furry friends get fresh – the complete low-down on the rad rodents.">
<META NAME="KEYWORDS" CONTENT="ham, pineapple, mozzarella, david attenborough">
```

…then you'd fare slightly better in searches including the keywords "ham" and "pineapple", and the searcher would see the "Furry friends…" description under your site's listing. For more information, see:

About.com html.about.com/cs/metatags

You should also add keywords and/or descriptions to the <alt> tags behind your images.

Search services

Whatever you do, don't respond to spam that claims to be able to "raise your ranking". These are usually scams. There are various genuine services that will optimize your search for Google and others, such as:

Did It Detective www.didit.com
Web Position Agent www.webposition.com

But the fees usually aren't worth it for small personal sites. Instead, do your own homework into the black art of search engines:

Search Engine Watch www.searchenginewatch.com

Measure your success

You'll also want to know how many people have stopped by your site. If you're paying for a Web hosting package, you'll probably find there's some kind of traffic-measuring system already up and running for your site. If not, grab some tracking tools, which are widely available. Explore the links from:

CounterGuide www.counterguide.com

The same sites also offer instant quizzes, polls, chat rooms, bulletin boards, guest books and much more. But if you want to add a free search engine to your site, turn to:

Free Find www.freefind.com
Google www.google.com/services

Or to find out what the big boys are talking about, try:

Webmaster World www.webmasterworld.com

19 Blogging & Podcasting

Online publishing made easy

The blogosphere

"Blogosphere" is the term that has come to be used to describe the entire phenomenon of blogging – all the blogs, all the links between the blogs, and all the topics being written about in blogs. It's the links between blogs that make the blogosphere such a dynamic, interrelated whole. One blog points to a news story or website, other blogs pick up the story and link to the original blog, and so on. In this way, a single interesting post can ripple throughout the blogosphere in a matter of hours. And, due to the fact that many blogs rank highly on search engines, many casual Internet surfers with no particular interest in blogs may come across the story, too.

A blog – or weblog – is a special kind of website, where the main page consists of short "posts", arranged with the most recent at the top. Many major sites feature blogs, sometimes written by teams of people. But the archetypal blog is composed by an individual – a daily log of a person's thoughts, life or online discoveries. Often described as the biggest publishing revolution since the advent of the World Wide Web itself, blogs have become a central part of Net culture. And it only takes a few minutes to set up your own.

Many of the most interesting and successful blogs are political or journalistic, reporting news from war-torn corners of the world or scrutinizing political happenings ignored by the mainstream media. Others are more personal, allowing an intimate and fascinating – or, in many cases, profoundly boring – glimpse into other people's lives. Blogs also form a key part of social networking websites such as MySpace and Friendster, which are covered in the following chapter (see p.237).

Traditionally, blogging has been mainly a text-based affair, but in recent years **audio and video blogging** has become increasingly popular. Audio blogs made available for subscription via RSS (see p.102) are known as Podcasts.

Becoming a blogger

If you so desired, you could create and maintain a blog manually, coding the HTML just as you would a standard webpage and uploading the pages via FTP. But the beauty of blogging is that you don't have to do any of this techie and time-consuming stuff. Creating a blog can be as simple as signing up with a free provider, logging in to their website, and typing a new post.

The easy option: sign up with a blog host

There are scores of **blog hosts** that will let you set up and update your weblog – the biggest being **Blogger**, part of the Google empire. When you sign up, you'll be asked to create a username, password and a name for your blog. Next, you'll need to choose a page template, which will determine how your blog will look. Many hosts allow you to create your own design from scratch, though you'll also be offered a set of existing templates to choose from.

Once all that's done, the provider will allocate a unique Web address for your blog and give you access to a webpage where you can post new entries and edit existing ones. Some blog hosts even

Blog Web addresses

When you sign up with a blog host, you'll be given a Web address within their "domain". For example, if you registered a blog called Rough Blog at LiveJournal, your address would be:

roughblog.livejournal.com

Or at Blogger, it would be:

roughblog.blogspot.com

However, some blog hosts, including Blogger, make it painless to use their service in combination with your own domain name, such as:

www.roughblog.com

For more on registering domain names, see p.220.

Changing templates

Templates are the blueprint for your blog, and give your main page and all of its subsequent archive pages a uniform look. Templates are written in HTML, with Javascript, XTML, CSS and other advanced programming languages providing additional bells and whistles.

Different templates can provide drastically different visual identities, so find one that reflects the personality and the tone of your blog. Templates are also referred to as skins, and changing a template is often called skinning. Your blog host will provide some stock skins for you, but there are many other sites that offer both free and paid alternatives. Changing your skin from time to time can keep your blog fresh and exciting, though too many changes might suggest some form of instability.

BlogSkins
www.blogskins.com
CreateBlog
www.createblog.com
Template Hunter
www.templatehunter.com

allow you to add a new post simply by sending an email to a special email address known only to you: the subject line becomes the article's title, and the message body becomes the post. Easy.

There are scores of blog hosts out there, but four are much more widely used than the rest:

Blogger www.blogger.com
LiveJournal www.livejournal.com
TypePad www.typepad.com
Xanga www.xanga.com

All of these – and most of the scores of others – offer a **free** service as well as more feature-packed pay-to-use options. Today, even the free packages supply most of the tools that no serious blogger can live without: a means for readers to leave **comments** about each post; **photo posting**; automatic **archiving** of your older posts, all linked from the homepage; space for a **blogroll** (a list of links to your own favourite blogs); and the ability to generate an RSS newsfeed (see p.102).

Server-side blogging

Blog hosts do an excellent job of making it a breeze to set up a blog and start posting. These days, most also offer a decent set of tools. However, if you want total control over your blog – and especially if you want to intergrate a blog into your existing website – then you might want to investigate **server-side blogging**.

This way, instead of managing your blog via the webpage of a blog host, you install special blogging software on a Web server that you have direct access to. Usually, this would be a server belonging to a Web host (see p.220), though it's also possible to use your own computer as a Web server (p.224).

The most popular server-side systems can be downloaded from:

Movable Type www.movabletype.org
WordPress wordpress.org

Extra tools

There are loads of other blogging tools out there – for tracking other bloggers linking to you, creating an email subscription option, adding a virtual community area… the list goes on. For many of the best tools, follow the links from:

Problogger.net www.problogger.net

Inspiration

Before you get stuck in, take a look online at what's already out there in the blog universe. A few of our favourites are listed on pp.292–293.

Audio, video & Podcasts

Audioblogs

An audioblog is a blog that primarily features audio entries. They have a similar format to blogs, with entries catalogued by time and date. The only difference is the presentation, which is aural as opposed to visual.

The quickest and easiest way to audioblog is through a blog host that lets you post via the telephone. You can also create your own audio files and post them manually – this requires recording equipment and your own hosting solution, but gets around the time limits imposed by most audioblog services.

Audio Blogger www.audioblogger.com
Blogger offers an easy way to create an audioblog. First, set up a Blogger account, then go to the Audio Blogger site and set up a free audioblog account. Once you've registered, you will be given a phone number to call where you can start making posts – just call the phone number and start talking. You can make unlimited posts up to five minutes in length.

Server requirements

Most server-side blogging software has certain minimum server requirements, such as a Perl installation or the ability to run CGI scripts. Free or inexpensive web hosts may not provide these.

Blogspeak

Over the years, the blogging community has developed its own language of labels, jibes and compliments. If you want to know the difference between a "blawg" and a "barking moonbat", stop off at:

Blog Glossary www.samizdata. net/blog/glossary.html

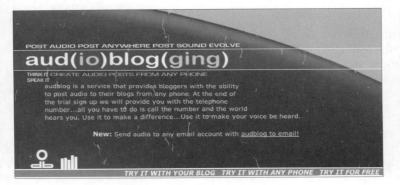

AudioBlog www.audioblog.com
Everything you'll need for audio, video and Podcasting in one easy interface for $5 a month.

AudBlog www.audblog.com
Enables audio posting to existing blogs (Blogger, TypePad, Movable Type and LiveJournal are all supported) via any telephone. After the free trial, it's $3 a month for up to twelve four-minute posts.

Podcasts

The terms Podcast and audioblog are often used interchangeably, but there is a difference. An audioblog is simply a blog with, or composed of, audio files. Podcasts, on the other hand, are stand-alone audio files with an RSS feed. You can create a Podcast by adding an RSS feed to an audioblog, though the resulting Podcast will consist of just the feed and the audio files – not the written components of the blog.

For more on subscribing and listening to Podcasts, see p.238. To learn how to create your own, see the box opposite.

Videoblogs

In the way that audioblogs and Podcasts focus on sound, videoblogs – also known as Vodcasts or video Podcasts – focus on video. They have so far taken a back seat to audioblogs, but they're getting more popular by the day thanks to the video-capable iPod and ever-faster broadband connections. They're generally five to ten minutes in length and feature anything from cooking lessons to hands-on product reviews. One of the best-known is Rocketboom (www.rocketboom.com), **an irreverent daily news show.**

Creating a Podcast

If you have a microphone, a computer, and a bit of technological savvy, it's pretty easy to set up a Podcast. The learning curve is not steep, and all the software you need can be downloaded for free from the Internet. To get really good sound quality, you'll need decent recording equipment, but you don't need anything special to get started. A full tutorial is beyond the scope of this book but, in brief, the process works like this…

▸ **Stage 1: Set up your hardware** You need to plug in a microphone to your computer. Most PCs and Macs have a socket for exactly this, but some don't, in which case you'll need either a USB microphone or an internal or external sound card.

▸ **Stage 2: Choose your audio editor** This is the program you'll use to record and edit your Podcast. If you've got a recent Mac, you may find you already have GarageBand, a fully featured tool that's ideal for the task. If you have a PC or an older Mac, grab an editor from the Web, such as:

Audacity audacity.sourceforge.net (free; PC & Mac)
Audio Recorder www.audio-tool.net (free; PC only)

▸ **Stage 3: Record and mix** Once you've got your audio recorded, cut it down to size using the editing tools and finally export it as an MP3 file. If your audio editor doesn't offer this feature, save it as a wave file and convert it to MP3 using iTunes (www.itunes.com). If you're asked to specify a bitrate for the MP3, experiment with different settings. The higher the number, the better the sound quality, but the bigger the resulting file.

▸ **Stage 4: Create your RSS feed** Once you've created your first Podcast, you need to think about getting your audio file online and creating an RSS feed so that listeners can subscribe. It's possible to create an RSS feed manually (see www.audiofeeds.org/tutorial.php) and simply upload it to some Web space along with the audio files. However, many people prefer to have the feed created automatically – often by an audio blog host in combination with **FeedBurner** (feedburner.com). There are also special Podcast services such as **Liberated Syndication** (www.libsyn.com), with which you upload audio and video files using a simple interface and the RSS feed appears automatically. The service starts at $5 a month for 100MB of storage space.

▸ **Stage 5: Publish your Podcast** Once you have your finished Podcasts and RSS file, to make them available to the world, grab iTunes (see p.191), open the Podcasts section of the Music Store, and click Submit a Podcast.

Currently, there are no turn-key solutions for creating video Podcasts, but any computer with a built-in webcam will more than likely have come with some software for recording video files from the camera … and short of a little imagination and a good script, that's pretty much all you need. If you use a Mac, and have a copy of QuickTime Pro, check out the tutorial to be found here:

Apple www.apple.com/quicktime/tutorials/videopodcasts.html

As for publishing and hosting video Podcasts, iTunes makes the whole process very straightforward, whether you are on a PC or a Mac. To find more advice on getting started:

Free Vlog www.freevlog.org

To find existing video Podcasts, search within iTunes, subscribe to a specific Podcast channel on YouTube, or visit:

MeFeedia mefeedia.com

For even more resources, try:

VideoBloggers videobloggers.org
VloggerCon www.vloggercon.com

Social networks

Facebook, MySpace, Friendster et al

Yet another way to create an online presence for yourself is to sign up with a social network – aka "friends network". With tens of millions of members around the world, these virtual common rooms are used for staying in touch and sharing music, photos and videos, as well as flirting and meeting new people. No surprise, then, that they're hugely popular with teenagers around the globe, though adults are increasingly catching the bug.

The details range widely between the various sites, but most work in a similar way. Once you're signed up to a site, you get your own page, complete with space for your thoughts, news, pictures and – all importantly – links to your "friends" on the network.

Your list of friends can include buddies from the real world (email and encourage them to sign up if they haven't done so already) or people on the site that you fancy getting to know. Once you've agreed to be friends, you can interact – leaving messages on each other's homepages, for example, or contacting friends of friends. Of course, your online friends can be just around the corner or on the other side of the planet.

The main problem with social networking sites is that they are thoroughly addictive and have a habit of taking over your life.

Safety issues

Social networking sites have received some bad press over the years in relation to the possible risks they can pose to children and teenagers. Most kids get by just fine, but if you're a parent you might want to talk to your offspring about issues such as approaches from unknown people and online bullying. Read the advice at www.wiredsafety.org or pick up a copy of *The Rough Guide to MySpace & Online Communities*.

Which site?

There are quite a few large social networking sites, each with a slightly different feel and demographic. If you're wondering which is for you, bear in mind that you don't have to align yourself with just one. Many people maintain active accounts with multiple networks to stay in touch with different groups of friends. There are sites out there for pre-teens and even dogs (see p.240).

Bebo www.bebo.com

▶ **Population** 40 million registered users

▶ **Demographic** 15–24 years old

Based in San Francisco and owned by AOL, this site has all the standard tools, including customizable "likes" and "dislikes", links to friends via their universities or secondary schools and extremely malleable "skins" (page design themes). You can also create and participate in polls and quizzes, blog your daily deeds and use instant messaging (IM) through Skype (see p.136). Within Bebo Music, the wing of the site for musicians, "friends" are automatically changed to "groupies", signed acts can converge on their label's page and thirty-second teaser tracks can be posted as downloadable MP3s.

Facebook www.facebook.com

▶ **Population** 140 million registered users

▶ **Demographic** 15–40 years old

Facebook takes its name from the American college practice of giving directories of student photos and profiles to incoming freshers. Today, though, it's by far the most popular social networking site in the UK as well as in the States, having overtaken MySpace in 2008. Far less chaotic than MySpace, Facebook is neat and clear, with a feed page allowing you to see at a glance updates from and about your friends. It is also very popular with professionals as well as students and has even been banned in many workplaces because of its detrimental affect on productivity. Running just behind Flickr (www.flickr.com), it's also the second most popular photo-sharing site on the Internet. You can post unlimited photos and "tag" friends who appear in those shots. There's even the option of uploading images straight from your mobile phone.

Friendster www.friendster.com

▶ **Population** 90 million registered users

▶ **Demographic** 21–30 years old

At just eight years of age, Friendster is the grandaddy of the social networking scene – the phenomenon on which the others were based. At its inception, Friendster was so popular that even in its unofficially released (beta) state, there were close to a million new users signing up each month. As the first of its kind, and with such an easily manipulated monicker, it's since spawned copycat sites such as Hatester, Enemyster and Introvertster.

Back to school...

Online communities can form around any fascination or fancy, from knitting to engine repair to foot fetishes. But one of the most popular common bonds is a shared education. Accordingly, there are quite a few social networking sites based on school ties. These sites allow current students to discuss homework assignments and stay in touch during the holidays, while generations of alumni can share stories of Sister Bernadine rapping their knuckles with a ruler. MySpace includes school groups within its vast framework, but you might be more likely to discover old friends via:

Classmates.com www.classmates.com (US)
Friends Reunited www.friendsreunited.co.uk (UK & Aus)
myYearbook www.myyearbook.com (US)
The Student Center www.student.com (US, CA, UK & Aus)

hi5 www.hi5.com

▶ **Population** 60 million registered users

▶ **Demographic** 18–30 years old

Popular all over the world, but with a particularly large following in South America. While dedicated band sites aren't as well supported or as heavily cross-linked as on some other networks, musicians can still upload and share their original tracks, and any user can listen to a wide range of popular music with the hi5 Musicplayer.

LinkedIn www.linkedin.com

▶ **Population** 30 million registered users

▶ **Demographic** 25–45 years old

This business-oriented network is becoming increasingly popular, allowing its members to maintain a network of "trusted" contacts within any given industry. To become a member you need to receive an invitation from an existing member.

MySpace www.myspace.com

▶ **Population** 253 million registered users

▶ **Demographic** 14–35 years old

By far the most heavily populated of the social networks, MySpace is most popular among teenagers and musicians. Like all of the major sites, MySpace allows you to store and share photos, access or upload music, search for friends, mass-mail everyone in your online address book, join groups, post videos (see p.236), instant message and write blogs. MySpace also allows you to fully customise your personal Profile page using HTML (see p.245). The results are often chaotic and uneasy-on-the-eye, and some users complain that the site's architecture makes it very difficult to use. But it remains incredibly popular.

orkut www.orkut.com

▶ **Population** 67 million registered users
▶ **Demographic** 15–30 years old

Owned by Google, orkut has users around the globe but (for reasons that aren't entirely clear) has become particularly successful in Brazil and India. It offers all the standard services, though by far the most popular features are the "Communities" that gather users together in subgroups. There has, sadly, been controversy about "hate groups" focusing on white supremecy and the like. This has resulted in pressure on Google to strengthen orkut's internal accountability and keep such things in check.

Networks for children and animals

Some social networking sites, such as Club Penguin and Whyville, are aimed at younger children and designed to provide a safe and educational environment. Whyville requires its users to pass a "chat licence" test, teaching them about online safety, and both sites use filters to block foul language. Whyville even goes so far as to alert a moderator when "suggestive" phrases such as "pants", or "what's your phone number?" are used. Moreover, the sites don't include any image-posting options. Instead, children can create online cartoon representations of themselves called avatars.

Another children's site, Imbee, creates a more visible online presence for children, allowing them to post blogs and upload pictures, but it counters potential predation ("grooming") by limiting interaction to par-

ent-approved associates. Imbee requires credit card identity verification, and grants parents publishing approval for all blog posts, messages and pictures.

Club Penguin www.clubpenguin.com
Imbee www.Imbee.com
Whyville www.whyville.com

Apparently making new friends online no longer requires a set of opposable thumbs. Many pets have their "own" pages, with pictures and profiles listing everything from favourite toys to best tricks, on sites such as:

Catster www.catster.com
Dogster www.dogster.com
HAMSTERster www.hamsterster.com
Petster www.petster.com

Twitter www.twitter.com

▶ **Population** 5 million registered users

▶ **Demographic** 18–50 years old

Twitter is somewhere between a social networking service and a mobile blogging tool. It allows you to broadcast SMS-style posts of up to 140 characters. These "tweets" – like the status feeds on Facebook – are typically used to describe what you're doing or thinking at any one time. Other users can become your followers, which means they'll be able to read and reply to your twitters, and you can in turn follow them.

Despite historic problems with its servers, Twitter has shown itself to be a medium perfectly suited to the newest generation of mobile phones such as the BlackBerry and iPhone. It can be accessed directly via the Web, though phone users often prefer to use a third-party application. For example, the iPhone app Tweetie (pictured) allows photo posting from the phone's camera and location-specific twittering from GPS-enabled devices.

Having started as recently as 2006, Twitter looks set to multiply its population very rapidly over the coming years, with both individuals and organizations keen to use the RSS-like nature of the service to make themselves heard. It remains to be seen, however, if Twitter can survive without either a subscription charge or any onboard advertising.

Follow me...

Here are a few Rough Guides twitterers to get you started:

twitter.com/ben_coop
twitter.com/PeterBuckley
twitter.com/Simonster

And some worthwhile additions from the wider world:

twitter.com/BarackObama
twitter.com/BBCnews
twitter.com/stephenfry
twitter.com/twitterforpeace

Second Life www.secondlife.com

▶ **Population** 11 million registered users

▶ **Demographic** 18–30 years old

Created by Linden Lab, Second Life is not so much a social networking site as an entire virtual world, complete with clubs, shops and real estate. The idea is a variation on the Massively Multiplayer Online Role-Playing Game (MMORPG) genre made popular by titles such as EverQuest and Ultima Online. Instead of hunting for treasure and battling demons, however, Second Life offers a world more similar to our own in which users – called "residents" – can interact.

Second Life isn't a simple website, but a full program that you need to download and install. Each user has an avatar modelled after themselves or some fantasy version thereof, and can do anything from visiting a nightclub to starting a business. Most more involved

things – such as buying land and building a house – require payment with Linden Dollars, which have a real-world value.

Second Life does run on Macs and Linux, but some features only work well on Windows.

Windows Live Spaces spaces.live.com

▶ **Population** 120 million registered users

▶ **Demographic** 18–35 years old

As if the name wasn't a giveaway, Windows Live Spaces, or WLSpaces, is Microsoft's social networking community. Launched in 2004 as MSN Spaces, it has quickly grown to become one

of the bigger networking sites on the Web. The attraction for many has been its familiarity: it incorporates many long-established elements of other Microsoft services, such as Passport login and "Contact Cards" that integrate with MSN Messenger and Hotmail. However, the whole experience feels a little clinical, with Microsoft-provided "themes" that can only be partially customized.

Yahoo! 360° 360.yahoo.com

▶ **Population** 5 million registered users

▶ **Demographic** 18–35 years old

An immediate advantage of Yahoo! 360° is the way it integrates itself with Yahoo! email accounts – you can quickly connect a new 360° page to all the contacts in your Yahoo! address book, and you won't need to spend any time establishing a profile or "avatar" if you've already filled out the same fields in Yahoo! Messenger. Among its page personalization options are user-created or downloadable themes, a music, movie and book review section, quick-post thought-bubbles called "blasts" and an area dedicated to your favourite RSS feeds (see p.102). You can also blog to your heart's content, and then use the embedded RSS feed creator to alert friends to new posts.

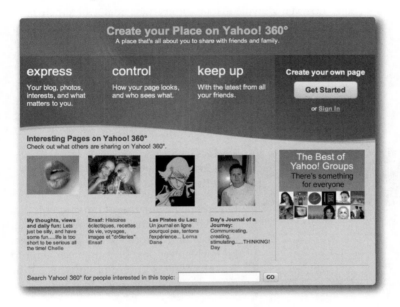

Customizing your homepage

Many online communities allow you a certain degree of control over the appearance of your homepage, or profile page. In most cases, such customizations are achieved through a series of online forms into which you can post HTML code (see p.212 for more on HTML). If writing code isn't up your street, don't worry, the FAQs, forums or support pages of your network will usually point to websites packed with code you can simply copy and paste. For example, MySpace users can drop into:

MySpaceSupport www.myspacesupport.com
PimpMySpace.org www.pimpmyspace.org

There are even downloadable applications that will pinch code from other pages that you like the look of and add it to yours.

If your network allows you to change the look of almost the entire page, you could try using a "layout generator". These let you click through a bunch of options for text colours, link colours, background colours, table colours and so on, and then present you with a large wad of code that you copy and paste into your homepage. Generators vary in terms of ease of use and the features on offer. Some of the better ones are:

FreeCodeSource freecodesource.com
GameSpot www.gamespot.com
Pimp-My-Profile pimp-my-profile.com

One problem with these kind of sites is that they have a nasty habit of throwing pop-up ads at you. If you can see a "Skip" button, hit it whenever possible, and never agree to download any software or plug-ins. To be extra safe, read the advice on p.167.

Things to
do online

Things to do online

21

The Web's your oyster

This book has already explained how to do scores of things on the Net, from making telephone calls via your broadband connection (see p.133) to setting up your own blog (see p.231). It's also provided tips on searching (see p.90) to enable you to find almost anything online quickly and efficiently. But if you fancy some further inspiration, or to cut straight to what we think are some of the very best sites on the World Wide Web, flick through this chapter. The following "things to do" cover everything from finding a satellite photo of your garden (see p.288), via re-igniting an old flame (see p.289) to setting up an online store (see p.253). Enjoy…

Dead link?

Some of the following sites will have moved or vanished altogether by the time you're reading this – it's simply the nature of the Web. But don't let that deter you. Even when a page appears to be gone, it's very often possible to track it down, either by looking for Google's cached copy of it, or by searching the domain of the site for pages containing relevant keywords. For advice on how to track down apparently absent pages, see p.85.

Things to do online: contents

Get diverted

If the only thing you're searching for is something new, cool and generally worth a diversion, then try StumbleUpon, Digg (see p.75) or one of the other social bookmarking sites to see what everyone else is getting excited about. There are also various websites dedicated to listing and ranking such things. Some concentrate on the good...

Cool Site of the Day www.coolsiteoftheday.com

...others focus on the bad and the ugly:

Worst of the Web www.worstoftheweb.com

Alternatively, cruise other people's lives, thoughts and links via some blogs, perhaps starting with our recommendations (see p.292) or by following the "top picks" links from a blogging directory, such as:

BlogCatalog www.blogcatalog.com

Once you've found some suitable distracting blogs, combine their feeds into the ultimate diversion machine using an RSS newsreader (see p.102). Alternatively, if randomness is more your thing, try:

Bleb.org bleb.org/random

Or for a random site that's more likely to be interesting, pull something unexpected out of Wikipedia's hat:

Wikipedia en.wikipedia.org/wiki/Special:Randompage

Wallow in the written word

Before you take the plunge with one of those old-fashioned paper things, you might find the book you want is available to read online. You'll find countless full texts – prose and poetry – at:

Bartleby www.bartleby.com
Bibliomania www.bibliomania.com
Classic Novels www.classic-novels.com
E Server www.eserver.org
The Internet Public Library www.ipl.org
Online Book Pages onlinebooks.library.upenn.edu
Shakespeare www.opensourceshakespeare.com

If you can't find what you're after, or you're craving a hard copy, why not use the Web to order it.

Amazon www.amazon.co.uk (UK)
Amazon www.amazon.com (US)
Barnes & Noble www.barnesandnoble.com (US)
Blackwell's www.blackwell.com (UK/US)
Waterstone's www.waterstones.co.uk (UK)
WHSmith www.bookshop.co.uk (UK)

These sites lay on all the trimmings: user ratings, recommendations, sample chapters, author interviews, bestseller lists, press clippings and gift-wrapping. To find the best deal across many stores simultaneously, try:

AddAll www.addall.com
BookBrain www.bookbrain.co.uk (UK)
Google Products www.google.com/products (US)

Or if the book in question is out of print, track it down via…

Abe Books www.abebooks.com (UK/US)

Still no joy? Locate a specialist bookshop via:

BookSellers www.booksellers.org.uk (UK)
BookWeb.org www.bookweb.org (US)

Or, if it's audio books you're in search of, you'll find thousands of titles available to download at sites such as:

Audible www.audible.com
BBC Shop www.bbcshop.com/icat/audio
iTunes Store Audiobooks tinyurl.com/csan6l

Or maybe you fancy publishing your own book using a Web-based print-to-order service. Look no further than:

Lightning Source www.lightningsource.com (UK)

Finished with a tome? Why not pass it on via Book Crossing? Print out a unique ID label, stick it on your book and then leave it on a train or park bench. If someone finds it and likes it, they'll follow the instructions on the label, go to the site, leave a message and review and then "release" it again. Some books have now changed hands more than a hundred times.

Book Crossing www.bookcrossing.com

Set up shop

These days, selling stuff via the Web is really not that difficult, and it doesn't have to mean finding any start-up capital – though don't expect a unique, bells-and-whistles superstore without investment of time and money. Whether you're already a small business thinking about moving onto the Web, or you have an idea for a Web-based enterprise, first think about the issues we discuss in this book's "Shopping" chapter (see p.145) but from the seller's point of view: does my product suit online sales? Is it easy to ship? And so on.

If you just want to sell merchandise, try the amazing Cafepress, which will generate an astonishing virtual store of everything from cups to bags to T-shirts bearing a company logo:

Cafepress www.cafepress.com

For anything more serious, you'll need to decide whether you want to sell things via your own discrete site, or set up a "store" within an established supersite such as **eBay** or **Amazon**. The latter option is *much* simpler, as everything from payment practicalities to the actual webpages will be taken care of automatically. Also, since these sites already get huge volumes of traffic, you won't need to worry so much about advertising or marketing.

Amazon www.amazon.com (or local branch)
eBay stores.ebay.com (or local branch)

That said, sending your customers to Amazon or eBay doesn't exactly make you seem like a very serious retail player. For that you'll need a "real" online store. First investigate some of the click-and-build store services and tools, such as:

BigStep www.bigstep.com (US)
BT Global Services www.globalservices.bt.com (UK)
Click and Build www.clickandbuild.com (UK)
Yahoo! store.yahoo.com (US)

Alternatively, if you're technically minded, you could create your own site from scratch (see p.209). You'll save money, though you'll have to work out how to accept payment. The easiest and least expensive option is to use a third-party payment systems such as PayPal. They provide a free shopping cart system and let you accept all common credit cards.

PayPal www.paypal.com

Be amused...

Looking for a chuckle or perhaps to extend your lunchbreak into the late afternoon? There's a never-ending ocean of amusement to be found online, much of it of a distinctly puerile nature and some downright offensive. A few to start with:

Coloring Pages
www.free-coloring-pages.com
Dean & Nigel Blend In www.deanandnigel.co.uk
Exorcist Bunnies www.angryalien.com
/0204/exorcistbunnies.html
The Flash Mind Reader www.flashpsychic.com
Fridge Magnets lunchtimers.com
Graffiti The Web www.yeahbutisitart.com/graffiti
Mini Pool www.fetchfido.co.uk/games
/minipool/minipool.htm
Online Etch-A-Sketch www.etchy.org
Rather Good www.rathergood.com
Hit Bush in the face with a shoe
www.sockandawe.com

For distractions with a more satirical bite, try one of the following, **The Onion** being the best stocked of the bunch:

The Onion www.theonion.com
Private Eye www.private-eye.co.uk
SatireWire www.satirewire.com

Perhaps you're simply at a loss as to why the chicken crossed the road. Find jokes galore at:

Humour Database www.humordb.com
Joke Index www.jokeindex.com

But if you're out to get revenge on the prankster who cling-filmed your toilet, inspiration awaits you at:

The Prank Insitute www.prank.org

If you have a fast broadband connection or are blessed with abnormal patience, you might like to investigate the world of online Flash games and animation. Offerings range from clones of old-school arcade games to feature-length Flash cartoons. Peruse the links from:

Assassin www.newgrounds.com/assassin
b3ta www.b3ta.com
Flasharcade www.flasharcade.com
The Pocket www.thepocket.com
Pop Cap www.popcap.com
Shockwave www.shockwave.com
Weebls www.weebls-stuff.com

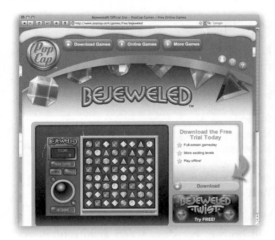

Or for those of you with a darker sense of humour:

David Shrigley www.mudam.lu/shrigley
Killer Cartoons www.killercartoons.com

Still not sated? Click through the following directory to enter a whole new dimension of time-wasting:

Open Directory dmoz.org/Recreation/Humor

And if that lot haven't tickled your funny bone, try these:

Real Ultimate Power www.realultimatepower.net
The official Ninja site.

Rec.humor.funny
www.netfunny.com/rhf
Archives of the rec.humor.funny newsgroup, updated daily.

Sissyfight
www.sissyfight.com
Scratch, tease and diss your way to playground supremacy.

Snowballing
www.3form.net/snowbawling/
Ever wanted to throw something at Jamie Oliver or Craig David? Now's your chance.

Star Wars Asciimation
www.asciimation.co.nz
The *Star Wars* saga rendered in vivid ASCII text.

Locate a masterpiece

Finding art online is very much a click-and-miss affair (www.museumofbadart.org) but there's no shortage of good stuff up there. Any artist who's at all switched on will have their work on the Web, and many of the major galleries display their entire collections.

If you want to find a specific famous painting, you could start with a Google image search (see p.96). Many of the results will be low resolution, however, so click on Large in the top-right corner to limit the search to decent-quality reproductions. Alternatively, try an art search engine, portal or directory, such as:

Artcyclopedia www.artcyclopedia.com
GalleryGuide www.galleryguide.org
World Wide Arts Resources www.wwar.com

These will point you towards hundreds of special online exhibitions and gallery sites, including:

American Museum of Photography
www.photographymuseum.com
ArtMuseum www.artmuseum.net
Frick www.frick.org
LACMA collectionsonline.lacma.org
Museum of Modern Art NY www.moma.org
Olga's Gallery www.abcgallery.com
Tate: Art On Demand tate.artgroup.com
Web Museum www.southern.net/wm

If you're in the market for some original art try an online auction at a specialist site such as iCollec-

tor; or go straight to eBay. To find out a little more about prices, see Gordon's.

Art4Auction www.art4auction.com
Auction Guide www.auctionguide.com/dir/Art
Gordon's www.gordonsart.com
iCollector www.icollector.com

For background and serious research, there's a huge amount of information at Grove Art Online. It's a pay-to-access site, though there is a free trial.

Grove Art Online www.groveart.com

Once that expires, **Wikipedia** makes a good base for further exploration (see p.287). Or for information on a specific big-name artist, and scans of most of their pictures, try:

Da Vinci www.leonardo.net
Matisse www.ocaiw.com/matisse.htm
Michelangelo www.michelangelo.com/buonarroti.html
Monet www.cmonetgallery.com
Picasso picasso.tamu.edu/picasso
Van Gogh www.vggallery.com

Of course, masterpieces aren't limited to canvas and bronze. For design and architectural wonders, start exploring at:

Architecture.com www.architecture.com
Design Addict www.designaddict.com
Great Buildings Collections www.greatbuildings.com

Plan a day out

Whether you are on holiday, taking a short break, or just trying to find a way to keep the kids entertained during those long school holidays, the Internet is a great place to find out what's going on nearby. If you are in a big city there will be no shortage of online listings and guides:

Citysearch www.citysearch.com (US)
Time Out www.timeout.com (London, New York, etc)
What's On When www.whatsonwhen.com (INT)
Yahoo! Local local.yahoo.com (US)
Zagat www.zagat.com (INT)

The various travel-publisher websites (see p.290) are also worth a scan for ideas. You could even download a city guide from **Vindigo** or **Rough Guides** and stick it on your iPod or PDA.

Rough Guides www.roughguides.com/mobile
Vindigo www.vindigo.com

And if you have an iPhone, try searching through the built-in Google Maps tool or use:

HearPlanet tinyurl.com/9se8s9
Rough Guides iphone.roughguides.com
Urban Spoon tinyurl.com/5t2rpb

To find museums and exhibitions by location or specialism:

Museums Around the World
www.icom.org/vlmp/world.html
24 Hour Museum www.24hourmuseum.org.uk (UK)

Or if you're planning a trip to a major museum, go straight to its own website – you may find it almost distracting enough to keep you at home. Good examples include:

British Museum www.thebritishmuseum.ac.uk
Guggenheim www.guggenheim.org
The Hermitage www.hermitagemuseum.org
Louvre www.louvre.fr
Metropolitan Museum of Art www.metmuseum.org
Museum of Modern Art www.moma.org
National Gallery www.nationalgallery.org.uk
National Portrait Gallery www.npg.org.uk
Natural History Museum www.nhm.ac.uk
Tate Gallery www.tate.org.uk
Victoria & Albert Museum www.vam.ac.uk

For more inspiration, visit one of these:

Castles Of Britain www.castles-of-britain.com (UK)
Castles.org www.castles.org (INT)
DaysOutUK www.daysoutuk.com (UK)
Theme Parks Online www.themeparksonline.org (US)
Theme Park Review www.themeparkreview.com (INT)
WalkLink www.walklink.com (UK)

Plan a night out

Finding out what's on in town, and booking your perch, has never been easier. For nightlife round the corner, it's worth checking out your local newspaper's site. But if you live in a big city, there's probably a major entertainments portal, such as:

CitySearch www.citysearch.com (US, Aus and more)
DigitalCity www.digitalcity.com (US)
Time Out www.timeout.com (London, New York, etc)

If you fancy the **big screen**, read reviews using the sites listed on p.268 and then find times here:

Guardian Film film.guardian.co.uk (UK)
Moviefone www.moviefone.com (US)

Or if you're in the mood for a serious night out, go straight to:

Club Planet www.clubplanet.com (US)
4 Clubbers www.4clubbers.net (UK)

Something more musical? Or cultural? For theatre, gigs and concerts, the following sites are useful sources of info about what's coming on – and you can book tickets online.

Aloud www.aloud.com (UK)
House Of Blues www.hob.com (US)
NME Tickets www.nme.com/gigs (UK)
See www.seetickets.com (UK)
Ticketmaster www.ticketmaster.com/international (INT)
Tickets.com www.tickets.com (US)
What's On Stage www.whatsonstage.com (UK)

You'll also find a surprising number of tickets up on **eBay**. There are bargains to be had, but be careful not to get sucked into a bidding war.

eBay Tickets tickets.ebay.co.uk (UK)
eBay Tickets tickets.ebay.com (US)

If you want to turn a night out into a weekend away, explore the possibilities of the festival scene. All tastes are catered for at:

Music Festival Finder www.festivalfinder.com (US)
Virtual Festivals www.virtual-festivals.com (UK)

These also cover opera festivals. But for in-depth info on operatic performances, past and present, head directly to:

Operabase www.operabase.com (INT)

Restaurants, too, have a strong presence online. If you know the name of the place you want to eat, a Google search may find either a homepage (if they have one) or a listings entry. But for inspiration – or an impartial opinion – try a restaurant review site such as:

Restaurants.co.uk www.restaurants.co.uk (UK)
Restaurants.com www.restaurants.com (INT)
TopRestaurants www.toprestaurants.com (US)
Zagat www.zagat.com (INT)

Also see the major travel publishers' websites (see p.290) for eating and nightlife recommendations the world over.

Plan a night in

What does a night in mean to you? A dinner party? Poker? A boardgame or two? Perhaps a sing-song around the old joanna…

BoardGameCentral www.boardgamecentral.com
Card Games Rules www.pagat.com
Traditional Games www.tradgames.org.uk
Victorian Recreation www.fashion-era.com/victorian_recreations.htm

…or perhaps a spot of light television consumption. The Web is a great place to find programme reruns, information and documentary follow-ups, often including live chats with the producers. And of course there's no shortage of listings:

Radio Times www.radiotimes.com (UK)
TV Guide www.tvguide.com (US)
TVZap www.tvzap.com (INT)
UKNetGuide www.uknetguide.co.uk/TV (UK)
Zap2It tv.zap2it.com (US)

UK viewers who want their listings a little more advanced and interactive should try:

Digi Guide www.digiguide.co.uk (UK)

Several sites specialize in TV episode guides:

Hu's Episode Guides www.episodeguides.com
Television Without Pity www.televisionwithoutpity.com

But if you want obsessive detail along with picture galleries, scripts, spoilers and rumours, search Google for a site dedicated to that show. If it's current and popular, you'll be confronted with hundreds of choices. For the strictly nostalgic:

Classic TV www.classic-tv.com (US)
TV Cream tv.cream.org (UK)

Postal DVD rental is an option if there's nothing on the box. You usually get an unlimited number of films for a monthly fee. Post back one film and another from your wishlist will promptly arrive.

Amazon www.amazon.co.uk/dvd (UK)
DVD Avenue www.dvdavenue.com (US)
Love Film www.lovefilm.com (UK)
Netflix www.netflix.com (US)
Reel.com www.reel.com (US)

Many of the above sites also offer movie rentals as downloads. Generally speaking, after downloading you have a fixed amount of time to view your film before it automatically deletes itself from your system. This service is also a feature of the iTunes Store:

iTunes Movie Rentals tinyurl.com/c7xzjc

Most rental sites also offer DVDs for sale, but check the selection at Amazon:

Amazon www.amazon.co.uk/dvd (UK)
Amazon www.amazon.com/dvd (US)

To compare prices across the board:

DVD Price Search www.dvdpricesearch.com (US)

Share your pictures

Whether you want to display your holiday snaps to everyone you know, or you're a wannabe artist looking to show off your portfolio, it's easy and inexpensive to post images online. Without too much trouble you could build yourself a website (see p.209), but it's much quicker and easier to use a photo-sharing service such as Flickr or FotoThing, or an online community such as Facebook (see p.238).

Facebook www.facebook.com
Flickr www.flickr.com
FotoThing www.fotothing.com

Windows users who have signed up for Microsoft's Windows Live services can use the Photo Gallery features to share their pictures with the world. Mac users, meanwhile, have several options open to them from the most recent version of the built-in iPhoto program. It allows you to publish your photos directly to Facebook and Flickr, or, when signed up with Apple's MobileMe service, you can upload directly to your pre-fab Web Galleries with the click of a button.

MobileMe www.apple.com/mobileme
Windows Live photos.live.com

You might also want to investigate Google's Picasa picture management application. Whatever you use to organize and store your photos at the moment, Picasa is worth looking at as an alternative, and its Web Albums feature gives those with a Google Account a wealth of online space for storing and displaying their snaps.

Picasa picasa.google.com (PC & Mac)

There are also many services that, for a small fee, will provide you with a ready-made photo gallery online. For instance:

Fotki www.fotki.com
Phanfare www.phanfare.com

If you need a bit of inspiration before you start snapping, see:

British Journal Of Photography www.bjphoto.co.uk
History Of Photography rleggat.com/photohistory
Photography Sites Online www.photographysites.com
Time Life Pictures www.timelifepictures.com

And before uploading any pics to the Web, process them to make them space-efficient (see p.216).

Buying a camera

Considering a new camera? Read some reviews:

Digital Photography Review www.dpreview.com
Photography Review www.photographyreview.com

To learn how to use it, see:

DCViews www.dcviews.com/tutors.htm
Photography Tips www.photographytips.com

Scan the business pages

Most of the prominent business newspapers and magazines offer much of their content on the Web, often complete with large back archives. Usually there's a fee to access these sites, though it still works out cheaper than buying the paper version.

Barrons www.barrons.com
Fast Company www.fastcompany.com
Financial Times www.ft.com
Forbes www.forbes.com
Wall Street Journal www.wsj.com

Naturally, there's a huge number of business-oriented sites that are unrelated to any old-fashioned paper or journal. A small sample of the better ones include:

AccountingWeb www.accountingweb.co.uk
Safe playpen for British bean-counters.

Business.com www.business.com
Attempting to become the king of business search engines. For European sites and trade data, see: www.europages.com

Clickz www.clickz.com
The Web as seen by the marketing biz.

Cluetrain Manifesto www.cluetrain.org
Modern-day translation of "the customer is always right". Read it or perish. Alternatively, if you'd prefer an update on "never give a sucker an even break", consult the Ferengi Rules of Acquisition: en.wikipedia.org/wiki/Rules_of_Acquisition

Companies House www.companieshouse.gov.uk (UK)
Get publicly available information on every registered company in the UK. For global data see: www.corporateinformation.com

Entrepreneur.com www.entrepreneur.com
Get rich now, ask us how.

The Foundation Center www.fdncenter.org
Find companies who might spare you a fiver.

Garage.com www.garage.com
Matchmaking agency for entrepreneurs and investors founded by Apple's Guy Kawasaki.

TrustNet www.trustnet.com
Keep track of your fund manager's performance.

US Patent and Trademark Office www.uspto.gov
Sift through a few decades of American patents, plus a gallery of obscurities. For UK patents and to learn how to see your own crackpot schemes through to fruition, see: www.patent.gov.uk

The Wonderful Wankometer
www.cynicalbastards.com/wankometer
Measure corporate hyperbole on this useful site. And if you want to know exactly what you should be saying to feel at ease in the corporate board room (whilst ensuring that you will be ostracized by the rest of the planet), pick up a few cliches from here: http://lifehacker.com/5091810/thirty-cliches-you-should-avoid-going-forward

Become a computer geek

As you'd expect, the Web is not short of sites devoted to reviewing, mending, buying and generally praising computers, the online world and other geekery. Well-written technology news can be found at:

CNet www.cnet.com
Internet Magazine www.internet.com
Newslinx www.newslinx.com
The Register www.theregister.co.uk
Wired News www.wired.com

Also explore **SlashDot**, a legendary website for computer-focused rumours, gossip, discussion and philosophy.

SlashDot www.slashdot.com

If your machine is giving you grief, the chances are that someone else has already had the same problem and posted a solution online. A Google search might lead you to an answer in a forum such as:

Computer Forum www.computerforum.com
Computing.net www.computing.net
Virtual Dr www.virtualdr.com

But don't forget to also try **Google Groups**, to see if someone has answered your question in a newsgroup (p.138).

Google Groups groups.google.com

No fix forthcoming? Try posting a question in a forum or newsgroup – you may be surprised how quickly you get an answer. If you're a PC user, it's not unlikely the problem is related to a deficiency in **Windows**, so make sure you've updated your system with the latest fixes. Then pop in to one of the many Windows sites, such as:

ActiveWin www.activewin.com
Annoyances www.annoyances.org
TweakWin7 www.tweakwin7.com
TweakXP www.tweakxp.com
WinOScentral www.winoscentral.com

Of course, you won't necessarily understand what the proper geeks on these sites are talking about. For jargon busting, point your browser at:

PCWebopedia www.pcwebopedia.com
What Is www.whatis.com
Wikipedia en.wikipedia.org/wiki/Computing

Or maybe the problem is related to a dodgy hardware **driver**. Download the latest versions from the manufacturers' websites or a driver site such as:

Driver Forum www.driverforum.com
Driver Guide www.driverguide.com
Drivers HQ www.drivershq.com
Windrivers www.windrivers.com

If none of this works and your computer has gone the way of the dodo, you're going to be in the market for a new machine or component. Use a price comparison agent (see p.152) to scan deals if you know what you're after. Otherwise browse the offerings at:

Amazon www.amazon.co.uk/electronics (UK)
Amazon www.amazon.com/computers (US)
CompUSA www.compusa.com (US)
Dabs www.dabs.com (UK)
Micro Direct www.microdirect.com (UK)
NewEgg www.newegg.com (US)

Or why not bite the bullet, buy the bits and build your own. It's easier than you might think.

Build an Easy PC www.buildeasypc.com
Build Your Own PC www.pcmech.com/byopc

By now you're probably approaching your nerd-ship brown-belt. Congratulations. A few more to explore:

Easter Egg Archive www.eeggs.com
Discover secret games and jokes hidden within your favourite software.

Linux Online www.linux.org
Tired of Windows woes? Get geek brownie points by switching to Linux.

MyFonts www.myfonts.com
Revel in the dark world of typography. Also see:
ilovetypography.com
www.1001freefonts.com

Old Computers www.old-computers.com
Re-live the heady days of Sinclairs, Amigas and cassette drives.

PC Mechanic
www.pcmech.com/byopc
How to build or upgrade your own PC. Also see:
arstechnica.com/tweak/hardware.html

Online storage

Whether you want to back up some files safely onto a remote server or transfer large amounts of data between two computers, consider signing up for some online storage. Some webspace may have come free with your Internet access account (ask your ISP). If it did, all you'll need is an FTP client to upload and download files to the space:

CuteFTP www.cuteftp.com (PC & Mac)
CyberDuck cyberduck.ch (Mac)

Other free options are Windows Live SkyDrive, ADrive's "Basic" package and Google's hotly anticipated GDrive.

ADrive www.adrive.com
GDrive .google.com/accounts
Windows Live SkyDrive skydrive.live.com

Alternatively, if you don't mind paying, sign up for a service such as Box.net, CloudFiles or Apple's MobileMe:

Box.net www.box.net
CloudFiles www.mosso.com/cloudfiles.jsp
MobileMe www.apple.com/mobileme

To find alternatives, read the reviews at:
online-storage-service-review.toptenreviews.com

If you simply want to send somebody files too large to email, try one of these services:

MailBigFile www.mailbigfile.com
YourFileLink www.yourfilelink.com
YouSendIt www.yousendit.com

Things to do online

PC Tweaking

www.anandtech.com

How to overclock your processor and tweak your BIOS to attract the opposite sex. Loads more at: www.arstechnica.com

Quiet PC

www.quietpc.com

Put a little peace and quiet back into your life. Quiet PC collects together fanless PSUs, giant CPU heatsinks, water cooling systems, acoustic treatments and everything else you could need short of earplugs. For silent fans visit: www.dorothybradbury.co.uk

Tech Dirt

www.techdirt.com

Keeping tabs on the dark underbelly of the Internet economy.

Tech Tales

www.techtales.com

Customers may always be right. But they sure ask the darndest things.

Tom's Hardware Guide

www.tomshardware.com

One of the most important sites on the Net, at least for the hardware industry. Tom and his reporters are credited with the delayed release of Pentium's 1GHz Pentium III processor because the site gave it a thumbs down. This is the best source for bug reports and benchmark tests. Try also: www.tech-pc.co.uk www.trustedreviews.com

WebReference

www.webreference.com

If you don't know your HTML from your XML or DHTML, try this reference and tutorials site. For more tips and tricks, try Webmonkey: webmonkey.wired.com/webmonkey

Widget Software

www.widget.co.uk

Selling all the latest handheld systems, EPOC devices, Palm OS, Windows CE and a selection of mobiles. Psion, Compaq, Hewlett Packard and Handspring dominate each section with high-street prices throughout.

Apple online

The Apple homepage is very useful (and, naturally, very pretty)…

Apple www.apple.com

…though the site offers access to a ton of very useful resources and of course the well-stocked Apple Store (which sells a lot more than just iPods and Mac-Books) the Apple site barely scratches the surface of online Mac obsession. For news and rumours about what the company is going to bring out next, grab your one-button mouse and navigate to:

MacAddict www.macaddict.com
Apple Insider www.appleinsider.com
MacNN www.macnn.com

MacSlash www.macslash.com
Mac Rumors www.macrumors.com
Tidbits www.tidbits.com

If you want to put your finger on the latest applications, hints and OS X news, visit:

Mac OSX Apps www.macosxapps.com
Mac OS Hints www.macosxhints.com

If you're still desperately clinging on to your old Quadra or Performa, try:

Low End Mac www.lowendmac.com

And to diagnose your ailing Apple:

Apple Discussions discussions.apple.com
MacFixit www.macfixit.com

If iPods and iTunes are your life blood, pop in to:

Apple/iPod www.apple.com/itunes
iLounge www.ilounge.com

And if you get a free minute, drop in at Red Light Runner, for Apple collectibles, from towels and sandals with the Apple logo to mugs, pens and even a "Steve Jobs for President" sticker. Also sells those classy "Think different" posters, featuring Miles Davis, Callas, Lucy & Desi and Martha Graham.

Red Light Runner www.redlightrunner.com

Alternatively, let us tell you everything you need to know and pick up a copy of *The Rough Guide to iPods & iTunes* or *The Rough Guide to Macs & OS X*.

Get educated

The Web is an unmatched educational resource, with thousands of sites offering help to students of all ages.

Youngsters will find support for every classroom subject, as well as endless educational games and puzzles, via major sites and directories such as:

About Homework homework.about.com (US)
Ask Kids www.askkids.com (INT)
BBC Schools www.bbc.co.uk/schools (UK)
Discovery school.discovery.com/students (US)
Homework Elephant
www.homeworkelephant.co.uk (UK)
Homework High www.channel4.com/homework (UK)
Homework Spot www.homeworkspot.com (US)
Infoplease www.infoplease.com/homework (US)

There are scores more subject-specific websites, of course, which are easily located via a Google search (see p.90). These range from the sensible to the less so. For example, you could learn the periodic table in either theory or practice:

Kid's Science Experiments
www.kids-science-experiments.com
Online Periodic Table www.webelements.com

Older school and college students will appreciate the huge number of free books that can be found online. And it's not just books – sites such as the Evil House of Cheat provide access to tens of thousands of other students' essays. You can either pay a fee to view them or submit your own in return.

Evil House of Cheat www.cheathouse.com

But you'll also find an amazing amount for free. Start with:

BBC Learning www.bbc.co.uk/learning
Academic Info www.academicinfo.net

Or use Google to find a good subject-specific directory, such as:

Maths archives.math.utk.edu/topics
English Literature www.english-literature.org/resources

If you're thinking of applying for college, you can do nationwide course searches and find out about funding at:

CollegeView www.collegeview.com (US)
Directgov www.direct.gov.uk (UK)
UCAS www.ucas.ac.uk (UK)

Or maybe you fancy going overseas:

International Education Site www.intstudy.com
Study Abroad www.studyabroad.com (US)

If campus life proves a little too distracting, you might be tempted by a dissertation writing service, such as those linked from Thesis.com. Tread carefully – many are rip-off merchants.

Thesis www.thesis.com

Land a job

The Web is an increasingly essential port of call for those seeking employment. Many **newspapers** that are popular for vacancy listings put all their job ads online, often with extra services such as email alerts: enter a keyword or company name and you'll receive a message if and when any relevant ads are placed. There are also many Web-only employment services, which list thousands of posts, both local and international. Equally numerous are online job agencies, with which you can post your CV, to be contacted when suitable things come up. Bear in mind, though, that your boss could find you up there. Some of the most popular job sites include:

UK/Eu
www.fish4jobs.co.uk
www.guardian.co.uk/jobs
www.jobsearch.co.uk
www.monster.com
www.reed.co.uk
www.topjobs.com

Aus
www.careerone.com.au
www.seek.com.au

US
www.ajb.dni.us
www.careerbuilder.com
www.flipdog.com
www.futurestep.com
www.hotjobs.com

INT
www.adecco.com
www.drakeintl.com
www.headhunter.net
www.monster.com

Furthermore, the Net is the ideal place for finding out about companies that you fancy working for. Most sites have a link for "jobs", "opportunities" or "vacancies", or at least an email address that you can use to enquire.

A bit of careful Google searching may also reveal a job site focusing on your specific area of interest, whether it's seasonal jobs in US resorts, national parks, camps, ranches or cruise liners…

Cool Works www.coolworks.com

…or more worthy employment in the UK:

Charity Jobs www.charityjob.co.uk

Naturally, however, employment sites do more than just list vacancies. Browse the following:

Check My Reference www.checkmyreference.com
Find out what your referees are saying about you.

Interview Advice interview.monster.com
Preparation for your grilling. Give the random question generator a spin.

I-resign.com www.i-resign.com
Quit now – while you're ahead.

The Riley Guide www.rileyguide.com
Messy, but massive, directory of job-hunting resources.

Salary Info www.salary.com
See what you're worth where you are, and then how much you'd be worth if you moved elsewhere:
www.homefair.com/calc/salcalc.html

Worst Job www.worstjob.com
Maybe being unemployed isn't so bad after all.

Become a movie bore

When it comes to movie info online, the **IMDb** rules. You'll be hard-pressed to find any work on or off the Net as comprehensive as this relational database of screen trivia covering more than 100,000 movies and a million actors. Within two clicks of finding your favourite movie, you can get full filmographies of anyone in the cast or crew, and then see what's in the cooker.

Internet Movie Database www.imdb.com

But IMDb isn't without competition. You'll find superior biographies and synopses at the colossal All Movie Guide. And there are some great genre- or region-specific equivalents. Chan, Li and Fat, for example, are best served at the HKMDB:

All Movie Guide www.allmovie.com
Hong Kong Movie Database www.hkmdb.com

All these sites provide opinion, but for reviews they're no match for the specialists. Search for a film at **Movie Review Query Engine** (repertoire) or **Rotten Tomatoes** (current releases) and you'll be presented with scores of critiques, including those from the major newspapers.

Movie Review Query Engine www.mrqe.com
Rotten Tomatoes www.rottentomatoes.com

There are at least a couple of good sites dedicated exclusively to the best of the big screen:

About Classic Film classicfilm.about.com
Greatest Films www.filmsite.org

But far more focus on the dire:

Bad Movie Night www.hit-n-run.com
Badmovies.org www.badmovies.org

Or the cultish:

Astounding B Monster www.bmonster.com

If you want to be that really annoying guy at parties, there are even sites that simply point out the blunders:

Movie Mistakes www.movie-mistakes.com
Nitpickers www.nitpickers.com

For the latest movie news and whispers of what's in production:

Ain't It Cool News www.aintitcool.com
CHUD www.chud.com
Dark Horizons www.darkhorizons.com
Empire Magazine www.empireonline.co.uk
Movies.com www.movies.com
Upcoming Movies www.upcomingmovies.com

Buy groceries & flowers

Online grocery ordering is now big business. Many of the major "real-world" food retailers will deliver for free. Obviously you don't get to feel the firmness of the avocados, or sniff the melons for ripeness, but you may decide that's a price worth paying for the time and effort saved – or perhaps use the Net solely for ordering bulky dry goods. Major online grocers include:

Australia
www.colesonline.com.au
www.greengrocer.com.au
www.homeshop.com.au
www.shopfast.com.au

UK
www.iceland.co.uk
www.ocado.com
www.sainsburystoyou.com
www.somerfield.co.uk
www.tesco.co.uk
www.waitrosedeliver.com

US & Canada
www.ethnicgrocer.com
www.netgrocer.com
www.peapod.com
www.telegrocer.com

For good quality and eco-friendly fresh fruit and vegetables, however, you might be better off exploring the possibility of an organic "box scheme". The UK is particularly well served in this area, thanks to the likes of:

Abel & Cole www.abel-cole.co.uk (London)
Organic Delivery www.organicdelivery.co.uk (National)
Riverford www.riverford.co.uk

But there are similar options in many countries – at least in the big cities. To track down one near you, try the links page at:

Organic Consumers Association
www.organicconsumers.org (US)
Organic Directory
www.theorganicsdirectory.com.au (Aus)
Soil Association www.soilassociation.org (UK)

Flowers are also easy to get online, though most services offer only pricey bouquets and won't let you design your own. Pop in to **About Flowers** (www.aboutflowers.com) to find out which flowers are right for which various occasions. Then proceed to one of the following. Many of these will arrange delivery to much of the globe, though you'll usually get better value ordering from a service within the country you're sending to.

Interflora www.interflora.com (INT)
0800flowers.com www.0800flowers.com (UK)
800Florals www.800florals.com (US)
Brant Flowers www.brantflorist.com (US)
Clare Florist www.clareflorist.co.uk (UK)
Teleflorist www.teleflorist.co.uk (UK)

They're all much the same, though Interflora features an organizer tool that will alert you to forthcoming anniversaries or birthdays.

Cook something special

Any decent search engine or recipe database will uncover more formulas for food than you could possibly cook in a lifetime. Start by casting your line here:

All Recipes www.allrecipes.com
Internet Chef www.ichef.com
Meals for You www.mealsforyou.com
Recipe Archives recipes.alastra.com
Recipe Goldmine www.recipegoldmine.com
Recipedia www.recipedia.org

Many of these will even suggest a meal based on the random miscellany of ingredients left in your fridge and larder.

When following recipes, note where they're from so you don't mix up the measures. An Australian tablespoon is four, not three, tea-spoons, for instance. If anything seems a little alien, look it up on Wikipedia (see p.287) or here:

Cooking Dictionary
www.cafecreosote.com/dictionary.php3
Recipe Glossary
www.recipegoldmine.com/glossary/glossary.html

With a little know-how, you can always convert obscure measurements using Google (see p.90). Looking for something more specific? Perhaps one of these sites will fill your pot:

An Ode to Olives www.emeraldworld.net/olive.html
Cheese www.cheese.com

Chile Headz www.chileheadz.com
Chocolate Lover's Page chocolate.scream.org
Curry House www.curryhouse.co.uk
Epicurious www.epicurious.com
Spice Advice www.spiceadvice.com/encyclopedia
Thai Recipes www.importfood.com/recipes.html
Tokyo Food Page www.bento.com
Vegetarian Society of the UK www.vegsoc.org

And for all things drink-related, try:

Bevnet www.bevnet.com
Cocktails www.barmeister.com
CoffeeGeek coffeegeek.com
The Espresso Index www.espresso.com
Home Distiller www.homedistiller.org
RealBeer www.realbeer.com
Tea www.tea.co.uk
Wine Spectator www.winespectator.com

Play games

The Internet is a game player's paradise. Whether you're into shoot 'em ups or chess, there are bound to be scores of sites catering to your interests. And where else can you find an opponent and get a game going at any minute of the day or night?

Serious video games are massive processor-hungry programs designed to run either on a turbo-powered PC or a console such as the PS2 or Xbox. All of these platforms can handle multiplayer games over the Internet, though latency – time lag – can make this a frustrating experience. Broadband (see p.29) is pretty-well essential and an ISP with a gaming server also helps.

For reviews of the latest video games and hardware, see:

Avault www.avault.com
Gamers.com www.gamers.com
GameSpot www.gamespot.com
Nintendo www.nintendo.com
GamesRadar www.gamesradar.com
PC Zone www.pczone.co.uk
PlayStation www.playstation.com
Planet Dreamcast www.planetdreamcast.com
Xbox Scene www.xbox-scene.com

Video gaming isn't all expense and hardware fetishism, however. For gentler diversions, such as card games, Flash-based puzzles and other browser-based games, try:

FreeArcade.com www.freearcade.com
Gamesville www.gamesville.com

MSN Zone zone.msn.com
iWin www.iwin.com
Pogo.com www.pogo.com

For something more interactive, try a server-side game. These often look simpler, but make up for it by allowing complex multiplayer modes. Some examples:

BattleMaster www.battlemaster.org
NationStates www.nationstates.net

To find more, download a game browser, which will enable you to locate the closest games with the lowest lag times.

GameSpy Arcade www.gamespyarcade.com

Or join the pony-tail gang in the universe of a MMORPG (massive multiplayer online role-playing game) such as:

Discworld discworld.imaginary.com
EverQuest www.everquest.com
Ultima Online www.uo.com

If non-video games are more your bag, there's bound to be a portal for you. The Internet Chess Club is particularly impressive, with at least a few grand masters online at any moment.

Go Base www.gobase.org
Internet Chess Club www.chessclub.com
Internet Scrabble Club www.isc.ro

Discover your roots

The Web is an invaluable tool for professional and amateur genealogists the world over. Don't expect to enter your name and produce an instant family tree, but if you're prepared to put a bit of time into it, you should have no problem filling in a few gaps – or digging up some dirt on your ancestors. Good places to start are:

Ancestry.com www.ancestry.com
Cyndi's List www.cyndislist.com
FamilyTreeMaker www.familytreemaker.com
GENUKI www.genuki.org.uk (UK)
Genealogy Home Page www.genhomepage.com
Genealogy Links www.genealogylinks.net
Genealogy Today www.genealogytoday.com
RootsWeb.com www.rootsweb.com
Surname Web www.surnameweb.org

Once you've found a name, you might even be able to put a face to it:

Ancient Faces www.ancientfaces.com

Public records are another obvious source of information, and there's no shortage online:

Archives.org
www.archives.gov/research_room/genealogy (US)
Census Records nationalarchives.gov.uk/census (UK)
General Register Office
www.gro.gov.uk/gro/content/research (UK)
Records.com www.records.com (US)

An alternative route is to conduct your research through newsgroups (see p.138). Try using a newsreader or Google Groups to access the various sub-groups of:

alt.family-names
alt.genealogy

For example, the authors of this book might investigate:

alt.family-names.buckley
soc.genealogy.surnames.clark

But be careful … who knows what you might uncover:

Prison Search
www.ancestorhunt.com/prison_search.htm

Develop hypochondria

While the Net's certainly an unrivalled medical library, it's also an unrivalled promulgator of the twenty-first-century equivalent of old wives' tales. So by all means research your ailment and pick up health tips online, but check with your doctor before putting any radical theories into practice.

To locate a doctor, dentist or specialist, go to:

American Medical Association www.ama-assn.org (US)
Dental Guide www.dentalguide.co.uk (UK)
Dentist Locator www.dentistlocater.com (US)
NHS Direct www.nhsdirect.nhs.uk (UK)

But before you trot off to see him or her, read up on your symptoms, starting at a health portal or government gateway such as:

Health Insite www.healthinsite.gov.au (Aus)
Healthfinder www.healthfinder.gov (US)
MedExplorer www.medexplorer.com
Medline Plus www.medlineplus.gov
NHS Direct www.nhsdirect.nhs.uk (UK)
Patient UK www.patient.co.uk
US National Library of Medicine www.nlm.nih.gov (US)

There are also many excellent self-help megasites, though the presence of sponsors may raise ethical questions. Their features vary, but medical encyclopedias, personal health tests and Q&A services are fairly standard fare. Try:

Dr Koop www.drkoop.com
HealthCentral www.healthcentral.com
HealthWorld www.healthy.net

Netdoctor.co.uk www.netdoctor.co.uk
24Dr.com www.24dr.com
WebMD www.webmd.com

Or for lots of information and links about global health issues, turn to:

World Health Organization www.who.int

For alternative remedies, therapies and practices, the best place to start is **About**. But don't buy anything until you've looked it up on **QuackWatch**, a good place to separate the docs from the ducks.

About altmedicine.about.com
Quackwatch www.quackwatch.com

And finally…

Alex Chiu's Eternal Life Device www.alexchiu.com
Live forever or come back for your money.

Ask the Dietitian www.dietitian.com
Eat yourself better.

Lifehacker lifehacker.com/tag/health
For solid general advice and an entertaining read, browse the archives found here.

Medicinal Herb FAQ www.henriettesherbal.com
If it's in your garden and doesn't kill you, it can only make you stronger.

RxList www.rxlist.com
Look up your medication to ensure you're not being poisoned.

Entertain the little ones

Kids these days are Web-savvy before they are out of the womb and there is no shortage of sites to keep them entertained. But there are also a whole bunch of things online that you really don't want your little angels stumbling across, so read the advice on p.83 and visit **Cybersmart Kids** before you let them near a mouse:

Cybersmart Kids Online www.cybersmartkids.com.au

Once your kids are connected, you'll find that almost every TV cartoon show and network has a formidable online presence. If you can handle the corporate tie-ins, they're as good a place as any to start and offer lots of fun and games with familiar faces:

Cartoon Network www.cartoonnetwork.com
CBeebies www.bbc.co.uk/cbeebies
PBS Kids www.pbskids.org

Alternatively, point them to one of these massive children's sites:

Kidscom www.kidscom.com
Kids Domain www.kidsdomain.com
Kids' Space www.kids-space.org
Yahooligans www.yahooligans.com

Still scribbling on the walls? Try:

The Bug Club www.ex.ac.uk/bugclub
Creepy-crawly fan club with pet-care sheets on how to keep your newly bottled tarantulas alive.

Children's Literature Web Guide www.ucalgary. ca/~dkbrown
Critical roundup of recent kids' books and links to texts.

eHobbies www.ehobbies.com
Separating junior hobbyists from their pocket money.

The Little Animals Activity Centre
www.bbc.co.uk/schools/laac
The second the music starts and the critters start jiggling, you'll know you're in for a treat.

Magic Tricks www.magictricks.com
Never believe it's not so.

Star Wars Origami
www.happymagpie.com/origami.html
Graduate from flapping birds to Destroyer Droids and Tie Fighters. Prefer something that will actually fly? See: www.bestpaperairplanes.com

The Yuckiest Site on the Internet
www.yucky.com
Fun science with a leaning towards the icky-sticky and the creepy-crawly.

Buy records and CDs

Shopping for music is another area where the Net not only equals but outshines its terrestrial counterparts. Apart from the convenience of not having to tramp across town, you can find almost anything, whether or not it's released locally, and in many cases preview tracks before you buy. You might save money, too, depending on where you buy, whether you're hit with tax and how the freight stacks up. Consider splitting your order if duty becomes an issue.

As far as where to shop goes, that depends on your taste. **Amazon** and its many associated **Amazon Marketplace** sellers (look out for the "New & Used" links on product pages) stands out. But then you can't go too far wrong with most of the big names:

Amazon www.amazon.co.uk (UK)
Amazon www.amazon.com (US)
CD Universe www.cduniverse.com (US)
Play.com www.play.com (UK)
Sam Goody www.samgoody.com (US)
Tower Records www.towerrecords.com (US)
Virgin Megastore www.virginmega.com (US)

All of these have a broad selection and will allow you to browse by genre. But you might get a deeper catalogue and more informed editorial from a specialist. The following will ship anywhere:

CD Roots www.cdroots.com (Folk/Roots)
eJazz Lines www.ejazzlines.com (Jazz)

Forced Exposure forcedexposure.com (Experimental)
MDT www.mdt.co.uk (Classical)
Reggae CD www.reggaecd.com (Reggae)
Stern's www.sternsmusic.com (African)

If you know the disc you're after is going to be hard to track down, you could try **eBay**, but also visit **GEMM** and **MusicStack**, extraordinary sites that offer immediate access to millions of new and used records from thousands of sources:

Global Electronic Music Market www.gemm.com
MusicStack www.musicstack.com

Alternatively, if it's obscure 45s or hard-to-find DJ material that you're after, check out:

Hard to Find Records www.htfr.com
Record Finder www.recordfinders.com

Keep up with the news

The Net is the greatest newswire that ever existed. Nearly every TV and print bugle – from local to global – has an online presence. And there's no shortage of online-only sources that are unencumbered by libel law, advertiser pressure and other such hurdles. Perhaps the single most respected news site in the world is Blighty's own:

BBC news.bbc.co.uk

Like most other TV news networks (all easily locatable via Google) the BBC allows you to watch the latest televised bulletins as streaming video (see p.188), and it also features a massive searchable archive.

For high-quality writing, however, the newspaper sites are better. Most put enough free content online for you to live without the hard copy – plus Web-only extras and a searchable back-issue archive (though this is often a subscription service). Google should take you directly to a particular publication. But if that doesn't work, or you want to scan a list of titles relating to a specific region or subject, try a directory like:

Metagrid www.metagrid.com
Publist www.publist.com

There are also sites that let you search multiple news sources simultaneously. The best free services include:

Google News news.google.com

Though the pay-to-access equivalents trawl even deeper:

FindArticles.com www.findarticles.com
HighBeam www.highbeam.com

For non-mainstream current-affairs coverage, tap into some news-focused blogs. Use a blog directory (see p.293) to browse the most popular, and an RSS aggregator (see p.102) to combine feeds from your favourite blogs and the major news services. Or track the hottest topics in the blogging universe at:

Blogdex blogdex.media.mit.edu
Technorati technorati.com

Like someone to monitor newswires and the Web for mention of your product or misdeeds? Or, indeed, any keyword of your choice? There are free and commercial options:

Google Alerts www.google.com/alerts
Webclipping.com www.webclipping.com

Or if you'd rather follow the headlines as they happen, slap a virtual newsticker on your desktop. For example:

BBC Newsline www.bbc.co.uk/newsline (news)
WorldFlash www.worldflash.com (customizable)

Or make use of the news Gadget built into more recent versions of Windows.

Get political

Governments, politicians, political aspirants and causes of all kinds maintain websites to spread the word and further their various interests. But probably the most useful politics sites on the Web are those which allow you to quickly find and contact your representatives. Simply enter your postcode or zip code and away you go:

Congress www.congress.org (US)
They Work for You www.theyworkforyou.com (UK)
UFCW www.ufcwaction.org/ufcwvoiceactivated (US)
Write to Them www.writetothem.com (UK)

To hear government propaganda unpolluted by comment, try:

Prime Minister www.pm.gov.uk (UK)
The White House www.whitehouse.org (US)

And for views from the opposite benches, plus all other types of party-political sites, check out the links directories at:

British Politics Links www.ukpolitics.org.uk (UK)
Political Resources www.politicalresources.com (US)

Government departments tirelessly belch out all sorts of trivia. So if you'd like to know about impending legislation and the like, go straight to the department. If a Google search doesn't deliver, try:

Open Directory
www.google.com/Top/Society/Government

For political poles and predictions:

Gallup www.gallup.com (US)
MORI www.ipsos-mori.com
PollingReport www.pollingreport.com (US)

But if it's stimulating debate, comment and dissent that you're after, then try:

Antiwar www.antiwar.com
Disinformation www.disinfo.com
Michael Moore www.michaelmoore.com
One World www.oneworld.net
The Progressive Review www.prorev.com
ZNet www.zmag.org

Or to find out who's oiling the wheels of US politics, explore:

Open Secrets www.opensecrets.org

Many of the best blogs have a political slant; proceed to a political weblog list such as:

eTalkinghead directory.etalkinghead.com

Feeling fired up by now? Fill your political action diary with dates from:

Protest.net www.protest.net (INT)

Or if you're determined to remain constructive, suggest and rate solutions to problems, political and otherwise, at:

Global Ideas Bank www.globalideasbank.org

Uncover "the truth"

Want the inside track on political assassinations, arms deals, Colombian drug trades, spy satellites, phone tapping, covert operations, government-sponsored alien sex cults and the X-Files? Then fire up your browser. The Web is the perfect medium for communicating everything that "they" don't want you to know about, and the Truth – often in various, wonderfully conflicting versions – can almost always be found.

For the ongoing low-down on the biggest cover-ups of all time, drop in here:

Above Top Secret www.abovetopsecret.com
Conspiracy Bomb www.conspiracybomb.com
The Emperor's New Clothes
www.emperors-clothes.com
From The Wilderness www.fromthewilderness.com
RINF.com www.rinf.com/conspiracy

But that's just the tip of the iceberg, allegedly. You also need to worry about, among other things, aliens…

Aliens And UFOs Among Us www.bright.net/~phobia
Roswell www.coverups.com/roswell/
UFO Seek www.ufoseek.com

Government agencies…

The Black Vault www.blackvault.com
FBI FOIA Reading Room foia.fbi.gov
Jane's IntelWeb intelweb.janes.com

And, um, Elvis Presley…

Elvis Sightings www.elvissightingbulletinboard.com

For scans of once-classified documents from the basements of the FBI, CIA and other agencies, released according to the Freedom of Information Act, drop into **Paperless Archives**. Included are files on such stars as John Wayne, The Beatles, Marilyn Monroe and the British royals:

Paperless Archive www.paperlessarchives.com

By now you should have learned that certain people are up to something and, what's worse, they're probably all in it together. But nothing is so exciting as a secret plot with you as the victim – or the conspirator. Generate your own hush-hush tales at:

Alchemica www.alchemica.co.uk/conspire

Find God

So many answers, so little time on earth. If you haven't yet signed up with a religious sect or are unhappy with the one passed down by your folks, here's your opportunity to survey the field at your own pace. Most are open to newcomers, though certain rules and conditions may apply. For a reasonably complete and unbiased breakdown of faith dealerships, try:

BeliefNet www.beliefnet.com
Wikipedia Religion en.wikipedia.org/wiki/Religion
Religious Tolerance www.religioustolerance.org

But don't expect such an easy ride from those demanding proof:

Atheism atheism.miningco.com
The Secular Web www.infidels.org

If you already know which heaven you're going to, take your pick from this selection:

Anglicans Online anglicansonline.org
The Bible Gateway bible.gospelcom.net
Catholic Online www.catholic.org
Chosen People www.chosen-people.com
Christians v Muslims debate.org.uk
The Hindu Universe www.hindunet.org
The Holy See www.vatican.va
Islamic Gateway www.ummah.net
Peyote Way Church of God www.peyoteway.org
Satanism www.churchofsatan.com
Totally Jewish www.totallyjewish.com
Zen www.do-not-zzz.com

And that's just the tip of the Web's religious iceberg. As well as the regular God-fearing sites there are oceans of much lighter fare to be found online. Here are a few of our favourites:

The Brick Testament
www.thebricktestament.com
And on the eighth day God created Lego.

Jesus and the dinosaurs
i27.tinypic.com/2h6yet5.jpg
The Web is littered with anomalous wonders waiting to be discovered – such as this page from the Beginner's Bible Colouring Book.

Jesus of the Week
www.jesusoftheweek.com
The original Mr Nice Guy in 52 coy poses per year.

Prophecy and Current Events
www.aplus-software.com/thglory
You'll never guess who's coming to dinner. Don't bother cooking, though – he's supposed to be a real whiz with food.

Ship of Fools
ship-of-fools.com
The lighter side of Christianity.

Skeptics Annotated Bible
www.skepticsannotatedbible.com
Contends that the Good Book is a misnomer.

Find a new home

Whether you're in the market for a mansion or a bedsit, the Web is the ultimate place for property listings. Start at…

Apartments.com www.apartments.com (US)
Find A Property www.findaproperty.com (UK)
HomeSeekers www.homeseekers.com (US)
Property Finder www.propertyfinder.co.uk (UK)
Realtor.com www.realtor.com (US)
Right Move www.rightmove.co.uk (UK)
Spring Street www.springstreet.com (US)

Wannabe celebrity? You'll love this:

Private Islands Online www.privateislandsonline.com

A new house – or indeed an archipelago – means a new mortgage. Compare rates and deals from lenders with a site such as:

Bankrate.com www.bankrate.com/mortgage (US)
HomeFair www.homefair.com (US)
Mortgages-Online www.mortgages-online.co.uk (UK)
UKmortgagesonline.com ukmortgagesonline.com (UK)

Or to rent (or rent out) a room, try an online matchmaker like:

Easy Roommate www.easyroommate.com (US)
Flatmate www.flatmateclick.co.uk (UK)

Once your lease or purchase is signed and sealed, you'll need to find someone to move your stuff from old home to new.

MovingHomeCheckList movinghomechecklist.com (UK)

And don't forget to prepare your houseplants for the change:

AtlasWorldGroup atlasworldgroup.com/howto/plants

If you're in the UK, you may also want to notify companies and services of your new address, and seek out a bargain on utilities:

Buy.co.uk www.buy.co.uk
I Have Moved www.ihavemoved.com

Next, plan your new interior using a virtual design tool such as Google's very own SketchUp:

SketchUp sketchup.google.com

Then grab hammer, shovel and round-leaf plant, and visit:

Do It Yourself www.doityourself.com
Feng Shui Ultimate Resource www.qi-whiz.com
GardenWeb www.gardenweb.com
HomeTips www.hometips.com

Become more productive

Throughout this book you'll find mention of useful online tools for everything from editing photos (see p.217) to storing files (see p.263), but there are many other Web-based applications and services out there that can make you more productive, more organized and also reduce the number of programs you have to buy and install on your computer. Who needs to fork out for Microsoft Office when you can achieve everything you want through your Web browser? Here are a few recommendations to get you started with so-called "cloud computing":

Evernote www.evernote.com
Amazingly versatile online note "capturing" service with text-recognition technology that can even read text from photos posted via a mobile or screen grabs added at your desk.

EyeOS eyeos.org
Create a free account here and access your very own Web-based operating system with built-in applications for handling contacts, calendars, RSS, spreadsheets, text documents and more.

Gliffy www.gliffy.com
Online flowchart creation tool. Sign up for a 30-day free trial and have a play.

Google Docs docs.google.com
Text documents, spread sheets and presentations, all integrated with your free Google account. Really useful for sharing projects between people in different locations.

MobileMe www.apple.com/mobileme
Apple's MobileMe subscription service has a very slick front end, but unfortunately it's not yet fast or stable enough to act as a full-time replacement for Apple Mail, Address Book and iCal.

Office Live Workspace workspace.officelive.com
Microsoft's burgeoning cloud suite features document sharing and note-making tools, with a swathe of Office applications being added soon.

Remember The Milk www.rememberthemilk.com
A great web-based "to-do list" service, with loads of extra features and reliable syncronization. There are also mobile apps and browser plug-ins available so that you can feel nagged wherever you are.

SeaMonkey www.seamonkey-project.org
Mozilla's SeaMonkey suite is very much a work in progress at the time of writing and will be of specific interest to web developers and "techier" readers.

Twiddla www.twiddla.com
Online white-boarding and brain-storming tool with integrated conference calling.

Zoho zoho.com
A comprehensive and free suite of office tools. If you get stuck, the Zoho community makes it easy to find the answers to your problems.

Tune in to Radio…

Radio on the Internet works pretty much like radio in the real world, except that – what with the Net being global and there being no online equivalent to radio stations fighting over frequency bands – the choice is almost infinite. You're limited neither by your geographical area nor your next-door neighbour's four-storey gazebo.

Radio online won't sound as good as straight off a "real" radio in Paris. But you might be surprised at just how good it does sound: somewhere between AM and FM would be a fair description.

Most online stations broadcast ("webcast") in RealAudio and/or Windows Media Format (see p.188). Both come with in-built station directories (as does iTunes) along with Web-based event guides. This is fine for starting out, but the listings are nowhere near complete. Instead, try one of the specialist radio directories listed below.

If you have a reasonably fast connection, radio streams are one of the great things the Net has to offer. Grab the latest media players (see p.188) and head off to the following directories:

Google Directory
www.google.com/Top/Arts/Radio/Internet
Live Radio www.live-radio.net
PenguinRadio www.penguinradio.com
RadioNow www.radio-now.co.uk
RadioTower www.radiotower.com
Real Guide radio.real.com
Virtual Tuner www.virtualtuner.com

Much of the best radio content in the world is still produced by the BBC. Most of their programmes can be found online. If you can't find what you're after, try a BBC-specific Google search (see p.94).

BBC Radio www.bbc.co.uk/radio

With so much online radio on offer, you're bound to find plenty of streams that suit your taste. But for something truly made-to-measure, check out Last.fm – "a personalized online radio station that plays the right music to the right people" and, in the US, Pandora. Both work out what music you like best and then create a customized radio station.

Last FM www.last.fm
Pandora www.pandora.com (US only)

...and to Podcasts

Unlike most online radio, which is "streamed" across the Net in real time, Podcasts are made available as files (usually MP3s) that can be downloaded to your computer and listened to at leisure through either a jukebox or on an MP3 player such as an iPod. Podcasts are usually free and often consist of spoken content – current affairs, poetry, cookery, etc – though there are many musical Podcasts, too,

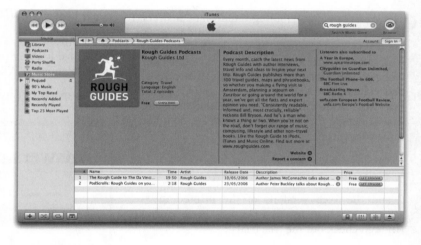

despite a grey area surrounding the distribution of copyrighted music in this way. And despite the name, they are not the exclusive domain of Apple iPod users.

It's usually possible to download an individual "show" directly from the website of whoever produced it, but the idea is to use an "aggregator" to subscribe to Podcasts that you're interested in and have them automatically downloaded to your jukebox – and digital music player. That way you have fresh news stories, debates, poems, music or whatever each day – ideal for the morning journey to work.

If you use iTunes you already have both an aggregator and a massive directory of Podcasts built-in – just hit the Podcasts button in the "Source list" on the left. If you use Windows Media Player as your jukebox, or don't like what's been made available by Apple, then Juice is the best way to find and subscribe to feeds.

Juice juicereceiver.sourceforge.net (PC & Mac)

Alternatively, visit audio.weblogs.com to browse the most recently posted Podcasts.

Creating a Podcast

Creating your own Podcast is a relatively simple process. See p.235 for more information.

Answer any question

The Web is a giant, bubbling cauldron of answers – many of them to questions you didn't even know you wanted to ask. We've already discussed many routes for seeking out facts online: via Google (see p.80), via newsgroups (see p.138), and via question and answer services (see p.92). For more context, try an online encyclopedia. These include the wonderful and up-to-date but rather unofficial…

Wikipedia www.wikipedia.org (see p.287 for more information)

…and the Web versions of the printed meg-atomes. You have to pay to access the following (though check out the free trials):

Britannica www.eb.com
World Book www.worldbook.com

But the *Columbia Encyclopedia*, along with scores of other top reference books – from the *Cambridge History of English and American Literature* via *Encyclopedia of World History* to *Strunk's Elements of Style* – can be found free online at the brilliant:

Bartleby www.bartleby.com

For access to over a thousand dictionaries and thesauri across almost every language:

Dictionary.com www.dictionary.com
One Look www.onelook.com

YourDictionary.com www.yourdictionary.com

Alternatively, enter a term into **Answers.com** and get a nice-looking page pulling together defini-tions, synonyms, Wikipedia entries and more:

Answers.com www.answers.com

A few more of the All-Electric InterWeb's key reference sites:

Acronym Finder www.acronymfinder.com
Ensure your prospective company name doesn't mean something blue.

Anagrams www.wordsmith.org/anagram
Recycle used letters.

Aphorisms Galore www.aphorismsgalore.com
Sound clever by repeating someone else's lines.

Babelfish Translator babelfish.altavista.com
Translate words or phrases from or into nearly any tongue.

Calculators Online www.math.com
Awesome collection of online tools.

Cliché Finder www.westegg.com/cliche
Submit a word to find out how not to use it.

InfoPlease www.infoplease.com
Handy, all-purpose almanac for stats and trivia.

Internet Archive www.archive.org
Wormhole your way into Web history. Huge and amazing.

Itools www.itools.com
All the search resources you need in one place.
More at refdesk:
www.refdesk.com

Librarian's Index www.lii.org
Naturally there are oodles of reference portals brimming with helpful reference tools. These are some of the best:
dir.yahoo.com/reference
dmoz.org/Reference
www.libraryspot.com
www.refdesk.com

Megaconverter 2 www.megaconverter.com/mega2
Calculate everything from your height in angstroms to the pellets of lead per ounce of buckshot needed to bring down an overcharging consultant.

Oxford Reference www.oxfordreference.com
Mind-blowing reference library of some one hundred titles now online. Unfortunately, you have to subscribe.

Questia www.questia.com
A contender for the title of world's biggest library, this site has the full contents of nearly half a million books and journals.

Quoteland www.quoteland.com
The best place to find out who said what.

RhymeZone www.rhymezone.com
Get a hoof up putting together a classy love poem.

Skeptic's Dictionary www.skepdic.com
Punch holes in mass-media funk and pseudo-sciences.

Symbols
www.symbols.com
Ever woken up with a strange sign tattooed on your buttocks? Here's where to find out what it means without calling in the FBI.

Get the latest scores

For live calls, scores, tables, draws, injuries and corruption inquiries across major sports, try any major news site or a sporting specialist such as:

BBC Sport news.bbc.co.uk/sport (UK)
CBS Sportsline www.sportsline.com (US)
Fox Sports www.foxsports.com.au (Aus)
SkySports www.skysports.com (UK)
Slam Sports www.canoe.ca/slam (CA)
Sports Illustrated sportsillustrated.cnn.com (US)
Yahoo! Sports UK sports.yahoo.com (UK)
Yahoo! Sports US sports.yahoo.co.uk (US)

Many of these sites feature RSS feeds (see p.102), which are a great way to get sports news as it happens. So look out for those orange buttons. Some of the above also offer streaming audio and video (notably the BBC), but there are also streaming specialists, such as:

Sportal www.sportal.com (UK)

But if your interest borders even slightly on obsession, you'll find far more satisfaction on the pages of something more one-eyed. A Web search should take you to clubs and fan sites, as well as countless sport-specific sites, complete with more stats than you could shake a snooker cue at. Alternatively, drill down through the terrifying links archive at:

Yahoo! Sport Directory
dir.yahoo.com/Recreation/Sports

This will lead to portals and stats archives for every conceivable game, from the popular…

Football365 www.football365.com (UK)
Major League Baseball mlb.mlb.com (US)

…to the obscure:

Amateur Gay Wrestling home.snafu.de/mitch
SledDog.com www.sleddog.com

Sports are also richly served by webloggers. Locate blogs related to your game of choice at:

Blogcatalog www.blogcatalog.com/directory/sports
Sports Blogs www.sportsblogs.org

And to find out who went furthest and fastest, when and where, there's always:

Guinness World Records
www.guinnessworldrecords.com

Discover the world of wikis

One of the best online developments of recent years has been the growing popularity of **wikis** – special webpages that can be immediately edited by any reader. The undisputed king of the wiki world, and one of the best things ever to happen on the Web, is **Wikipedia**: a vast, multi-language encyclopedia, written, edited and updated by its users.

Common sense dictates that such a thing would be unreliable, badly written and highly opinionated, but in fact nearly all the articles are erudite, balanced and tightly composed – amazing proof of the power of globally pooled knowledge and skills. Best of all, Wikipedia articles – which now number more than a million – are released under a special "copyleft" licence (just like open-source software) meaning that they will remain freely accessible forever.

Wikipedia www.wikipedia.org

Contributing is easy, though obviously you should only add or edit anything if you're a good writer and you're really sure of your facts. If an article is incomplete or inaccurate, simply click the "edit this page" link, tweak the text and then choose "save this page". Naturally, you can also start an article from scratch. To find out how, see; en.wikipedia.org/wiki/Wikipedia:About

The Wikimedia Foundation, who run the Wikipedia site, have applied the same formula to these sites:

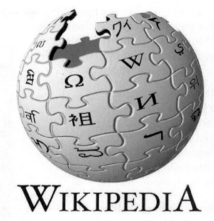

WIKIPEDIA

Wikibooks www.wikibooks.org
Wikiquote www.wikiquote.org
Wikispecies species.wikimedia.org
wiktionary www.wiktionary.org

What's more, a wiki is very easy to set up, and their uses are only really limited by your imagination. Many hosting companies (see p.220) offer so called "wiki-farm" packages. A couple you might consider are:

DreamHost www.dreamhost.com
Peanut Butter Wiki pbwiki.com

And for a full list of wiki-farms, visit:
en.wikipedia.org/wiki/Comparison_of_wiki_farms

Map things out

There are lots of sites on the Web that will give you maps of the entire Western world (and much of the rest), often complete with route-planning tools, Wi-Fi hotspot locators and much more:

Expedia maps.expedia.com
Google Maps maps.google.com
MapBlast www.mapblast.com
MapQuest www.mapquest.com
Multimap www.multimap.com (UK/Eu)
Streetmap www.streetmap.co.uk (UK)
Whereis www.whereis.com (Aus)

Probably the best of these are **Google Maps** and **Multimap**, which let you overlay detailed satellite photographs over your map (see if you can spot your room). For more aerial imaging, see:

Globe Explorer www.globexplorer.com
NASA worldwind.arc.nasa.gov
Terraserver www.terraserver.com

If you like the whole satellite-view thang, consider downloading Google's free Google Earth tool – it's a 3D modelling application that zooms you around the globe and offers all sorts of great tools to play with.

Google Earth earth.google.com

Or if you require highly detailed US topographic maps, visit:

Trails.com www.trails.com/maps.aspx

And if it's old maps you're after:

HipKiss www.hipkiss.org/data/themaps.html
Old Maps www.old-maps.co.uk (UK)

For more cartographical resources, follow the links from:

About geography.about.com
Open Directory dmoz.org/Reference/Maps

Cultivate relationships

Friends, colleagues, sweethearts, likeminded odd-balls… they can all be found on the Web – though don't assume that your online relationships will necessarily blossom in the real world. Why not start by checking out what some old classmates are up to these days, and maybe organizing a reunion…

ClassMates.com www.classmates.com (US, CAN)
Friends Reunited www.friendsreunited.co.uk (UK)
School Friends www.schoolfriends.com.au (Aus)

Or to meet friends of friends of friends, explore some **social networks** (see p.237):

Facebook www.facebook.com
Friendster www.friendster.com
MySpace www.myspace.com
Orkut www.orkut.com

These might lead to romance (or turn you into a drummer in a band), but if not, don't worry. The Net is the world's biggest singles bar, responsible for the uniting of many happy couples (see www.cyberlove101.com). But bear in mind that, like the offline world, the Web isn't short of hustlers, leeches and other unsavoury characters; keep your wits about you. Some of the biggest dating agencies include:

Dating Direct www.datingdirect.com (INT)
Friendfinder www.friendfinder.com (US)
Lavalife www.lavalife.com (INT)

Match.com www.match.com (INT)
SocialNet www.relationships.com (US)
UDate www.udate.com (INT)
UK Singles www.uksingles.co.uk (UK)

For something more exclusive, try and get yourself accepted at:

Beautiful People www.beautifulpeople.net (INT)

Naturally, there are scores more friendship and relationship sites out there. A few to get you started…

Infidelity.com www.infidelity.com (US)
They're all no-good, lying, cheating slime. But at least there's help.

So There www.sothere.com
A place to post your parting shots.

Weddings in the Real World www.theknot.com
Prepare to jump the broom. Or if you want to untie the knot, try:
www.divorcesource.com

Book a trip

Whether you're planning an itinerary, shopping for a ticket or already mobile, everything you could possibly hope for is online somewhere. If it's background and ideas you're after, probably the best place to start is the major guidebook publishers:

Fodors www.fodors.com
Frommers www.frommers.com
Insiders www.insiders.com
Let's Go www.letsgo.com
Lonely Planet www.lonelyplanet.com
Rough Guides www.roughguides.com

Some of these – including yours truly – publish nearly the full text of their guidebooks online. This might seem like commercial suicide, but the reality is that books are still more convenient, especially on the road, when you need them most. If you'd like to order a paper version – or a map – you'll find plenty of opportunities either from the above publishers or any online bookshop (see p.252). For the biggest selection, try a specialist such as:

Get Lost www.getlostbooks.com (US)
Stanfords www.stanfords.co.uk (UK)

For further inspiration, try the user-submitted travelogues at:

IgoUgo www.igougo.com
TravelBlog www.travelblog.org
Travel Library www.travel-library.com

Or for general destination guides and location-specific advice on planning your trip, drop into:

About Travel travel.about.com

Once you've decided where you want to go, you'll probably be in the market for a flight. There are loads of places to try, with varying levels of usability and flexibility, but one stands out:

Skyscanner www.skyscanner.net (Eu; Aus)

Skyscanner pulls together flight information and quotes from a range of companies and even lets you view a graph of price variations over a week or month to help you work out the best time to travel.

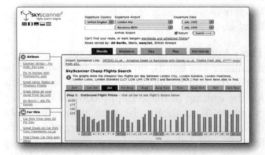

The alternatives are to go straight to an airline's website, or to search with one of the online ticketing systems. Unless you're spending someone else's money, you might want to sidestep the full fares offered on these major services:

Expedia UK www.expedia.co.uk (UK)
Expedia US www.expedia.com (US)
Travelshop au.travelshop.com (Aus)

And head to a discount specialist such as:

1Travel.com www.1travel.com (INT)
Bargain Holidays www.bargainholidays.com (UK)
Cheap Flights www.cheapflights.com (UK)
Ebookers.com www.ebookers.com (UK, Eu)
Lowestfare.com www.lowestfare.com (US)
Opodo www.opodo.co.uk (UK)
Travel Zoo www.travelzoo.com (US)

Most of the above will also offer you hotels, car rental and full tour packages. But you might get better value on a last-minute all-in trip from a special deal like:

Lastminute.com www.lastminute.com (UK)
Lastminutetravel.com www.lastminutetravel.com (US)

More bargain places to lay your head at:

Bed and Breakfast.com www.bedandbreakfast.com
Hostels.com www.hostels.com
Hotel Discount www.hoteldiscount.com

Alternatively, if you already know the tour operator you want to travel with, you should be able to track down their home page through **Google**. Or browse for a company via:

ABTA www.abta.com (UK)
Travel Hub www.travelhub.com/agencies (US)

To swat up on jabs, bugs and disease before departure, visit:

CDC www.cdc.gov/travel
World Health Organisation www.who.int

If you still have time to kill before you leave for the airport, check out a few of these useful resources:

Art of Travel www.artoftravel.com
How to see the world on $25 a day.

Climate Care www.co2.org
Offset the global warming that your trip is about to cause. Also visit:
www.carbonneutral.com

Electronic Embassy www.embassy.org
Directory of foreign embassies in DC, plus Web links where available.

How Far Is It? www.indo.com/distance
Calculate the distance between any two cities.

International Student Travel Confederation
www.istc.org
Save money with an authentic international student card.

The Man in Seat 61 www.seat61.com
Times and fares from London to anywhere in the world by rail and sea, courtesy of an ex-station manager at Charing Cross.

Responsible Travel www.responsibletravel.com
Agent for scores of travel companies, all screened for ethical soundness.

Explore the blogosphere

Adam Curry's Weblog
live.curry.com
Audio and text blog from former MTV VJ.

Apparently Nothing
www.apparentlynothing.com
Regular photographic postings and commentary.

Belle de Jour
belledejour-uk.blogspot.com
The diary of a London call girl; but is it fact or fiction?

The Best Page in the Universe
maddox.xmission.com
Beneath the onion layers of misanthropy and delusions of grandeur you'll find a soulless husk.

Call Centre Confidential
callcentrediary.blogspot.com
Though no longer updated (presumably a better job was found) this is still a good read – the gripping diary of a call centre team leader.

Coolfer
www.coolfer.com
A Big Apple blog covering "for the most part" music and the music industry, and, of course, NYC.

The Daily Report
www.zeldman.com
Web guru Jeffrey Zeldman dishes up tech advice and links, and the wickedly funny "If the great movies had been websites".

The Diary of Samuel Pepys
www.pepysdiary.com
Every day brings an entry from the renowned 17th-

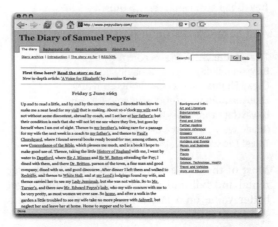

century diarist. If you've missed his exploits to date, there's a "story so far" page.

Doubletakes
www.doubletakesblog.com
A great blog, mostly of images that fall under the category of "things that make you look twice".

Going Underground
london-underground.blogspot.com
Adventures below the streets of London.

Hippy Shopper
www.hippyshopper.com
Ethical consumerism in a weblog.

KICK-AAS
kickaas.typepad.com
Campaign blog devoted to "Kicking All Agricultural Subsidies" in the name of fair trade for poor nations.

Librarian.net
www.librarian.net
A crucial insight on the subterranean world of the librarian.

Lifehacker
lifehacker.com
A wonderful collection of posts and articles that offer tips and tricks for navigating "this mortal coil". Other worthwhile self-improvement blogs include:
www.dumblittleman.com
zenhabits.net

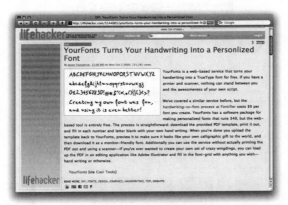

The Londonist
www.londonist.com
Award-winning blog covering all sorts of stuff, from news and reviews to cinema and culture. Well laid out and funny.

MetaFilter
www.metafilter.com
Long-standing community weblog.

nyclondon
www.nyclondon.com/blog
Stunning photoblog.

Pop Culture Junk Mail
pcjm.blogspot.com
Your guide to the flotsam of post-industrial society.

Talking Points Memo
www.talkingpointsmemo.com
All the dirt from the Washington DC Beltway.

World Changing
www.worldchanging.com
Interesting site based on the premise that the tools, models and ideas for building a better future lie unconnected all around us, and which aims to bring some of those elements together to promote change.

And more...

For thousands more, covering just about every subject under the sun, try a blog search engine or directory, such as:

BlogSearchEngine blogsearchengine.com
Eatonweb Portal portal.eatonweb.com

Shiny Shiny
shinyshiny.tv
What the world has been waiting for – a girls' guide to gadgets.

Or for historical and technological background, follow the links from:

Wikipedia en.wikipedia.org/wiki/Weblog

Check the forecast

Most news sites report the weather, with click-throughs to destination forecasts worldwide. Particularly good services include:

BBC www.bbc.co.uk/weather
CNN Weather www.cnn.com/WEATHER
Yahoo! Weather weather.yahoo.com

For general weather resources, links to regional meteorology sites, and the fanatical extremes of weather-watching, scan these specialists:

About Weather weather.about.com
Open Directory dmoz.org/News/Weather
Weather.com www.weather.com
Wildweather www.wildweather.com
WMO Members www.wmo.ch/web-en/member.html

If weather is your hobby then you'll probably want to stock up with something a little more high tech than a pine cone and some seaweed:

Ambient Weather www.ambientweather.com
Anemometers www.anemometers.co.uk
UK Weather Shop www.ukweathershop.co.uk

Become dazed and confused

This is what happens when you set up a global computer network that every lunatic on the planet with a bit of spare time on his hands has access to. Enjoy…

Absurd.org www.absurd.org
Please do not adjust your set.

Bizarre www.bizarremag.com
Updates from the print monthly that takes the investigation of strange phenomena more seriously than itself.

Cats Who Throw Up Grass
www.catswhothrowupgrass.com
So, you think your cat wants to kill you? This website agrees. Scroll down to the bottom of the page for more home truths.

Circlemakers www.circlemakers.org
Create crop circles to amuse New Agers (and the press).

A Citizen from Hell www.amightywind.com
/hell/citizenhell.htm
If Hell sounds this bad, you don't want to go there. Of course, you could try the virtual tour before taking the plunge:
www.riverstyx.com

Clonaid www.clonaid.com
Thanks to the Raelians, we now know life on Earth was created in extraterrestrial laboratories. Here's where you can buy genuine cloned human livestock for the kitchen table. Ready as soon as the lab's finished.

Corrugated Iron Club www.corrugated-iron-club.info
It's metal. It's wavy. It rocks.

The Darwin Awards www.darwinawards.com
Each year the Darwin Award goes to the person who drops off the census register in the most spectacular fashion.

Derek's Big Website of Wal-Mart Purchase Receipts
blacksunn.net/receipts
Discuss everything from other people's shopping to Wal-Mart's product abbreviation policy. Trust us – it's better than it sounds.

Derm Cinema www.skinema.com
Know your celebrity skin conditions.

Dr MegaVolt www.drmegavolt.com
The Doc sure sparked right up when they switched on the power, but could he cut it in the big league?
www3.bc.sympatico.ca/lightningsurvivor

Entrances To Hell www.entrances2hell.co.uk
Damnation is to be found in the strangest of places.

Flashpedia flashpedia.net/linesuperfollow.swf
Keep clicking and dragging until you feel completely "weirded out man".

Furniture Porn www.furnitureporn.com
See well-upholstered chairs getting wood. And if that's not hard enough for you, visit:
drew.corrupt.net/bp

Future Horizons www.futurehorizons.net
Snap off more than your fair share through solid-state circuitry.

Gallery of the Absurd
captainpackrat.com/Misc/galleryoftheabsurd.htm
Strange ways to sell strange stuff.

Gum Blondes www.gumblondes.com
Portraits of your favourite blondes fashioned from chewed bubblegum.

Halfbakery www.halfbakery.com
Somewhere to deposit those great invention ideas that keep you awake at night. "Hover Hats" or "Water Duvets", anyone?

I Hate Clowns www.ihateclowns.com
A website for all of you out there who are scared of clowns – drop in and order the "Can't sleep, clowns will eat me" T-shirt.

Illuminati News www.illuminati-news.com
Storm into secret societies and thump your fist on the table.

International Ghost Hunters Society
www.ghostweb.com
They never give up the ghost. Nab your own with:
www.maui.net/~emf/TriFieldNat.html

Japanese Rabbit Balancing shorterlink.com/?W2VGS5
Oolong sure can make a donkey of himself. Or if yawning rabbits are your thing…
www.talkingegg.com/humor/bunnyyawns.html

Man In The Dark
www.maninthedark.com
Drag the man through the dark … no, that's it … really.

News of the Weird www.thisistrue.com
Dotty clippings from the world's press.

Nobody Here www.nobodyhere.com
Sometimes things with the least purpose are the most enthralling.

Scanwiches www.scanwiches.com
Feeling peckish? You won't be after looking at this site and its daily dose of sliced and scanned sandwiches.

Contexts

A brief history of the Internet

Who'd have thought it?

The concept of the Net might not have been hatched in Microsoft's cabinet war rooms, but it did play a role in a previous contest for world domination. It was 1957, at the height of the Cold War. The Soviets had just launched the first Sputnik, thus beating the USA into space. The race was on. In response the US Department of Defense formed the Advanced Research Projects Agency (ARPA) to bump up its technological prowess. Twelve years later, this spawned ARPAnet – a project to develop a military research network or, specifically, the world's first decentralized computer network.

In those days, no one had PCs. The computer world was based on mainframe computers and dumb terminals. These usually involved a gigantic, fragile box in a climate-controlled room, which acted as a hub, with a mass of cables spoking out to keyboard/monitor ensembles. The concept of independent intelligent processors pooling resources through a network was brave new territory that would require the development of new hardware, software and connectivity methods.

The driving force behind decentralization, ironically, was the bomb-proofing factor. Nuke a mainframe and the system goes down. But bombing a network would, at worst, remove only a few nodes. The remainder could route around it unharmed. Or so the theory went.

Wiring the world

Over the next decade, **research agencies** and **universities** flocked to join the network. US institutions such as UCLA, MIT, Stanford and Harvard led the way and, in 1973, the network crossed the Atlantic to include University College London and Norway's Royal Radar Establishment.

The 1970s also saw the introduction of **electronic mail**, **FTP**, **Telnet** and what would become the **Usenet** newsgroups. The early 1980s brought **TCP/IP**, the **domain name system**, Network News Transfer Protocol and the European networks **EUnet** (European **UNIX** Network), **MiniTel** (the widely adopted French consumer network) and **JANET** (Joint Academic Network), as well as the Japanese **UNIX** Network. **ARPA** evolved to handle the research traffic, while a second network, MILnet, took over US military intelligence.

An important development took place in 1986, when the US National Science Foundation established **NSFnet** by linking five university supercomputers at a backbone speed of 56Kbps. This opened the gateway for external universities to tap into superior processing power and share resources. In the three years between 1984 and 1988, the number of host computers on the **Internet** (as it was now being called) grew from about 1000 to over 60,000. NSFnet, meanwhile, increased its capacity to T1 (1544Kbps). Over the next few years, more and more countries joined the network, spanning the globe from Australia and New Zealand to Iceland, Israel, Brazil, India and Argentina.

It was at this time, too, that **Internet Relay Chat** (IRC) burst onto the scene by providing an alternative to CNN's incessant, but censored, Gulf War coverage. By this stage, the Net had grown beyond its original charter. Although ARPA had succeeded in creating the basis for decentralized computing, whether it was actually a military success was debatable. It might have been bombproof, but it also opened new doors to espionage. It was never particularly secure, and it is suspected that Soviet agents routinely hacked in to forage for research data. In 1990, ARPAnet folded and NSFnet took over administering the Net.

Coming in from the cold

Global electronic communication was far too useful and versatile to stay confined to academics. Big business was starting to notice. The Cold War looked as if it was over and world economies were regaining confidence after the 1987 stock market savaging. In most places, market trading moved from the pits and blackboards onto computer screens. The financial sector expected fingertip real-time data, and that desire was spreading. The world was ready for a people's network. And, since the Net was already in place, funded by taxpayers, there was really no excuse not to open it to the public.

In 1991, the NSF lifted its restrictions on enterprise. During the Net's early years, its "**Acceptable Use Policy**" specifically prohibited using the network for profit. Changing that policy opened the gates to commerce, with the greater public close behind.

However, before anyone could connect to the Net, someone had to sell them a connection. The **Commercial Internet eXchange (CIX)**, a network of major commercial access providers, formed to create a commercial backbone and divert traffic from the NSFnet. Before long, dozens of budding ISPs began rigging up points of presence in their bedrooms. Meanwhile, NSFnet upgraded its backbone to T3 (44,736Kbps).

By this time, the Net had established itself as a viable medium for transferring data, but with one major problem. You had to know where to look. That process involved knowing a lot more about computers and the UNIX computing language than most punters would relish. The next few years saw an explosion in navigation protocols, such as WAIS, Gopher, Veronica and, most importantly, the now-dominant **World Wide Web**.

The gold rush begins

In 1989, Tim Berners-Lee of **CERN,** the Swiss particle physics institute, proposed the basis of the World Wide Web, initially as a means of sharing physics research. His goal was a seamless network in which data from any source could be accessed in a simple, consistent way with one program, on any type of computer. The Web did this, encompassing all existing infosystems such as FTP, Gopher and Usenet, without alteration. It remains an unqualified success.

As the number of Internet hosts exceeded one million, the **Internet Society** was formed to brainstorm protocols and attempt to coordinate and direct the Net's escalating expansion.

Mosaic – the first graphical **Web browser** – was released and declared to be the "killer application of the 1990s". It made navigating the Internet as simple as pointing and clicking, and took away the need to know UNIX. The Web's traffic increased 25-fold in the year up to June 1994, and domain names for **commercial organizations** (.com) began to outnumber those of educational institutions (.edu). As the Web grew, so too did the global village. The media began to notice, slowly realizing that the Internet was something that went way beyond propeller-heads and students. Almost every country in the world had joined the Net. Even the White House was online.

Of course, as word of a captive market got around, entrepreneurial brains went into overdrive. Canter & Seigel, an Arizona law firm, notoriously "**spammed**" Usenet with **advertisements** for the US green card lottery. Although the Net was tentatively open for business, cross-posting advertisements to every newsgroup was decidedly bad form. Such was the ensuing wrath that C&S had no chance of filtering out genuine responses from the server-breaking level of hate mail they received. A precedent was thus established for

how not to do business on the Net. Pizza Hut, by contrast, showed how to do it subtly by setting up a trial service online. Although it generated wads of publicity, it too was doomed by impracticalities. Nevertheless, the ball had begun to roll.

The homesteaders

As individuals arrived to stake out Web territory, businesses followed. Most had no idea what to do once they got their brand online. Too many arrived with a bang, only to peter out in a perpetuity of "under construction" signs. Soon business cards not only sported email addresses, but Web addresses as well. And, rather than send a CV and stiff letter, job aspirants could now send a brief email accompanied with a "see my webpage" for further details.

The Internet moved out of the realm of luxury into an elite necessity, verging towards a commodity. Some early business sites gathered such a following that by 1995 they were able to charge high rates for advertising banners. A few, including Web **portals** such as **InfoSeek** and **Yahoo!**, made it to the Stock Exchange boards, while others, like **GNN**, attracted buyers.

But it wasn't all success. Copyright lawyers arrived in droves. Well-meaning devotees, cheeky opportunists and info-terrorists alike felt the iron fists of Lego, McDonald's, MTV, the Louvre, Fox, Sony, the Church of Scientology and others clamp down on their "unofficial websites" or newsgroups. It wasn't always a case of corporate right but of might, as small players couldn't foot the expenses to test **new legal boundaries**. The honeymoon was officially over.

Point of no return

By the beginning of 1995, the Net was well and truly within the public realm. It was impossible to escape. The media became bored with extolling its virtues, so it turned to **sensationalism**. The Net reached the status of an Oprah Winfrey issue. New tales of hacking, porn, bombmaking, terrorist handbooks, homebreaking and sexual harassment began to tarnish the Internet's iconic position as the great international equalizer. But that didn't stop businesses, schools, banks, government bodies, politicians and consumers from swarming online, nor the major **Online Services** – such as CompuServe, America Online and Prodigy, which had been developing in parallel since the late 1980s – from adding Internet access as a sideline to their existing private networks.

As 1995 progressed, **Mosaic**, the previous year's killer application, lost its footing to a superior browser, **Netscape**. Not such big news, you might imagine, but after a half-year of rigorous beta-testing, Netscape went public with the third-largest-ever NASDAQ IPO share value – around $2.4bn.

Meantime, Microsoft, which had formerly disregarded the Internet, released **Windows 95,** a PC operating platform incorporating access to the controversial **Microsoft Network.** Although **IBM** had done a similar thing six months earlier with **OS/2 Warp** and its **IBM Global Network**, Microsoft's was an altogether different scheme. It offered full Net access, but its real product was its own separate network, which many people feared might supersede the Net, giving Microsoft an unholy reign over information distribution. But that never happened. Within months, Microsoft – smarting from bad press and finding the Net a larger animal even than itself – about-turned and declared a full commitment to furthering the Internet.

Browser wars

As Microsoft advanced, Netscape continued pushing the envelope, driving the Web into new territory with each release. New enhancements arrived at such a rate that competitors began to drop out as quickly as they appeared. This was the era of "This page looks best if viewed with Netscape". Of course, it wasn't just Netscape, since much of the new activity stemmed from the innovative products of third-party developers such as **MacroMedia (Shockwave), Progressive Networks (RealAudio), Apple (QuickTime) and Sun (Java).** The Web began to spring to life with animations, music, 3D worlds and other tricks.

While Netscape's market dominance gave developers the confidence to accept it as the de facto standard, treating it as a kind of Internet operating system into which to "plug" their products, Microsoft (an old hand at taking possession of cleared territory) began to launch a whole series of free Net tools. These included **Internet Explorer,** a browser with enhancements of its own including **ActiveX,** a Web-centric programming environment more powerful than the much-lauded **Java** but without the same platform independence, and clearly geared toward advanc-

ing Microsoft's software dominance. Not only was Internet Explorer suddenly the only other browser in the race, unlike Netscape it was genuinely free. And many were not only rating it as the better product, but also crediting Microsoft with a broader vision of the Net's direction.

By mid-1997, every Online Service and almost every major ISP had signed deals with Microsoft to distribute its browser. Even intervention by the US Department of Justice over Microsoft's (logical but monopolistic) bundling of Internet Explorer as an integral part of Windows 98 couldn't impede its progress. Netscape looked bruised. While it continued shipping minor upgrades, it no longer led either in market share or innovation. In desperation, it handed over the project of completely reworking the code to the general programming public at **Mozilla.org.** When AOL bought Netscape in early 1999, little doubt remained: Netscape had given up the fight.

Found on the Internet

Skipping back to late 1995, the backlash against Internet freedom had moved into full flight. The expression **"found on the Internet"** became the news tag of the minute, depicting the Net as the source of everything evil – from bomb recipes to child pornography. While editors and commentators, often with little direct experience of the Net, urged that "children" be protected, the Net's own media and opinion shakers pushed the **freedom of speech** barrow, claiming that the very foundations of democracy were at stake.

At first politicians didn't take much notice. Few

could even grasp the concept of what the Net was about, let alone figure out a way to regulate its activities. The first, and easiest, target was **porn**, resulting in raids on hundreds of **private bulletin boards** (BBSs) worldwide and a few much-publicized convictions for the possession of child porn. BBSs were sitting ducks, being mostly self-contained and run by someone who could take the rap. Net activists, however, feared that the primary objective was to send a ripple of fear through a Net community that believed it was bigger than the law, and to soften the public to the notion that the Internet, as it stood, posed a threat to national wellbeing.

In December 1995, at the request of German authorities, **CompuServe** cut its newsfeed to exclude the bulk of newsgroups carrying sexual material. But the groups cut weren't just pornographers: some were dedicated to gay and abortion issues. This brought to light the difficulty in drawing the lines of obscenity and the problems with publishing across foreign boundaries. Next came the **US Communications Decency Act**, proposed legislation to forbid the online publication of "obscene" material. It was poorly conceived, however, and, following opposition from a very broad range of groups (including such mainstream bodies as the American Libraries Association), it was overturned, the decision later being upheld in the Supreme Court.

Outside the US, more authorities reacted. In **France,** three ISP chiefs were temporarily jailed for supplying obscene newsgroups, while in **Australia** police prosecuted several users for downloading

child porn. NSW courts introduced legislation banning obscene material with such loose wording that the Internet itself could be deemed illegal – if the law is ever tested. In **Britain,** the police tried a "voluntary" approach in mid-1996, identifying newsgroups that carried pornography beyond the pale and requesting that providers remove them from their feed. Most complied, but there was unease within the Internet industry that this was the wrong approach – the same groups would migrate elsewhere and the root of the problem would remain.

But the debate was, and is, about far more than porn. For **Net fundamentalists**, the issue is about holding ground against any compromises in liberty and retaining the global village as a political force – one that is potentially capable of bringing down governments and large corporations. Indeed, they argue that these battles over publishing freedom have shown governments to be out of touch with both technology and the social undercurrent, and that in the long run the balance of power will shift towards the people, towards a new democracy.

Wiretapping

Another slow-news-day story of the mid-1990s depicted **hackers** ruling networks, stealing money and creating havoc. Great reading, but the reality was less alarming. Although the US Department of Defense reported hundreds of thousands of network break-ins, they claimed it was more annoying than damaging, while in the commercial world little went astray except the odd credit card file. (Bear in mind that every time you hand your credit card to a shop assistant they get the same information.) In fact, by and large, for an online population greater than the combined size of New York, Moscow, London, Calcutta and Tokyo, there were surprisingly few noteworthy crimes. Yet the perception remained that the Net was too unsafe for the exchange of sensitive information such as payment details.

Libertarians raged at the US government's refusal to lift export bans on crack-proof **encryption algorithms**. But cryptography, the science of message coding, has traditionally been classified as a weapon and thus export of encryption falls under the Arms Control acts. Encryption requires a secret key to open the contents of a message and often another public key to code the message. These keys can be generated for regular use by individuals or, in the case of Web transactions, simply for one session upon agreement between the server and client. Several governments proposed to employ official authorities to keep a register of all secret keys and surrender them upon warrant – an unpopular proposal, to put it mildly, among a Net community who regard invasion of privacy as an issue equal in importance to censorship, and government monitors as instruments of repression.

However, the authorities were so used to being able to tap phones, intercept mail and install listening devices to aid investigations, they didn't relish giving up that freedom either. Government officials made a lot of noise about needing to monitor data to protect national security, though their true motives probably involve monitoring internal insurgence and catching tax cheats

– stuff they're not really supposed to do but we put up with anyway because if we're law-abiding it's mostly in our best interests.

The implications of such obstinacy went far beyond personal privacy. Business awaited browsers that could talk to commerce servers using totally snooper-proof encryption. Strong encryption technology had already been built into browsers, but it was illegal to export them from the US. At any rate, **the law was finally relaxed in mid-2000**.

The entertainment arrives

While politicians, big business, bankers, telcos and online action groups such as **CommerceNet** and the **Electronic Frontier Foundation** fretted over the future of privacy and its impact on digital commerce, the online world partied on regardless. If 1996 was the year of the Web, then 1997 was the year the **games** began. Netizens had been swapping chess moves and struggling with the odd network game over the Net for years, but it took id Software's **Quake** to lure the gaming masses online. Not to miss out, Online Services and ISPs took steps to prioritize game traffic, while hard-core corporate data moved further back on the shelves.

Music took off, too. **Bands** and **DJs** routinely streamed concerts over the Net, while celebrities such as Michael Jackson, Joe Dolce and Paul McCartney bared their souls in public chat rooms. Webpages came alive with the sound of music, from cheesy synthesized backgrounds to live radio feeds. Many online music stores like

CDNow reported profits, while **Amazon** became a major force in bookselling.

And then there was the Net as a prime news medium. As **Pathfinder** touched down on Mars, millions logged into NASA sites to scour the Martian landscape for traces of life. China marched into Hong Kong, Tiger Woods rewrote golfing history, Australia regained the Ashes and Mike Tyson fell from grace – all live on the Net. In response to this breaking of news on websites and newsgroups, an increasing number of **print newspapers** began delivering online versions before their hard copies hit the stands. In 1997, if you weren't on the Net, you weren't in the media.

The casualties

Not everyone had reason to party in 1997. **Cybercafés**, touted the height of cool in 1995, tended to flop as quickly as they appeared – at least in Western countries – as did many small **Internet Service Providers** (if they weren't swallowed by larger fish). From over thirty **browsers** in early 1996, less than a year later only two real players – Netscape and Microsoft – remained in the game. The also-ran software houses that initially thrived on the Net's avenue for distribution and promotion faded from view as the two browser giants ruthlessly crammed more features into their plug-and-play Web desktops. Microsoft and scores of other software developers declared that their future products would be able to update themselves online, either automatically or by clicking in the right place. So much for the software dealer.

Meanwhile, **Web TV** arrived delivering webpages and email onto home TV screens. It offered a cheap, simple alternative to PCs, but found its way to a smaller niche market than its fanfare predicted.

The whole **Web design industry** was due for a shakeout. Web cowboys who'd charged through the teeth for cornering the homepage design scam – yet lacked the programming skills to code, the artistic merit to design or the spelling standards to edit – were left exposed by the emerging professionalism. **New media** had come of age. The top Web chimps reworked their CVs and pitched in with online design houses. Major ad agencies formed new media departments and splashed Web addresses over everything from milk cartons to toothpaste tubes.

Bizarrely, though, 1997's best-known Web design team, **Higher Source**, will be remembered not for HTML handiwork but for publishing their cult's agenda to commit suicide in conjunction with the passing of the Hale-Bopp comet. This was the Internet as major news story. Within hours of the mass suicide, several sites appeared spoofing both its corporate pages as well as its cult, **Heaven's Gate**. Days later, there were enough to spawn four new Yahoo! subdirectories.

Back in the real world of **business and money**, major companies have played surprisingly by the book, observing **Netiquette** – the Net's informal code of conduct. The marriage has been awkward but generally happy. Even the absurd court cases between blockbuster sites such as **Microsoft Sidewalk v TicketMaster** and **Amazon v Barnes** and Noble (over the "biggest bookstore in the world" claim) did little to convince Netizens that they were witnessing anything more than carefully orchestrated publicity stunts. Indeed, many felt launching a website without some kind of legal suit was a waste of free publicity. It seemed like just a bit of fun. And as big money flowed in, **bandwidths** increased, content improved, ma and pa popped aboard and the online experience richened.

Alas, the same couldn't be said for the new-school entrepreneurs. Low advertising costs saw **Usenet newsgroups and email in-trays** choked with cross-posted get-rich schemes, network marketing plans and porno adverts. Further, unprecedented **banks of email** broke servers at AOL, MSN and scores of smaller providers. Netcom was temporarily forced to bar all mail originating from **Hotmail**, the most popular free Web email service and thus a safe haven for fly-by-night operators, due to the level of spam originating from its domain.

At the same time, in July 1997, a misplaced digger ripped up a vital US backbone artery and darkened large parts of the Net – something many had presumed impossible – and reduced the worldwide network to a crawl. The Net was nuclear-proof, maybe, but certainly not invulnerable.

The world's biggest playground

By the end of 1997, the Net's population had skyrocketed to well over a hundred million. The media increasingly relied on it for research and, in the process, began to understand it. It could no longer be written off as geek-land when it was

thrust this far into mainstream consciousness. Notable among the most recent arrivals were the so-called "**silver surfers**", predominantly retirees. Indeed, the Net was looking not only useful but essential, and those without it had good reason to feel left behind.

This new maturity arrived on the back of email, with the Web hot on its heels. As toner sales plummeted, surveys indicated that email had not only overtaken the fax but possibly even the telephone as the business communication tool of choice. However, at the same time, it could also lay claim to being the greatest time-waster ever introduced into an office – with staff spending large chunks of the day reading circulars, forwarding curios and flirting with their online pals.

The speed that email offered, and the ease with which entire address books could be carbon-copied, altered the six degrees of separation. Something with universal appeal – like the infernal **dancing baby animation** that did the rounds in 1999 – could be disseminated to millions within a matter of hours, potentially reaching everyone on the Net within days. And, as most journalists were hooked in by this stage, whatever circulated on the Net often found its way into other media formats. Not surprisingly, the fastest-moving chain emails were often hoaxes. One such prank, an address of sensible old-timer advice supposedly delivered by Kurt Vonnegut to MIT graduates (but actually taken from Mary Schmick's *Chicago Tribune* column), saturated the Net within a week. The director of *Romeo + Juliet*, Baz Luhrmann, was so taken he put it to music resulting in the cult hit "Sunscreen", which even more incredibly was re-spoofed into a XXXX beer advert. All within six months.

On a more annoying note, almost everyone received **virus hoaxes** that warned not to open email with certain subject headings. Millions took them seriously, earnestly forwarding them to their entire address books. An email campaign kicked off by Howard Stern propelled "Hank, the ugly drunken dwarf" to the top of **People**'s 100 Most Beautiful People poll as voted on the Net. Meanwhile, the Chinese community rallied to push Michelle Kwan into second place. But the biggest coup of all was **Matt Drudge**'s email leaking Bill Clinton's inappropriate affair with Monica Lewinsky, which sent the old-world media into the biggest feeding frenzy since the OJ trial. Although it might not have brought down the most powerful man in the world, it showed how in 1998, almost anyone, anywhere, could be heard.

The show must go on

In May 1998, the blossoming media romance with hackers as urban folk heroes turned sour when a consortium of good-fairy hackers, known as the **L0pht**, assured a US Senate Government Affairs Committee that they, or someone less benevolent, could render the Net entirely unusable within half an hour. It wasn't meant as a threat, but a call to arms against the apathy of those who'd designed, sold and administered the systems. The Pentagon had already been penetrated (by a young Israeli hacker), and though most reported attacks

amounted to little more than vandalism, with an increasing number of essential services tapped in, the probability of major disaster loomed.

Undeterred, Net commerce continued to break into new territories. **Music**, in particular, looked right at home with the arrival of DIY CD compilation shops and several major artists such as Massive Attack, Willie Nelson and The Beach Boys airing their new releases on the Net in MP3 before unleashing them on CD. However, these exclusive previews weren't always intentional. For instance, Swervedriver's beleaguered "99th Dream" found its way onto a Net bootleg almost a year before its official release.

By now, celebrity chat appearances hardly raised an eyebrow. Even major powerbrokers like Clinton and Yeltsin had appeared before an online inquisition. To top it off, in April 1998, Koko, a 300lb gorilla, fronted up to confess to some 20,000 chatsters that she'd rather be playing with Smokey, her pet kitten.

The red-light district

Despite the bottomless reserves of free Web space, personal vanity pages and Web diaries took a downturn in 1998. The novelty was passing, a sign perhaps that the Web was growing up. This didn't, however, prevent live Web cameras, better known as **webcams,** from enjoying a popularity resurgence. But this time around they weren't so much being pointed at lizards, fish, ski slopes or intersections, but at whoever connected them to the Net – a fad which resulted in numerous bizarre excursions in exhibitionism from some very ordinary folk. Leading the fray was the entirely unremarkable **Jennifer Ringley**, who became a Web household name simply for letting the world see her move about her college room – clothed and (very occasionally) otherwise. She might have only been famous for being famous, but it was fame enough to land her a syndicated newspaper column about showing off and, of course, a tidy packet from the thousands of subscribers who paid real money to access Jennicam.

But this was the tame end of the Net's trade in voyeurism. These were boom times for pornographers. Research suggested that as much as ninety percent of network traffic was consumed by porn images. That's not to suggest that anywhere near ninety percent of users were involved, only that the images consume so much bandwidth. The story in Usenet was even more dire, with more than eighty percent of the non-binary traffic hogged by spam and spam cancel messages. Meanwhile, the three top Web search aids, **HotBot**, **AltaVista** and **Yahoo!**, served click-through banners on suggestive keywords. However you felt about pornography from a moral standpoint, it had definitely become a nuisance.

The bottleneck

As 1998 progressed, **cable Internet access** became increasingly available – and, in the USA, even affordable. New subscribers could suddenly jump from download speeds of 56Kbps at best to as high as 10Mbps. Meanwhile several telcos, such as PacBell and GTE, began rolling out **ADSL**, another broadband technology capable of mega-bit access, this time over plain copper telephone wires. However, even at these speeds, users still had to deal with the same old bottleneck; namely, the Internet's backbone, which had been struggling to cope with even the low-speed dial-up traffic.

The power to **upgrade the backbone** (or more correctly backbones) lies in the hands of those who own the major cables and thus effectively control the Net. It's always seemed inevitable that the global telecommunication superpowers would starve the smaller players out of the market – and the emergence of Internet telephony forced telcos to look further down the track at the broader scenario where whoever controls the Internet not only controls data but voice traffic as well. They recognized that their core business could be eroded by satellite and cable companies. To survive, telcos realized, they needed to compete on the same level, provide an alternative or join forces with their rivals.

The dust clears, the fog remains

As the world packed up shop for the millennium, fretting over double-digit date blunders, the Internet settled into a **consolidation phase**. For the most part, what was hot got hotter while the remainder atrophied. Broadband cable, ADSL and satellite access forged ahead, particularly in the US and Australia. Meanwhile, in the UK, British Telecom stooped to an eleventh-hour exploit on its unpopular metered local call system, weaselling deals with local ISPs to enable free access by divvying up its phone bill booty. Surprisingly, instead of torching 10 Downing Street for allowing the situation to exist in the first place, browbeaten Brits snapped it up, propelling free-access pioneer **Freeserve** (later Wanadoo, then Orange) to the top of the ISP pops within months. BT refused to budge on unmetered local calls but, in response to increasingly vocal dissent, finally launched fixed-rate modem access in 2001, with unmetered ADSL following soon after.

Interest in **online commerce** surged with explosive growth in stock trading, auctions, travel booking and mail order computers. Big-budget empire builders such as AOL, Amazon, Cisco, Disney, Excite, Microsoft and Real Networks hit overdrive, announcing intertwined strategic mergers, and continued swallowing and stomping on smaller talent. Most notably AOL, with little more than a dip into petty cash, wolfed down Netscape – not, as many assumed, for its revolutionary browser, but for the sizeable user-base still buzzing its browser's default homepage.

This, however, wasn't the Netscape of the mid-1990s, but a defeated relic that had lost its way, ceased innovating and appeared unable to ship products. Its legacy had been passed over to **Microsoft**, which remained in court squabbling over Internet Explorer, Windows 98 and its success in cornering all but some five percent of the operating system market share. Apart from whatever voyeuristic pleasure could be gained from king-hitting computing's tallest poppy, the Department of Justice's case grew increasingly meaningless against the broader backdrop. The computer-wielding public weren't too worried

about lack of choice, but lack of quality. Even Apple's allegedly foolproof **iMac** fell way short of a sturdy carriage to traverse the Net, play games and make life generally more push-button-friendly.

By this stage the Internet was ready to become a public utility, but both the computing and access provision industries remained rooted within a hobbyist mindset. As PC dealers shamelessly crammed their systems with interfering utilities, ISPs continued to supply inadequate bandwidth, unreliable software and irresponsible advice. Yet no alternative existed, and governments appeared incapable of intelligent input. As the twentieth century bit the dust, you didn't have to be a geek to get on the Net, but it sure didn't hurt to know your stuff.

The American dream

Doomsday was not televised live as daylight broke across the year 2000. Planes didn't crash, Washington wasn't nuked and ATMs did not randomly eject crisp banknotes. Instead, attention turned to the ever-inflating Internet stock bubble. The new tech stocks were driving the biggest speculative frenzy since Tulipmania. Every grandmother and her cabbie wanted in on the **dotcom** action. **Cisco Systems**, a network hardware supplier and hardly a household name, celebrated its tenth birthday by briefly becoming the world's biggest company (in terms of market cap). To add further insult to the old world order, AOL, foster home to twenty million chirpy AOLers, offered its hand to the **TIME–Warner** cross-media conglomerate. Meanwhile **Bill Gates,** the billionaire icon of the new American dream, continued defiantly delivering his own brand of truth, justice and the Microsoft way to the desktops of nineteen out of twenty computers. What could possibly go wrong?

Too much gold for one gringo

Enter US **District Judge Thomas Penfield Jackson,** who declared that Microsoft had maintained its monopoly by anticompetitive means, and that it should sever both physical and corporate ties between its Internet software and Windows. Microsoft had made few friends outside the fans of Ayn Rand, particularly within the Mac-monopolized media, so any public spanking was welcomed. Yet, in reality, it was an unsatisfying outcome for all concerned. Not least for investors, whose tech share portfolios crumbled. And so that was it for the speculative dotcom startups. As the house of Gates fell, so too did the bricks around it. By the time **Boo.com** folded in May 2000, "dotcom" was already a dirty word.

With an appeal pending in the Supreme Court, Microsoft brazenly released **Me,** yet another version of Windows with Internet Explorer inside, and furthermore announced that its future applications would be delivered on demand across the Net. What little sympathy remained for Bill and his merry cast of outlaws was almost completely eroded.

Nobody can stop the music

As wave after wave of email-borne viruses sneezed from Outlook address books, it seemed clear that most office workers lacked basic computer training. Overlooked in the mass media hysteria was the simple truth that **Melissa, Happy 99, I Love You** and similar Internet worms could only be propagated by the grossly incompetent. It also seemed certain that it would happen again.

But viruses weren't the only source of mischief. A 15-year-old Canadian, going by the cute name of "Mafiaboy", unleashed a bevy of **Denial of Service** attacks, temporarily knocking out several high-profile websites such as Yahoo!, Amazon and eTrade. Despite his relatively low level of technical expertise he was able to outwit the FBI for almost three months. Even then it was only his chat room confession that triggered the arrest.

With pirate **MP3 music tracks** hogging the bulk of college network bandwidth, legal action inevitably followed. **Napster** faced the music against stadium rockers Metallica, and the Recording Industry Association of America sued **MP3.com** over its ingenious Beam-It service. While the holders of copyright won in the courts of law, back in the real world it was business as usual – with the added extra that the publicity drew millions of new music lovers into the file-trading loop. As mounting legal pressure pummelled Napster into the commercial reality of blocking copyrighted material from its servers, traders merely migrated to decentralized networks such as **WinMX** and **Gnutella.**

Dumb money

As the **new economy** lay gutted on the screens of the NASDAQ and beyond, many predicted a global meltdown in 2001. Yet, despite ninety percent falls in dotcom blue-chips like Cisco, Amazon and Yahoo!, the broader economy remained surprisingly intact. So too did Microsoft, with the DC Court of Appeals overruling Judge Jackson's remedy to split the company (Microsoft managed to wriggle out of the case on a technicality, though they did have to pay AOL three-quarters of a billion dollars in a related out-of-court settlement in 2003).

Hard cash failures ushered in hard cold facts, and one of those was no secret to those who'd been online since the BBS days. The Net's popularity had been largely driven by the lure of something for nothing. Few wanted to pay when so much was free. Few wanted to click on banner ads. And even fewer could profit from advertising in someone's diary. As we waved goodbye to the dumber dotcoms, we also bid farewell to a romantic delusion called **cyberspace**. The Internet was no longer an exotic frontier but a ubiquitous utility like the telephone.

And it certainly was everywhere. Suddenly it seemed mandatory to cast anything online that could be cast online, from inane Coke vending machines to inane reality TV experiments like **Big Brother**. So, of course, it seemed logical that celebrity bomber Timothy McVeigh should exit the jeering hordes live via RealVideo. When a federal judge refused the Entertainment Network's request to webcast the execution in April 2001, it was the surest sign we'd entered a brave new era – one where common sense still stood a chance.

Still rocking in the free world

When outright war was declared on a small army of Islamic revolutionaries in September 2001, interest plummeted in the plight of those suffering in the aftermath of the new media revolution. According to the papers, the Internet was henceforth last year's news. Full-colour IT lift-outs became mono spreads as sponsors cut staff and budgets to match.

But a quick trip to any backpacker ghetto would quickly dispel notions of a Net fallen from grace. Strings of cybercafés bid freshly tattooed teens to book tickets, Instant Message and Hotmail their oldies for cash. Meanwhile, back home, their chums were sampling the pleasures – and frustrations – of high-speed access via ADSL, cable and Wi-Fi.

As broadband exploded, so too did **P2P** (peer to peer) file-sharing. What began as a trickle of MP3s was now a torrent of music, movies and software gushing across the FastTrack and eDonkey networks, seemingly impervious to legal intervention. Labels were already hurting, claimed the International Federation of the Phonographic Industry, pointing to a global drop in CD sales of five percent during 2000. Considering the economic downturn, these figures didn't seem all that bad, but as millions of new tracks hit the networks daily, no one doubted their reasoning.

So many sites, so little time

With storage freebies in freefall, independent webmasters became more concerned with staying afloat than trying to be clever. Unfortunately, popularity didn't guarantee survival in **dot-pessimistic 2002**. Rather, it meant higher hosting costs, which were rarely offset by the nugatory return on click-thru banner ads and occasional subscriptions. And its wasn't just the small sites feeling under pressure to make the books balance. Even spam magnet **Hotmail**, the original free stooge, began busking for cash to help fund its massive server farms. And soon even the big and respectable sites began employing new-style **JavaScript banners** which move across the page and block the content until the user works out how to close them.

Yet despite the squeeze and the talk of doom, gloom and dot-bust, the Internet was actually beginning to live up to its claims. Astute organizations started recognizing the Web as a media expense, rather than revenue raiser, and began to make it work in their favour. And so did the ever-growing number of clickees, who were increasingly using the smartest site – **Google** had become ubiquitous, for example, so no more stumbling through long lists of links.

Sharing feeds and files

In 2003, as the US-led invasion of Iraq temporarily re-politicized the Western populace, the Web became more than ever before a provider of **cross-border news**. As Americans became dissatisfied with their local press's reluctance to criticize the government, they turned elsewhere; in January, without precedent, half the users accessing the UK's left-of-centre *Guardian* newspaper website were situated across the Atlantic. The Net also became the centre of a massive propaganda war, with campaigners on both sides hacking into and **blocking opposition websites** – from **Al-Jazeera** to **10 Downing Street**. And more than ever before, the actual combat unfolded live on news sites around the world.

The Iraq war also raised the profile of weblogs, or **blogs** as they had become more widely known. The so-called "Baghdad Blogger" and many others brought coverage directly from the scene, while back in the West, journalists, teenagers and geeks alike signed up with Google's Blogger service. A new era of online publishing had begun.

In April 2003, soon after the war officially ended, the record labels took an in-court blow as a US judge ruled that **P2P file-sharing** programs/networks weren't inherently illegal, as they could serve a legitimate function. They responded by issuing subpoenas for individual file-sharers – winning huge resentment from the press and music fans – and Madonna felt compelled to take action personally, flooding the networks with files purporting to be her tunes but actually containing a hate message from the singer (an outraged hacker left a rude reply on her official homepage). With broadband now in many millions of homes – and **KaZaA** becoming the most downloaded program ever – the film and software industries were also getting seriously jittery.

While copyright holders were struggling to

come to terms with the fact that tech-savvy users will probably always find a way to share their files for free, Apple kick-started what proved to be a more successful approach. Their **iTunes software/store** – offering any track for 99¢, complete with cover art and legality – sold 275,000 songs in its first day. By 2004, many had followed suit, from major corporations such as Sony, to charities such as Oxfam, whose **Big Noise Music** began selling tunes to fight world poverty.

But the illegal file-sharing continued unabashed, helped along by a Canadian judge's conclusion that making an archive of copyrighted material available via a file-sharing service was no worse than placing a photocopier in a public library.

Open source gets serious

If Microsoft thought it had won the browser wars back in the 1990s, it got a rude awakening in late 2004 when the global community of open-source programmers, headed up by the Mozilla Foundation, released **Firefox**, a browser that quite comfortably knocked the socks off Internet Explorer. Twenty-five million copies were downloaded within 100 days of its release. This wasn't enough to make a serious inroad into IE's dominance, but it doubtless raised eyebrows at Microsoft HQ, not least because the open-source alternatives to Windows and MS Office (Linux and OpenOffice respectively) were also gaining download popularity – and because the unstoppable success of the iPod and iTunes Music Store was powering on sales of Apple Macs.

Where open-source software was making an impact like never before, so too was open-source information. By 2005, **Wikipedia**, the free encyclopedia that any user can contribute to, had proved its doubters wrong to become one of the most useful, reliable and well-written sites online. A bottom-up revolution was taking place in the world of broadcasting, too. Audio blogging, aka Podcasting, saw thousands of individuals making radio-style shows available as free MP3 files.

While all this was making the online world seem less of a corporate domain, August 2004 did the opposite, with **Google**, now commanding a near monopoly in the field of Web searching, making its initial public offering on the stock market. The sale raised more than $1.5 billion – a financial order of magnitude unseen since the height of the Internet boom. By June 2005, with its armada of services now including webmail and maps, the California-based search engine was pronounced the most valuable media company in the world. What had once been a refreshingly off-beat website was gradually redefined among many Net observers as a dangerously dominant force, with some commentators predicting an era when people would employ Google as their ISP and no longer access the Web directly – only Google's cached copy of it.

It's good to talk

By 2006, millions of Internet users had respectable broadband connections – and it was showing. Apple sold its billionth song via iTunes, and *King Kong* became the first blockbuster to be offered as a legal download at the same time as its DVD release. But the fastest-growing sector in the broadband world wasn't music or video but telephony – and mainly thanks to **Skype**, a free program for making phone calls over the Internet. Online telephony wasn't anything new, of course, but Skype brought together excellent sound quality and foolproof technology with the ability to call (for a small fee) landlines and mobile phones across most of the world. Auction website **eBay**, now one of the most popular and profitable sites on the Web, had seen the light back in late 2005 and snapped up Skype for a cool $1.8 billion. By April 2006, there were 100 million registered Skype users and plenty more signing up every day.

If the success of Skype suggested a boost to the Internet's role as a communications tool, so did the rapid growth of **social networking** sites. Friendster and Orkut led the way, with **MySpace,** Bebo, Facebook and others following soon after. Teenagers and students used them to flirt or stay in touch, musicians to show off their wares, and everyone else to find out what their old school friends were up to. By 2007, hundreds of millions of people had signed up.

The same year also saw big developments in the world of mobile Internet. First came laptops with wide-area broadband access; then came Apple's iPhone, the first pocket-sized device to make Web browsing and email a pleasure to use. These sold in large numbers in 2008 and 2009, ensuring that growing numbers of people are never more than a few seconds away from the Web even when out and about.

Looking forward, looking back

With futuristic handheld devices and vast swathes of people connected via virtual social networks, the online world seems to be finally delivering something akin to the Utopian vision imagined by its early proponents. But even at the age of thirty-something, the Internet is still only in its infancy. So be patient, enjoy it for what it is today, and complain – but not too much. One day you'll look back and get all nostalgic about the days when you logged on through copper telephone wires. It's amazing it works at all…

Glossary

What does it all mean?

A

AAC Apple's compressed audio file format.

ActiveX Microsoft concept that allows a program to run inside a webpage.

Add/Remove Programs Correct place to uninstall programs from Windows. Found in the Control Panel.

ADSL (**A**synchronous **D**igital **S**ubscriber **L**ine). Broadband over the phoneline.

Antivirus scanner Program that detects, and usually removes, computer viruses.

AOL (**A**merica **O**nline). A major ISP that encourages subscribers to use its own Web browser and email software.

Applet A small program.

Archive File that bundles a set of other files together under a single name for transfer or backup. Often compressed to reduce size, or encrypted for privacy.

Attachment File included with email or other form of message.

B

Backbone Set of paths that carry long-haul Net traffic.

Bandwidth In effect, the speed of an Internet connection. Increased bandwidth means more data can flow at once.

Binary file Any file that contains more than plain text, such as a program or image.

BinHex Method of encoding, used on Macs.

Blog See Weblog.

Bookmarks Netscape file used to store Web addresses.

Bounced mail Email returned to sender.

Bps (**B**its **p**er **s**econd). Basic measure of data transfer.

Broadband High-speed Internet access.

Browser Program for viewing Web pages such as Internet Explorer or Firefox.

Buffer Temporary data storage for ensuring the smooth flow of data (eg in an online radio stream).

Bug Logical, physical or programming error in software or hardware that causes a recurring malfunction.

C

Cache Temporary storage space; or the "snapshot" copy of a Webpage stored by your browser, a search engine, etc.

Client Program that accesses information across a network, such as a Web browser or newsreader.

Cloud computing Using Web-based storage and applications instead of those installed locally.

Context menu See Mouse menu.

Crack Break a program's security, integrity or registration system, or fake a user ID.

Crash When a program or operating system fails to respond or causes other programs to malfunction.

Cyber In IRC, may be short for "cybersex", that is, the online equivalent of phone sex. Otherwise, a prefix for anything to do with the Internet – eg cybercafé.

Cyberspace Coined by science-fiction writer William Gibson to describe the virtual world that exists within the marriage of computers, telecommunication networks and digital media.

D

Default The standard settings.

Dialog box Window that appears on the screen to ask or tell you something.

Dial-up connection Temporary network connection between two computers via a telephone line and an analogue modem.

Digital signing Encrypted data appended to a message to identify the sender.

DNS (Domain Name System) The system that locates the numerical IP address corresponding to a host name.

Domain Part of the DNS name that specifies details about the host, such as its location and whether it is part of a commercial (.com), government (.gov) or educational (.edu) entity.

Donationware Software that, in return for using it, encourages you to make a donation to the developers, or a named charity.

Download To copy files from a remote computer to your own.

Downstream The flow of data from your ISP (the server) to your computer (the client).

Glossary

Driver Small program that acts like a translator between a device and programs that use that device.

DRM (Digital Rights Management). The encoded protection of compressed audio formats purchased from some music download sites.

DSL (Digital Subscriber Line). Also called xDSL. A type of broadband connection that comes in various flavours, the most popular is ADSL.

E

Email Electronic mail carried on the Net.

Email address The unique private Internet address to which email is sent. Takes the form: user@host

Encryption Processing of encoding data so that it cannot be understood by unauthorized people.

F

FAQ (Frequently Asked Questions). Document that answers the most commonly asked questions on a particular topic.

File Anything stored on a computer, such as a program, image or document.

File compression Reducing a file's size for transfer or storage.

File extension Set of characters added to the end of a filename (after a full stop) intended to identify the file as a member of a category (file type). For example, the extension .TXT identifies a text file.

Firefox Free, open-source Web browser.

Firewall Network security system used to restrict external and internal traffic.

Firmware Software routines stored in a hardware device.

FTP (File Transfer Protocol) Common method for moving files across the Internet.

G

GIF (Graphics Interchange Format). Compressed graphics format widely used on the Web, especially for buttons and icons.

Google Popular Web search engine and online email and services provider, located at: www. google.com

Gopher Defunct menu-based system for retrieving Internet archives, usually organized by subject.

GPRS (General Packet Radio Service). Technology used to transmit mobile phone data.

H

Hacker A computer programmer, especially one who gets off on breaking through computer security and limitations. A cracker is a criminal hacker.

Header Pre-data part of a packet, containing source and destination addresses, error checking, and other fields. Also the first part of an email or news posting which contains, among other things, the sender's details and time sent.

Homepage Either the first page loaded by your browser at startup, or the main Web document for a particular group, organization or person.

Host Computer that offers some sort of services to networked users.

HTML (HyperText Markup Language.) The language used to create Web documents.

HyperText links The "clickable" links or "hotspots" that interconnect pages on the Web.

I

ICQ A popular Instant Messaging program: www.icq.com

Image map A Web image that contains multiple links. Which link you take depends on where you click.

IMAP (Internet Message Access Protocol). Standard email access protocol that's superior to POP3 in that you can selectively retrieve messages or parts thereof as well as manage folders on the server.

Infinite loop See Loop.

Install To place a program's working files onto a computer so that it's ready to be set up and used. Normally done by clicking on a setup-file (often called setup.exe).

Instant Messaging Point-to-point chat such as ICQ.

Internet Cooperatively run global collection of computer networks with a common addressing scheme.

Internet connection sharing (ICS) Allows a networked computer to access the Internet through another's connection. A feature of recent Mac and Windows operating systems.

Internet Explorer Microsoft's Web browser bundled with the operating system since Windows 98.

Internet Favorites Internet Explorer folder for filing Web addresses.

Internet Shortcut Microsoft's terminology for a Web address or URL.

IP (Internet Protocol). The most important Internet protocol. Defines how packets of data get from source to destination.

Glossary

IP address Every computer connected to the Internet has an **IP address** (written in dotted numerical notation), which corresponds to its domain name. Domain Name Servers convert one to the other.

IRC (Internet Relay Chat). Internet system where you send text, or audio, to others in real time.

ISDN (Integrated Services Digital Network). International standard for digital communications over telephone lines. Allows data transmission at 64 or 128Kbps.

ISP (Internet Service Provider). Company that sells access to the Internet.

J

Java Platform-independent programming language designed by Sun Microsystems.

JPEG/JPG Graphics file format widely used online as it combines good data compression (making images quicker to transfer) with good compatibility (all browsers can handle them).

K

Kbps (Kilobits per second). Standard measure of data transfer speed.

Kill file Newsreader file into which you can enter keywords and email addresses to stop unwanted articles.

L

LAN (Local Area Network). Computer network that spans a relatively small area such as an office.

Latency Length of time it takes data to reach its destination.

Leased line Dedicated telecommunications link between two points.

Line-splitter Device used to separate ADSL broadband data from telephone data coming through a phoneline.

Link A pointer to another document or file. When you click on a link in a webpage, the linked file will be retrieved and displayed, played or downloaded, depending on its type.

Linux Freely distributed implementation of the UNIX operating system.

LLU "Local Loop Unbundling" – the deregulation of local telephone exchanges to aid the supply of highspeed ADSL broadband.

Log on/Log in Connect to a computer network.

Loop See Infinite loop.

M

Malware Any application or piece of code designed for malicious purposes – viruses, Trojans, etc.

Meta tag An HTML tag that gives some information about the contents of a webpage, such as keywords and a description.

MIME (Multipurpose Internet Mail Extensions). Standard for the transfer of binary email attachments.

Mirror Replica FTP or website set up to share traffic.

Modem (**Mo**dulator/**Dem**odulator). Device that allows a computer to communicate with another over a standard telephone line, by converting the digital data into analogue signals and vice versa.

Mouse menu Useful custom menu that pops up when you right-click (by default) on-screen items such as icons, Web links and taskbars.

Mouse wheel Rolling wheel positioned between the right and left mouse buttons on suitably equipped mice. Invaluable for scrolling pages and selecting weapons in first-person shooters.

MP3 A compressed music format.

MPEG/MPG A compressed video file format.

MTU (Maximum Transfer Unit) The maximum size in bytes of a packet of data that can be sent over a given broadband Internet connection.

Multithreaded Able to process multiple requests at once.

N

Name server Host that translates domain names into IP addresses.

The Net The Internet.

Netscape Web browser – and the company that produces it, now owned by AOL.

Newbie Newcomer to the Net, discussion or area.

Newsgroups Usenet message areas, or discussion groups, organized by subject hierarchies.

NNTP (Network News Transfer Protocol). Standard for the exchange of Usenet articles across the Internet.

Node Any device connected to a network.

O

Offline The state of being disconnected from a network, typically the Internet.

Online 1. The state of being connected to a network, typically the Internet. 2. Describes a resource that is located on the Internet.

Outlook Microsoft's business email program incorporated into MS Office. Includes scheduling and contact tools, but no Usenet reader.

Outlook Express Leaner version of the above that's bundled free with Internet Explorer, Windows 98 and later.

Glossary

P

Packet Unit of data. In data transfer, information is broken into packets, which then travel independently through the Internet.

Packet loss Failure to transfer units of data between network nodes. A high percentage makes transfer slow or impossible.

Patch Temporary or interim add-on to fix or upgrade software.

Ping Echo-like trace that tests if a host is available.

Platform Computer operating system, such as Mac OS, Windows or Linux.

Plug-in Program that fits into another.

POP3 (Post Office Protocol). Email protocol that allows you to pick up your mail from anywhere on the Net, even if you're connected through someone else's account.

Podcast An audio blog, usually in the form of an MP3 file.

POPs (Points of Presence). An ISP's range of local dial-in points.

Port number The numerical address of a process running on a computer attached to the Internet.

Portal Website that specializes in leading you to others.

Post To send a public message to a Usenet newsgroup, blog, etc.

Protocol Agreed way for two network devices to talk to each other.

Proxy server Sits between a client, such as a Web browser, and a real server. Most often used to improve performance by delivering stored browser caches and to filter undesirable material.

Q

QuickTime Apple's proprietary multimedia standard. Commonly used to preview movies online. Download the Windows player from: www.quicktime.com

R

README file A last-minute document, included with program set-up files, that gives installation instructions and other messages from the developers. Sometimes useful when things go wrong.

RealAudio A standard for streaming compressed audio over the Internet. See: www.real.com

Registry Windows database for system and software configuration settings. Edit (at your own risk) by typing Regedit at the Run command in the Start menu.

Robot Program that automates Net tasks such as collating search engine databases or automatically responding in IRC. Also called a **Bot**.

Router A hardware device (or sometimes a piece of software) that distributes information "packets" between two computers or networks.

RSS (Really Simple Syndication) The means by which websites and blogs enable individuals to subscribe to their newsfeeds, Podcasts, etc.

S

Safari Email program bundles with Apple's OS X operating system.

Search engine Database of webpage extracts that can be queried to find reference to something on the Net. Example: Google (www.google.com).

Serial port An old-school socket that allows data transfer one bit at a time.

Server Computer that makes services available on a network.

Shareware Software with a free trial period, sometimes with reduced features.

Signature file 1. Personal footer that can be attached automatically to email and Usenet postings. 2. Database used by virus scanners to keep track of strains. Update regularly.

Silverlight Microsoft-built browser plug-in that enables certain animation and interactive effects on a webpage.

Spam (n & v). Junk email or Usenet postings.

Streaming Delivered in real time instead of waiting for the whole file to arrive, eg RealAudio.

Stuffit Common Macintosh file compression format and program.

Surf Skip from page to page around the Web by following links.

T

TCP/IP (Transmission Control Protocol/Internet Protocol). The protocols that drive the Internet.

Telnet Internet protocol that allows you to log on to a remote computer and act as a dumb terminal.

Temporary Internet Files Special system folder used by Internet Explorer to store webpages' contents for quick recall when backtracking. It's wise to empty contents regularly through Internet Properties, General tab.

3G Technology used to transmit mobile-phone and Internet data to mobile devices.

Trojan (horse) Program that hides its true (usually sinister) intention.

Troll Prank newsgroup posting intended to invoke an irate response.

Tweet An individual post to the timeline of the Twitter micro-blogging service.

U

UNIX Operating system used by most ISPs and colleges. So long as you stick to graphic interfaces, you'll never notice it.

Update To bring a program, program version, operating system or data file (such as a virus scanner signature) up to date by installing a patch, revision or complete new version.

Upgrade A newer, and presumably improved version of a hardware or software system, or the process of installing it.

Upload Send files to a remote computer.

Upstream The flow of data from your computer (the client) to your ISP (the server). Also see "Downstream".

URL (Uniform Resource Locator). Formal name for a Web address.

USB/USB2 (Universal Serial Bus). High-speed serial bus standards that allows for the connection of up to 127 devices and offers advanced plug-and-play features. Gradually replacing the serial, parallel, keyboard and mouse ports.

Usenet User's Network. A collection of networks and computer systems that exchange messages, organized by subject into newsgroups.

Utility program A small program that extends, supplements or enhances the functionality of the operating system.

UUencode Method of encoding binary files into text so that they can be attached to mail or posted to Usenet. They must be UUdecoded to convert them back. Most mail and news programs do it automatically. Alternative to MIME.

V

Vaporware Rumoured or announced, but non-existent, software or hardware. Often used as a competitive marketing ploy.

VDSL (Very high bit rate Digital Subscriber Line) An up-and-coming member of the DSL family capable of transmitting data downstream at speeds up to 52 Mbps over short distances.

Version number Unique code used to distinguish between product releases.

W

WAN (Wide Area Network) A computer network that encompasses a large geographical area.

WAP (Wireless Application Protocol). Refers to a set of standards that determine the way in which mobile phones and other devices connect to the Internet.

Warez Slang for software, usually pirated.

The Web The World Wide Web or WWW. Graphic and text documents published on the Internet that are interconnected through clickable "HyperText" links. A webpage is a single document. A website is a collection of related documents.

Web authoring Designing and publishing webpages using HTML.

Weblog A journal-like personal webpage.

Webmaster Person who maintains a website.

Wi-Fi The friendly name for the 802.11b protocol that allows nearby computers and other devices to communicate wirelessly.

Wider-Fi A developing wireless standard similar to Wi-Fi but with the wider range of a few miles.

Wiki An open-source, editable webpage.

World Wide Web See The Web, above.

WYSIWYG (What You See Is What You Get). What you type is the way it comes out.

Y

Yahoo! The original Web portal: www.yahoo.com

Z

Zip PC file compression format that creates files with the extension .zip, usually using the WinZip program (www.winzip.com). Frequently used to reduce file size for transfer or storage on floppy disks.

Still confused?

Then try:

Netlingo www.netlingo.com
PC Webopedia www.webopedia.com
What Is? www.whatis.com
Wikipedia www.wikipedia.org

Index

Index

Index

Index

Index

Index